Fortress Shield, 2026 Edition

Step-by-Step Identity Protection with Zero-Cost Cybersecurity Tools That Actually Work

Published by SPIRE Value Stream Press,

An imprint of Value Stream Learning Group, L.L.C.

Weaverville, NC, USA

© 2025, 2026 SPIRE Value Stream Press. All Rights Reserved.

No part of this publication may be reproduced, stored, or transmitted in any form or by any means, electronic, mechanical, photocopying, recording, or otherwise, without prior written permission of the publisher, except for brief quotations in reviews or educational use.

ISBN: 979-8-9935398-1-2

First Edition October 2025

This publication is provided for educational and informational purposes only.

It does not constitute legal, financial, or cybersecurity advice.

Readers assume full responsibility for their actions and must comply with all applicable laws and regulations.

Fictional Disclaimer:

CMSgt Alan Palmer (USAF, Ret.) is a narrative persona used for educational storytelling and authenticity.

No endorsement, sponsorship, or representation by the United States Air Force or Department of War is implied.

For corrections, permissions, or additional resources, visit

FortressShieldBook.com

Printed in the United States of America

Dedication

To my wife,
My dearest, best friend, and the kindest person I know.
You've been my compass in every storm and the calm that keeps me steady.
This mission —and everyone before it — was possible because of you.

Table of Contents

Chapter 1: Lock Your Digital Front Door _____ 7

Chapter 2: Catch Breaches Before They Catch You _____ 23

Chapter 3: Freeze Your Credit in 15 Minutes ___ 41

Chapter 4: Daily Habits That Take Seconds ____ 61

Chapter 5: Stay Current with 2026 Updates ____ 83

Chapter 6: Secure Your Home Network _____ 101

Chapter 7: When Paid Services Make Sense __ 123

Chapter 8: Password Command - Your One Key to the Fortress _____ 143

Chapter 9: ALERT - Early Warning Systems ____ 171

Chapter 10: Credit Armor - Fortifying Your Financial Identity _____ 195

Chapter 11: Community - Building Collective Defense _____ 217

Chapter 12: Red Team - Thinking Like the Enemy _____ 245

Chapter 13: Recovery - What to Do After a Breach _____ 271

Chapter 14: Maintain & Future-Proof - Keeping Your Fortress Current _____ 329

Chapter 15, Law & Policy: Knowing Your Rights and Using the System _____ 373

Chapter 16: Phishing & Social Engineering - Recognizing the Human Attack _____ 399

Chapter 17: Closing Orders - Your Mission Continues _____ *431*

Appendix A: Guided Setup for Helping Parents and Elders _____ *469*

Appendix B: Teen Starter Pack - Essential Digital Defense _____ *483*

Appendix C: Fortress Shield Reference Materials _____ *491*

About the Author _____ *504*

FORTRESS SHIELD 2026: ESSENTIAL DIGITAL DEFENSE FOR REGULAR PEOPLE

Step-by-Step Identity Protection with Zero-Cost Cybersecurity Tools That Actually Work

---

Welcome to Fortress Shield

This book is written for ordinary people who want extraordinary digital safety. It bridges the gap between cybersecurity professionals and everyday users, providing a clear path to comprehensive protection without requiring technical expertise or expensive software.

Whether you are confident with technology, overwhelmed by it, or helping someone else stay safe online, Fortress Shield guides you step by step to secure your identity and privacy. The approach is practical, not theoretical. Every recommendation has been tested with real people facing real threats.

Each chapter follows a mission-based format combining narrative storytelling with practical instruction. You'll read real stories from families who faced security challenges, then learn exactly how to implement the defenses that protected them. The structure includes clear objectives, realistic time estimates, and step-by-step procedures you can follow immediately.

How to Use This Book

You can follow the chapters in sequence for comprehensive defense setup, building your fortress layer by layer from foundation to completion. Alternatively, you can skip directly to chapters addressing your most urgent concerns, whether that's recovering from a breach, protecting elderly parents, or teaching teenagers about digital safety. Each chapter stands alone while contributing to the complete system.

Every chapter includes a Mission Time estimate so you know the time commitment before starting, a clear Objective stating what you'll accomplish, and a Call Sign providing the core principle in memorable form. Supporting materials including detailed procedures, templates, and quick-reference guides appear in three appendices. Appendix A provides guided setup instructions for helping parents and elderly relatives who find technology overwhelming. Appendix B offers a teen starter pack covering essential digital defense in language and format designed for younger users. Appendix C contains fortress shield reference materials including emergency response procedures and maintenance checklists.

Additionally, practical implementation tools including current URLs, fillable forms, printable checklists, and detailed battle plans are available as a free companion PDF titled Strategic Defense Plans. Download it at FortressShieldBook.com/plans before you begin. This separation allows the main book to work in any format, audiobook, e-reader, or print, while implementation materials remain accessible and current through semi-annual updates.

About the Author

Chief Master Sergeant Alan Palmer, USAF (Ret.), is a narrative persona combining thirty years of military cybersecurity leadership with a passion for teaching everyday people how to protect themselves online. His direct, mission-based style reflects decades of training service members, civilians, and families in digital readiness across some of the most sensitive facilities in the United States Air Force.

The character of Chief Palmer represents the accumulated wisdom of career cybersecurity professionals who've defended critical systems against sophisticated adversaries and then translated that expertise into practical guidance for civilian life. His focus remains clear: teaching cybersecurity that works in the real world, not just in theory.

The stories, procedures, and recommendations throughout this book draw from real experiences helping families recover from breaches, teaching elderly relatives to recognize scams, and building sustainable security practices that protect people without overwhelming them. The military framework provides structure and discipline, but the content addresses civilian threats and uses civilian tools accessible to everyone.

Join the Fortress Shield Community

To stay informed with updates, current tool recommendations, and threat alerts, visit **FortressShieldBook.com**. Download the free Strategic Defense Plans companion PDF at **FortressShieldBook.com/plans** for implementation materials including step-by-step setup guides with current URLs, fillable forms and templates, printable checklists and worksheets, and detailed battle plans for every security procedure.

Before You Begin: Get Your Implementation Tools

This book teaches you principles and strategies of digital security through seventeen comprehensive chapters. The practical implementation tools, step-by-step setup guides with current URLs, fillable forms and templates, printable checklists and worksheets, and detailed battle plans for every procedure are available as a free companion PDF titled **Strategic Defense Plans**.

Download it now at **FortressShieldBook.com/plans** before you start building your fortress. You'll want these materials accessible as you work through each chapter. The PDF is completely free, includes semi-annual updates with current information, and contains everything you need to execute what you're about to learn.

Don't skip this step. The book teaches you what to do and why. Strategic Defense Plans show you exactly how to do it with tools that work today.

Join the Fortress Shield Community

To stay informed with updates, additional guides, and new tool comparisons, visit **FortressShieldBook.com/plans**. There, you'll find downloadable worksheets, printable quick start plans, and ongoing community discussions to help you stay protected.

Mission Complete: *Your decision to act begins with the shield. Stay informed, stay secure.*

"The best time to plant a tree was twenty years ago. The second-best time is now. The same is true for digital security."

- Chief Palmer

Chapter 1: Lock Your Digital Front Door

⏱ 15 minutes | Essential

CALL SIGN: GATEKEEPER, ONLY ONE KEY OPENS THE GATE. PROTECT IT WITH YOUR LIFE.

Let me tell you about the phone call that made me realize we're sending civilians into battle without armor.

It was a Tuesday morning, six months before I hung up my uniform. I'd just finished briefing some profoundly serious people about very serious threats when my phone rang.

"Uncle Alan?" The voice was shaky. My niece Emma, a senior at Colorado State, is studying accounting. Sharp kid, dean's list, the kind of person who color-codes her class schedules.

"What's wrong, Em?"

"Someone got into everything. My email, my bank account, my student loans. They changed all my passwords, and I can't get back in. The bank says someone tried to transfer my entire savings to some account in Romania."

When you've spent your career thinking about how bad actors operate, your mind immediately goes to sophisticated scenarios. Social engineering, maybe. Advanced reconnaissance. The kind of thing that takes weeks of planning.

"Walk me through exactly what happened," I said, pulling out my notebook.

Emma's problem wasn't sophisticated at all. She'd used the same password for everything: "Emma1997!" Her birth year. Her name. An exclamation point because some website told her passwords needed special characters.

One data breach at a random clothing website, and criminals had the key to her entire digital life.

You know what you learn standing watch in places where details matter? The biggest threats aren't always the sophisticated ones. Sometimes, it's the simple things that get you. Emma had essentially left her house key under the doormat with a sign pointing to it.

Why This Step Matters

Picture your home with ten doors, each with a weak lock. That's how most people live online: one password used everywhere. Crack it once, and the enemy has full access.

In my 30 years of serving in Air Force cyber operations, I've seen adversaries repeatedly exploit this mistake. They didn't storm the gates; they found one careless weakness and slipped inside. Once they were in, they moved silently, spreading deeper with every unlocked door.

That's why this first step is mission-critical: if you secure your accounts with one master key, you close off the most common path that attackers take.

The Reality Nobody Talks About

I've spent three decades protecting systems that absolutely cannot be compromised. But civilians face something we never did in the military: you're fighting the same adversaries with none of the infrastructure.

Where I worked, if someone wanted to cause trouble, they had to get past multiple checkpoints, background-checked personnel, and monitoring systems that would make Hollywood jealous. The barriers to entry were enormous.

You? You're defending against the same threats with whatever password you made up when you signed up for Netflix five years ago.

The criminal organizations targeting your family today used to focus exclusively on government and military targets. They've figured out something important: it's easier to steal from a thousand civilians than to penetrate one secure facility. And frankly, they're right.

Fortress Shield - 2026 Edition

⚠ THREAT ALERT

Passphrases are no longer invincible.

AI-powered cracking tools and spoofing scams make even clever passphrases vulnerable. If someone spoofs your bank or company's IT help desk, they can trick you into handing over sensitive information. Once they have it, they own everything: email, bank accounts, even access to your boss.

Emma's Real Problem

After we spent three weeks recovering her accounts (more paperwork than getting a security clearance, I swear), I asked her why she'd used the same password everywhere.

"I tried to use different ones," she said, "but I couldn't remember them all. I wrote them down once, but then I lost the paper. This seemed easier."

That's when it clicked for me. Emma isn't careless; she's human. Human brains are fantastic at recognizing faces and remembering stories, but asking your brain to memorize fifty random character strings is like asking a pianist to perform surgery. Wrong tool for the job.

The solution isn't to get better at memorizing passwords. The solution is to stop trying.

Chapter 1: Lock Your Digital Front Door

The One Password Rule

Your fortress begins with one master password. This is the only password you will need to memorize. Every other login, email, bank, streaming service, will be encrypted in a password manager.

The enemy thrives on chaos and repetition. Reusing the same password across accounts is like giving them the master key to your entire life. Once one site is breached, they use automated tools to test that same password across dozens of others.

So, the mission is straightforward: eliminate password reuse by entrusting your accounts to a secure, free password manager.

The Password Manager: Your Personal Weapons Locker

In the Air Force, we didn't ask people to memorize combinations to every secure container on base. We gave them one master key that opened the weapons locker, and the locker secured everything else.

That's precisely what a password manager does.

Instead of trying to remember fifty passwords, you remember one excellent password that unlocks a vault containing fifty passwords no human brain could memorize.

The criminals who got into Emma's accounts? If she'd been using a password manager, they would have gotten one random 20-character password that worked only on that clothing website. Everything else would have stayed locked down tight.

My Brother-in-Law's Conversion

Mike runs a plumbing business here in the Springs. A good guy who works with his hands, doesn't think of himself as "technical." When I started talking about password managers, his eyes glazed over.

"Alan," he said, "I can barely remember to charge my phone. You want me to learn some complicated computer program?"

So, I showed him instead of explaining. I pulled out my phone and went to log into my bank account. I tapped the password field, selected my password manager, used my fingerprint, and logged in. Three seconds, no typing.

"That's it?"

"That's it. The manager remembers the impossible passwords, so you don't have to."

Six months later, Mike called me. Someone had tried to hack his business banking. Because he was using unique passwords for everything, they got nowhere. "That password thing you showed me just saved my business."

Mike isn't technical. But he understands tools that work.

🔒 FORTIFY PROTOCOL

One master password, two-factor authentication.

- Install Bitwarden Free (or Proton Pass)
- Create your master password: a long, memorable phrase.
- Enable two-factor authentication (2FA) on your vault.
- Store your most important accounts first: email, bank, Amazon.

The End of the Passphrase Era

For years, we told people, "Make a long passphrase and you're safe." That advice worked until the attackers became more skilled. Now:

- AI cracking tools can brute-force long phrases faster
- Social engineering can trick you into revealing them
- Spoofing can make a fake login page look real, stealing your passphrase in seconds.

This is why relying solely on memory, even with a strong passphrase, is no longer sufficient. You need a password manager protecting unique credentials for every account, backed by two-factor authentication.

Step-by-Step: Building Your Digital Defense

Step 1: Choose Your Password Manager (2 minutes)

I recommend two options, both completely free for personal use:

Bitwarden - Open source, which means security experts worldwide examine the code. Great free tier works everywhere.

Proton Pass - Swiss privacy laws, made by people who understand what "secure" actually means. Includes features we'll discuss later.

Both are like having a secure container that you control entirely.

What to avoid: Chrome's built-in manager, Safari's keychain, anything made by companies that profit from advertising. If it's free and has ads, you're not the customer, you're the product.

Step 2: Create Your Master Password (5 minutes)

This is the one password you'll memorize perfectly. Make it count.

Good example: "Coffee!Mountain!Sunrise!2024"
Bad example: "password123" or "Mike1965!"

Think of it like the combination to a safe holding everything valuable. You want something you'll remember under pressure, but no one could guess even if they knew you well.

Take four unrelated words that mean something to you, add some numbers and punctuation. Make it long enough that even computers will need decades to crack it.

Choose a phrase at least sixteen characters long. Make it personal but not guessable.

Example: "Sunsets in Colorado are brighter than city lights 77."

Write it down on paper until you've memorized it completely. Then destroy the paper. This password never gets stored digitally anywhere.

Critical backup step: Most password managers offer emergency access options. Set up at least two recovery methods (like a trusted family member or recovery codes stored separately) before you start relying on the manager entirely.

Step 3: Install Everywhere (3 minutes)

Your password manager only works if it's available when you need it.

On your phone:

- **iPhone**: App Store → search for your chosen password manager
- **Android**: Play Store → same process

On your computer:

- Install the browser extension from the official store.
- Chrome Web Store, Firefox Add-ons, Safari Extensions

Test it: Make sure you can access your vault from every device you use regularly.

Step 4: Import and Upgrade (5 minutes)

Most browsers have been saving your passwords, but not in a secure manner. Let's fix that.

Import existing passwords: Your password manager can typically import passwords that your browser has saved. This gives you a starting point.

Upgrade critical accounts: Start with email and banking. Log into each account, go to security settings, let your password manager generate a new 20+ character random password. Save it and test that it works.

The beautiful part: You'll never need to remember these new passwords. That's the manager's job now.

 MISSION CRITICAL

Email is your command center.

If attackers breach your email, they can reset your bank logins, impersonate you to coworkers, and spread malware as if it came from you. Secure your email account in your password manager FIRST, with 2FA. Everything else comes after.

Two-Factor Authentication (2FA): Your Security

Checkpoint

You know what we never did with anything important? Relied on just one security measure. If someone got past the perimeter, there were guards. Past the guards, there were locks. Past the locks, there were alarms.

Two-factor authentication (2FA) works the same way for your accounts.

Why 2FA Changes Everything

Last year, my neighbor Dave received an alert that someone had attempted to log into his Gmail account from Russia. Thanks to 2FA, the criminal had Dave's password but couldn't get in without the second factor, a code from Dave's phone.

Without 2FA, that would have been game over. With it, Dave just changed his password and went about his day.

Setting Up 2FA the Right Way

Essential accounts:

- Email (this protects everything else)
- Banking and investment accounts
- Your password manager

How to do it:

1. Go to account security settings.
2. Look for "Two-Factor Authentication" or "2FA"
3. Choose "Authenticator App" (NOT text messages)
4. Download Microsoft Authenticator, Google Authenticator, or Authy
5. Scan the QR code.
6. Test it by logging out and back in

Critical point: Whenever possible, avoid using SMS codes. I've seen too many people lose accounts because text messages can be intercepted or phone numbers transferred.

Never use SMS codes; they can be intercepted.

Essential backup step: Always maintain at least two independent authenticators (your phone plus a tablet, or phone plus a hardware key). Save backup codes in your password manager as soon as possible after setup.

Passkeys: The Future Is Here

Something that would have sounded impossible when I started my career: you can now log into accounts without typing any password at all.

Passkeys use your phone or computer as a physical key. Instead of typing a password, you approve the login with your fingerprint or face.

Where they work: Google, Apple, Microsoft, many banks, government websites.

How to enable: Look for "Sign in with a passkey" in account settings. When you see it, enable it. It's more secure than even the strongest password.

Think of it like the biometric scanners we used for secure areas. Your fingerprint becomes the key, and it can't be stolen, guessed, or forgotten.

Many sites now support passwordless login. Turn them on, your manager will store them securely.

▨ RED TEAM INSIGHT

During Cold War training, we tested "secure" systems by playing the enemy. We never went through the front door. Instead, one phone call pretending to be an IT officer, or one email disguised as urgent orders, got us the access we wanted. Today's cybercriminals use the same tricks, just dressed in new uniforms. Don't let them in.

Why This Works

Think of your password vault like a hardened command bunker: thick steel doors, multiple layers of checks, and no entry without clearance.

By putting your accounts inside this fortress, you:

- Eliminate password reuse risk.
- Make phishing less effective.
- Add resilience with 2FA.
- Future-proof with passkeys.

And it costs you nothing.

Common Mistakes That Keep Me Awake

After helping family and friends set up password managers, I see the same errors repeatedly:

Using your master password anywhere else: This password should never unlock anything except your password manager. Ever.

Writing passwords on sticky notes: If you need to write something down, make it a hint about your master password, not the password itself.

Trusting text messages for 2FA: SMS can be intercepted. Use an authenticator app.

Forgetting mobile installation: You'll need access when you're away from your computer.

Skipping backup procedures: Set up recovery methods before you need them, not after you're locked out.

When Things Don't Go According to Plan

"I Forgot My Master Password"

This is why we write it down until it's memorized and set up recovery options. If you forget it before setting up recovery, you might need to start over. Better to lose access to a new password manager than to your actual accounts.

"The Password Manager Isn't Working"

Usually, the browser extension isn't enabled. Check your extensions, ensure they're active. If a website rejects the generated password, adjust the settings (remove special characters or change length).

"I Can't Access My 2FA Codes"

This is why you maintain multiple authenticators and save backup codes when setting up two-factor authentication (2FA). They're your emergency access when your phone dies or disappears.

SITREP: Threat Assessment

- Passphrases are no longer sufficient.
- 2FA is mandatory.
- Without a password manager, you are leaving multiple doors wide open.

Your Mission Parameters

Week 1:

- Password manager protecting your top 5 accounts.
- Master password memorized with backup plan.
- 2FA enabled on email and banking.

Month 1:

- All-important accounts use unique, strong passwords.
- Password manager feels automatic.
- Login process is effortless and secure, instead of stressful.

Checkpoint: Can you access your three most essential accounts using just your password manager and 2FA? If yes, you've built digital defenses that would make security professionals proud.

Mission Complete

By the end of this chapter, you should have:

- Installed a password manager.
- Created and memorized one master password.
- Secured your vault with 2FA.
- Loaded your first accounts.

Emma's call was my wake-up moment. After decades of protecting classified systems, I realized the biggest threat to people I care about wasn't foreign governments or sophisticated hackers.

Nobody had taught them how to protect themselves.

You've just changed that. In fifteen minutes, you've built defenses that will protect you for years. The same principles that secure the most sensitive facilities now secure your digital life.

The criminals who target easy victims? You're no longer one of them.

Congratulations, Gatekeeper. Your Fortress door is locked, the enemy is outside, and you've taken the first step in protecting yourself and your family.

Call to Action

Use free tools to form your Fortress, protect everything with one password.

This isn't just advice. It's your operational doctrine. Without it, your fortress crumbles. With it, your defenses stand ready.

Reference Materials: Print the Quick Start Checklist for Day 1-2 setup steps you can follow offline.

Next up: Chapter 2 shows you how to know about data breaches before the bad guys can exploit them, because early warning is half the battle.

Alan Palmer is a retired Chief Master Sergeant who spent his Air Force career protecting critical systems at locations including Schriever Space Force Base (formerly Falcon Air Force Station) and Cheyenne Mountain Complex. He now helps civilians apply proven security principles to their personal digital lives.

Chapter 2: Catch Breaches Before They Catch You

⏱ 10 minutes setup + ongoing alerts | Essential

CALL SIGN: SENTINEL, ALWAYS WATCHING.

ATTACKERS CAN'T HIDE FROM WHAT YOU CAN SEE.

My sister-in-law, Janet, called me last spring, and I could hear the fear in her voice before she even said a word.

"Alan, I think someone's watching me. These people keep calling, they know things about me they shouldn't know. They knew Tom's name" (that's her late husband), "they knew what kind of car I drive, even knew that Sarah went to CU Boulder."

Janet's not paranoid. She's the kind of person who locks her car in her own driveway and checks her credit report religiously. But she was convinced someone was physically surveilling her.

"What kind of things are they saying?" I asked.

Turns out these callers were running classic scams, fake Medicare updates, bogus car warranty extensions, "security alerts" about her bank account. But they weren't just using generic scripts. They had details that made her think the calls might be legitimate.

I had to explain something that surprised her: nobody was following her around with binoculars. Her personal information was being sold in bulk to anyone with a credit card, and scammers were using those details to make their pitches sound authentic.

"How is that legal?" she asked.

That's when I realized most people have no idea, they're fighting a war they don't even know exists.

Why This Step Matters

In the field, the sentinel is the one who sees the first smoke on the horizon and raises the alarm. In digital life, breach monitoring is your sentinel, the system that watches the horizon for signs that your data has been exposed and sold into underground markets.

Every day, companies leak data. Some breaches make headlines; most do not. Stolen usernames, emails, and passwords end up in shadow marketplaces where buyers test and resell credentials. The damage isn't always in the initial break; it's in the way it's repurposed. A credential from a small forum can become the first domino that knocks down your email, then your bank, then your workplace.

The Sentinel's mission is clear: detect exposure early, respond fast, and deny the enemy the momentum they need to cause real damage.

Chapter 2: Catch Breaches Before They Catch You

The Day Emma Became a Target

Remember my niece Emma from Chapter 1? Three months after we fixed her password situation, she got a text message that looked like it came from her bank:

"ALERT: Suspicious activity detected on account ending in 4491. Click here to verify [link]"

The scary part? Her account really did end in 4491. Six months earlier, she would have clicked that link immediately.

Instead, she paused (that two-second rule we talked about) and called me.

"Uncle Alan, this looks real, but something feels off."

"What feels off about it?"

"My bank never texts me. They always email. And why would they put my account number in a text?"

That's when I knew she got it. Emma had developed what we call "situational awareness." She wasn't just looking at what the message said, she was thinking about whether it made sense.

We called her bank directly. No suspicious activity. No alerts. Just another criminal trying to fish for login credentials.

25

⚠ THREAT ALERT

Your data is likely already for sale somewhere.

If you've used an email address for more than a year, it probably appears in at least one leaked dataset. These datasets get repackaged and traded quickly. Awareness is your first defense.

Your Sentinel Tools: What They Actually Do

You don't need a black-ops budget to gain early warning. A handful of well-regarded tools give ordinary people sentinel-level visibility into leaks and dark web circulation.

Have I Been Pwned (HIBP) - The Public Sentinel

HIBP maintains a public index of known breaches and allows you to register email addresses for notification. When your email appears in a newly discovered breach, you receive the alarm, and that alarm is your opportunity to act.

Password Manager Health Checks - The In-Vault Sentinel

Modern password managers include a "health" or "breach check" feature that cross-references the logins saved in your vault against known leaks. This alerts you when a saved credential is compromised and walks you through generating and storing a new, secure password. Detection and remediation happen in the same workflow.

Browser/Email-Integrated Monitors - Consumer-Friendly Alternatives

Some browsers and consumer privacy tools offer built-in breach monitoring. They provide a simple interface: if a stored or entered email appears in a known breach, you're notified and guided on next steps.

Paid Dark-Web Monitoring & Identity Services - The Extended Sentinel

Some paid services advertise deeper dark-web coverage: scanning private marketplaces, closed forums, or trading channels for Social Security numbers, credit info, and other sensitive PII. They may bundle identity-theft insurance and restoration support. The appeal is convenience and broader coverage; the tradeoff is cost and a trust decision, you're giving a company more of your data to scan for problems.

Fortress Shield - 2026 Edition

🔒 FORTIFY PROTOCOL

What the sentinel tools accomplish:

- Detection: Spot if your email or username appears in known leaks
- Prioritization: Show which exposed credentials are tied to high-value accounts
- Integration: When paired with your password manager, remediation is fast change, generate, and save a new password in minutes
- Escalation: If you choose a paid provider, gain broader scans and sometimes insurance/restoration support

Building Your Early Warning Network

In military operations, you never rely on one source of intelligence. You want multiple sensors giving you different perspectives on the same threats.

Your personal early warning system works the same way.

Step 1: Set Up Breach Monitoring (3 minutes)

Think of this as having a scout watching enemy movements. When criminals steal databases containing passwords, you want to know immediately if yours were in the haul.

Primary system: Have I Been Pwned

Go to haveibeenpwned.com and do this:

1. Check your current status - Enter your email address to see if you're in any known breaches.

2. Don't panic if you see results - It means you need to change passwords for those services.
3. Click "notify me" at the top of the page.
4. Enter your email and confirm through the link they send.
5. Repeat for all email addresses - work, personal, that old Hotmail account you forgot about.

When Troy Hunt (the guy who runs this service) finds your email in a new breach, you'll know within hours instead of months.

Secondary system: Password manager monitoring

Your password manager is already watching for you:

- **Bitwarden users:** Check Tools → Reports → "Data Breach Report."
- **Proton Pass users:** Settings → Security → Toggle "Dark Web Monitoring" to ON.

These services automatically cross-reference your saved passwords against known breaches.

Checkpoint: You should get confirmation emails for each address you register. Save them, they prove your early warning system is active.

Step 2: Add Firefox Monitor (Optional but Smart)

For extra coverage, set up monitor.firefox.com. Sometimes they catch breaches before other services do, and having multiple sources provides redundancy.

The process is similar: enter your email, confirm, and enable ongoing monitoring.

Fortress Shield - 2026 Edition

🚨 MISSION CRITICAL

If your primary email is exposed, act immediately.

Email is the command center of your identity. An attacker with access to your email can reset logins across services, impersonate you, and move laterally into other systems. If an alert shows your email in a breach: treat it like a red alarm. Change the credential, verify 2FA, and scan for suspicious activity.

When Your Early Warning System Activates

Last year, my neighbor Dave got a breach alert at 6 AM about a service he'd forgotten he'd even used. Some photo printing website from 2018. He followed the response protocol we'd practiced:

Within the first hour:

1. Read the alert carefully - What specific data was exposed?
2. Change the password immediately - Don't wait, don't research, just change it.
3. Check your password manager - Were you using that password anywhere else?
4. Enable 2FA if the account didn't have it already.

Within 24 hours:

1. Review account activity - Look for unauthorized access.
2. Update security questions if they were part of the breach.

3. Save the breach notification - Screenshot or forward it to yourself.

Dave was protected because he acted fast. The criminals who stole that database tried to use his old password on other sites, but he'd already changed everything.

Speed matters in breach response. The window between "data stolen" and "criminals using it" keeps shrinking as criminal operations become more automated.

SITREP: What You Must Know About Dark-Web Markets

These marketplaces aren't random noise; they're organized economies. Vendors list, categorize, and sell stolen data. Buyers test credentials en masse with automated tools. Private networks, closed forums where trusted members swap access and "recipes", amplify the speed and scope of reuse. Understanding that stolen credentials are a commodity explains why time-to-detection and response is the operational priority.

▩ RED TEAM INSIGHT

In exercises, we observed how quickly a leaked dataset can turn into an active compromise. A list labeled "retail_exposed_2023" would be picked up, and automated scripts would attempt access at hundreds of services within hours. The problem wasn't the initial theft; it was the time gap before defenders noticed and rotated credentials. That gap is the window you must close.

Creating Your Digital Aliases

You know what we never did in sensitive operations? Use our real names and addresses when we didn't have to. The same principle applies to your online life.

Email and phone aliases are like having different identities for different purposes. When one gets compromised, it doesn't affect the others.

Email Alias Strategy

Think of aliases like having different business cards for different situations:

- **Your real email:** Banking, healthcare, government, work, family.
- **Shopping alias:** Online purchases, retail accounts, delivery services.
- **Social alias:** Social media, forums, gaming accounts.
- **Newsletter alias:** Subscriptions, promotional emails.
- **Testing alias:** Free trials, one-time signups, anything suspicious.

Setting Up Email Aliases (5 minutes)

Proton Pass users:

- Generate aliases directly in your password manager
- Format: random@pass.proton.me
- Track which alias goes with which service

DuckDuckGo Email Protection:

- Go to duckduckgo.com/email.
- Get unlimited aliases like yourname@duck.com.
- They strip tracking from forwarded emails.

Firefox Relay:

- Visit relay.firefox.com.
- Get up to 5 free aliases.
- Format: randomname@mozmail.com.

All of these forward to your real email, but you can disable any alias that starts getting spam.

Phone Number Alias

Google Voice gives you a free second phone number:

1. Go to voice.google.com.
2. Choose a number in your area code.
3. Link it to your real phone.
4. Use this number for online shopping, public listings, services you don't fully trust.

Calls and texts forward to your real phone, but you can block spam numbers permanently without affecting your real number.

My brother Mike's experience: He started using his Google Voice number for Craigslist sales and contractor quotes. When spam calls started coming to that number, he just got a new Google Voice number and updated the few legitimate contacts. Try doing that with your real phone number.

Stopping Spam and Scams at the Source

Your phone and email already have defensive systems; most people don't know how to activate them.

Phone Protection (2 minutes setup)

iPhone users: Settings → Phone → "Silence Unknown Callers" (ON)

This sends unknown numbers straight to voicemail. Your contacts, recent calls, and Siri suggestions still ring through.

Android users: Phone app → Settings → "Filter spam calls" (ON)

All carriers offer free basic protection:

- Verizon: Text "BLOCK" to 7726.
- AT&T: Download "ActiveArmor" app.
- T-Mobile: "Scam Shield" app.

Email Protection (1-minute setup)

iPhone: Settings → Messages → "Filter Unknown Senders" (ON)
Android: Messages app → Settings → "Spam protection" (ON)

For spam texts: Forward them to 7726 (SPAM). This helps carriers improve their filters for everyone.

Recognizing Scam Patterns

After helping family members deal with various scams, I've noticed the same patterns:

Phone call red flags:

- Urgent threats about account closure or arrest.
- Requests for passwords, SSN, or verification codes.
- Pressure to pay with gift cards or wire transfers.

- Claims to be from "the fraud department," but they called you.

Email/text red flags:

- Generic greetings ("Dear Customer")
- Suspicious links that don't match the claimed company.
- Urgent action required with tight deadlines.
- Too-good-to-be-true offers or prizes.

The universal rule: When in doubt, verify through a separate channel. Hang up and call the official number. Go directly to the website instead of clicking links.

Your Monthly Intelligence Brief

Set a calendar reminder for the first of each month: 15 minutes to maintain your early warning systems:

Breach response (5 minutes):

- Check for any breach alerts from the past month.
- Change passwords for any flagged services immediately.
- Update 2FA on newly compromised accounts.

Alias management (5 minutes):

- Review alias performance (any getting too much spam?).
- Disable problematic aliases and create replacements.
- Update your password manager notes with new alias assignments.

System check (5 minutes):

- Verify monitoring services are still active.
- Test that aliases are still forwarding properly.
- Check spam filter effectiveness.

This routine keeps you ahead of the vast majority of internet users. Most people are reactive, they deal with problems after they happen. You're being proactive.

When Things Go Wrong (And How to Fix Them)

"I'm getting too many breach alerts."

This usually means you have accounts scattered across the internet from years of online activity. Focus on the accounts you still use actively. Consider closing accounts you no longer need.

"The breach notification email looks like spam."

Legitimate breach notifications often do look suspicious. Always verify by going directly to haveibeenpwned.com or your password manager, never by clicking links in alert emails.

"My alias stopped working."

Check if forwarding is still enabled in your alias service dashboard. Some free services quietly disable aliases after periods of inactivity. Switch to a different provider if needed.

"I think I'm being targeted specifically."

You probably are, it means your information is circulating in criminal networks. Don't engage with suspicious communications at all. Block aggressively, report spam, and remember that your aliases are protecting your real contact information.

Chapter 2: Catch Breaches Before They Catch You

Signs Your System Is Working

Week 1:

- Breach monitoring confirmation emails received.
- Spam calls decrease noticeably on your real number.
- Email aliases forward properly to your inbox.

Month 1:

- You catch and respond to your first breach alert quickly.
- Scammers start targeting your aliases instead of your real accounts.

Quarter 1:

- You recognize scam attempts easily across multiple platforms.
- Your real phone and email stay significantly cleaner.

Checkpoint: Are you receiving breach alerts and using aliases for new signups? If yes, you've just built an intelligence network that most criminals can't penetrate.

Mission Complete

By the end of this chapter, you should:

- Understand the different classes of sentinel tools and their roles.
- Have active monitoring set up on all your email addresses.
- Be using aliases to protect your real contact information.
- Be ready to act when an alert arrives.

The most effective intelligence operations are those that the enemy is unaware of. You've just built exactly that, an early warning system that spots threats before they spot you, combined with operational security that makes you a more challenging target.

Janet no longer worries about answering her phone. Emma pauses and thinks before clicking links. Dave responds to breach alerts like someone prepared, rather than panicking.

You're no longer fighting blind. You have eyes on the battlefield and the tools to respond appropriately.

You are now the Sentinel, watching the horizon, understanding the markets your data flows into, and able to respond faster than the buyers who test stolen credentials.

Call to Action

Use free tools to form your Fortress, protect everything with one password, and detect exposure before it becomes damaged.

Reference Materials: Use the Monthly Maintenance Routine to maintain your breach monitoring systems consistently.

Next up: Chapter 3 shows you how to lock down your financial identity so completely that even criminals with all your personal information can't open new accounts in your name.

When Chief Palmer isn't helping friends and family with cybersecurity, he volunteers with local veteran organizations and occasionally consults on security awareness training. He believes that thirty years of protecting national assets means nothing if he can't help protect the people he cares about.

Chapter 3: Freeze Your Credit in 15 Minutes

⏱ 15 minutes | Essential

CALL SIGN: SHIELD WALL, HOLD THE LINE. NO ENEMY CROSSES WITHOUT YOUR COMMAND.

My daughter Sarah called me from her dorm room at Colorado State, sobbing. It was her junior year, finals week, and she'd just gotten a call from a debt collector about a car loan she'd never taken out.

"Dad, they say I owe $23,000 on a BMW. I drive that beat-up Honda you helped me buy freshman year. They won't believe me when I tell them I didn't buy a car."

While Sarah was studying for her accounting exams, someone had used her name, Social Security number, and address to finance a luxury car in Denver. They'd also opened three credit cards and applied for a personal loan. By the time she found out, her credit score had dropped over two hundred points.

The campus financial aid office informed her that this happens to college students frequently. "Their information is everywhere," the counselor explained. "Student directories, scholarship applications, alumni databases. They're easy targets."

That's when I learned something that still makes me angry: the most effective identity theft protection in America costs absolutely nothing, takes fifteen minutes to set up, and most people have never heard of it.

Why This Step Matters

A credit freeze is not a gimmick. It's your legal right as a U.S. citizen, guaranteed by federal law. The Fair Credit Reporting Act requires all three major credit bureaus, Equifax, Experian, and TransUnion, to provide freezes at no cost. This right exists because lawmakers recognized the truth: identity theft thrives when consumers cannot control who has access to their credit.

When you freeze your credit, you take command of your financial perimeter. You deny criminals the ability to open new accounts in your name. You deny lenders the ability to pull your file without your consent. You establish a protective wall that remains in place until you decide to lift it.

⚠ THREAT ALERT

Fraudsters don't need your bank login to steal your identity.

They apply for new accounts in your name. A freeze, that's free, permanent, and federally guaranteed, blocks them completely.

Chapter 3: Freeze Your Credit in 15 Minutes

The Turning Point: The Equifax Breach

In September 2017, Equifax admitted it had been breached. The scale was staggering: 147 million people had their personal information exposed. Names, birth dates, Social Security numbers, and in some cases driver's license data were stolen.

Equifax's failure became a national wake-up call. Congress acted, amending the law to require the bureaus to make credit freezes free and permanent. What had once cost money now became a right.

The breach taught us a hard lesson: we cannot rely on institutions to safeguard our data. A credit freeze is how you regain control.

Why Credit Freezes Are Your Financial Nuclear Option

You know what we did with the most sensitive materials when I was stationed at missile sites? We didn't just put them behind one lock. We put them in secure containers, inside secure rooms, inside secure buildings, with multiple people required to access anything important.

A credit freeze works the same way for your financial identity. It locks your credit file so tight that even you can't open new accounts without explicitly unlocking it first.

Think about how identity theft actually works: criminals don't usually drain your existing bank accounts (banks have fraud detection for that). Instead, they open new accounts in your name. Credit cards, car loans, mortgages, cell phone contracts. They build a whole financial life using your identity, and you don't find out until the bills come due.

A credit freeze stops this completely. When someone tries to open an account in your name, the lender can't access your

43

credit file. No credit file access means no approved application. It's like putting a steel door between criminals and your financial future.

Lisa's Story: When the Shield Wall Was Missing

Lisa was a working mother in Ohio who never froze her credit. When her Social Security number was stolen in a healthcare breach, someone used it to buy a $30,000 car in her name. She discovered the fraud only after collection agencies started calling.

It took six months, multiple police reports, and countless hours on the phone with lenders and lawyers before she cleared her name. Her credit score was damaged, her mortgage refinance was delayed, and the emotional toll was overwhelming.

If Lisa had placed a credit freeze, when the thief's loan application reached the lender, the bureau would have returned a straightforward answer: file frozen, no report available. The loan would have been denied immediately. Lisa would never have known an attempt had been made.

The difference between months of misery and total peace of mind was one free, federally guaranteed action she had never taken.

The College Campus Hunting Ground

After helping Sarah recover her credit (which took three weeks and more paperwork than a security clearance application), I started asking around. Identity theft on college campuses is practically an epidemic.

Students have their information scattered across dozens of databases: admissions records, financial aid applications, student directories, scholarship programs, alumni networks. They often live in dorms with unattended mail, use public Wi-Fi for everything, and haven't yet learned to be suspicious.

Sarah's roommate had the same thing happen six months earlier. Different criminals, same pattern. Someone got her information from a data breach at a scholarship website and went shopping for luxury items on her credit.

The frustrating part? Both Sarah and her roommate could have prevented the entire mess with fifteen minutes of effort.

What a Freeze Is, and Is Not

A credit freeze is a block placed on your file at each of the three bureaus: Equifax, Experian, and TransUnion. With the freeze in place:

- No lender can access your credit without your authorization.
- No new account can be opened in your name.
- Existing accounts remain active and unaffected.

What a freeze is not:

- It's not a fraud alert. Fraud alerts only warn lenders; they don't stop accounts from being opened.

- It's not credit monitoring. Monitoring notifies you after damage occurs. A freeze prevents it.
- It's not the same as a "credit lock." Locks are app-based, sometimes paid, and legally weaker. A freeze is the stronger, no-cost option written into law.

The Three-Bureau Reality

Most people don't understand, there isn't one credit reporting system in America. There are three independent companies (Equifax, Experian, and TransUnion), and they don't talk to each other.

When someone applies for credit, the lender usually checks with just one of these bureaus. If that bureau's file is frozen, the application gets rejected. But if the other two aren't frozen, criminals can simply try to find a different lender that checks a different bureau.

It's like having three separate locks on your front door. Locking one doesn't protect you if burglars can walk through the other two.

This is why credit monitoring services (those that charge monthly fees) are often security theater. They tell you after someone steals your identity. Freezes prevent the theft from happening in the first place.

Chapter 3: Freeze Your Credit in 15 Minutes

My Neighbor's Wake-Up Call

Dave, who lives two houses down from me, learned this the hard way. He'd been paying $20 a month for credit monitoring for years. I felt pretty good about his protection.

Then someone opened a Home Depot credit card in his name and charged $8,000 worth of tools and materials. His monitoring service sent him an alert three weeks later.

"Alan," he said, "What good is knowing someone stole my identity after they already did it?"

That's when I walked him through the freeze process. It took longer to explain than to actually do it.

🔒 FORTIFY PROTOCOL

The shield wall has three panels.

- Contact Experian.com, follow their instructions, and place a freezer.
- Contact Equifax.com, repeat the process.
- Contact TransUnion.com, complete the set.
- After your freezes are in place, practice unlocking and re-freezing at one bureau, so you know how to act quickly when you legitimately need new credit.

- Important: Don't be tricked into paying for "credit lock" services unless you fully understand the difference and decide the convenience is worth it. The freeze you already have a right to is stronger, and it's free.

Step-by-Step: Locking Down All Three Bureaus

You need to create an account with each credit bureau and freeze your file. Each one is independent, so you'll do this three times with slight variations.

Phase 1: Equifax (5 minutes)

Start with Equifax, they've had enough security breaches that they've actually made their freeze process pretty straightforward.

1. Go to myequifax.com
2. Click "Sign Up" (top right corner)
3. Create your account with personal information
4. Navigate to "Credit Lock & Alerts" in the main menu
5. Find the "Equifax Credit Lock" section
6. Click "Lock It" or toggle the switch to "On"
7. Save your PIN in your password manager immediately

What you'll see: A confirmation screen saying "Your Equifax credit is locked" with a green shield icon.

Save this in your password manager: Create an entry called "Equifax Credit Freeze" with your login credentials and PIN.

Phase 2: Experian (5 minutes)

Experian's process involves answering security questions based on your credit history. These can be tricky, they're designed to trip up people who aren't really you.

1. Go to experian.com/freeze/center.html
2. Click "Add a Security Freeze"
3. Create an account or log in if you have one
4. Answer the security questions (based on your actual credit history)
5. Submit your freeze request
6. Save your 10-digit PIN in your password manager

Security question tips: These come from your credit file, so they might reference old addresses, previous loans, or accounts you've forgotten about. If none of the multiple-choice answers seem right, "None of the above" is often correct.

What confirms success: Email with subject line "Security Freeze Confirmation"

Phase 3: TransUnion (5 minutes)

TransUnion is slightly different, they use login credentials instead of PINs for freeze management.

1. Go to transunion.com/credit-freeze.
2. Click "Add freeze."
3. Create an account and complete identity verification.
4. Submit your freeze request.
5. Save your login credentials in your password manager.

Identity verification: TransUnion might ask you to upload a photo ID or answer additional questions. This is normal, they're trying to verify you're really you.

Success indicator: Dashboard shows "Security freeze: Active" with a lock icon.

Critical backup steps: Each bureau has different recovery procedures if you lose access. Set up security questions you can remember, consider designating a trusted family member for emergency access, and save all confirmation emails in a separate location from your password manager.

Verification: Making Sure It Worked

After freezing all three bureaus, you should have:

- Three confirmation emails (one from each bureau).
- Three password manager entries with all access credentials.
- Visual confirmation on each bureau's website showing frozen/locked status.

Field test: Try signing up for a free credit monitoring service like Credit Karma. It should tell you that your credit files are locked and can't be accessed. That's precisely what you want to see.

Chapter 3: Freeze Your Credit in 15 Minutes

When Sarah Tested Her Freezes

After we got Sarah's credit cleaned up and frozen, she decided to test the system by applying for a store credit card during a back-to-school promotion.

The application was rejected immediately. "Unable to access credit file," the system said.

Sarah called me, worried she'd done something wrong. "Dad, I can't get approved for anything now."

"That's the point," I told her. "Now you control who gets access to your credit, not criminals."

🚨 MISSION CRITICAL

Freeze your credit now, before you need it.

Waiting until after identity theft is like building a wall after invaders are already inside. Freeze your credit today and stop attackers cold.

Living with Frozen Credit: Temporary Lifts

The beautiful thing about credit freezes: you have complete control over them. When you need to apply for legitimate credit (car loan, apartment rental, new phone service), you can temporarily lift the freeze.

The process:

1. Log into the bureau's website (use your password manager)
2. Select "Temporarily lift freeze."
3. Choose duration: anywhere from 1 hour to 30 days.
4. Effect is usually immediate.

Which bureau to lift? When in doubt, lift all three. Some lenders only check one bureau, but you won't know which one ahead of time. Better safe than sorry.

Practical Lessons: Living with a Freeze

A freeze is powerful, but it's also practical. Common questions:

Will a freeze affect my existing credit cards? No. You can keep using your cards as usual. The freeze only blocks new accounts from being opened.

What if I need new credit? You can temporarily lift a freeze. Options:

- **Time-based lift:** Unfreeze your file for a specific number of days.
- **Lender-specific lift:** Unfreeze only for a single creditor.

Both can be done online in minutes with a PIN or password.

Does a freeze affect job applications, rentals, or insurance? Sometimes. Employers, landlords, or insurers may need access to your credit file. In those cases, you temporarily lift the freeze, then reapply it when the check is complete.

Is a freeze permanent? It stays until you remove it. Unlike fraud alerts, it doesn't expire.

Real-world example: When my son bought his first house last year, his mortgage broker told him to lift all three freezes for two weeks during the underwriting process. He did it online in about three minutes, got his loan approved, then re-froze everything. Total cost: zero. Total time: less than five minutes.

Recovery planning: Test the lift/restore process on one bureau before you need it for a real application. Make sure you can access all three accounts and understand each system. Document the process for family members who might need to help you in an emergency.

Why This Works

Lenders are gatekeepers. They won't approve credit without seeing your file. By freezing your file, you've locked the gate. Even if a thief has your Social Security number, the system won't open for them.

Criminals look for the easiest target. If your credit file is frozen, they move on.

Common Misconceptions That Drive Me Crazy

After helping family and friends set up freezes, I keep hearing the same worried questions:

"Won't this hurt my credit score?"
No. Freezing has zero impact on your credit score. Your score is based on how you handle credit you already have, not whether new credit can be opened.

"What if I need credit in an emergency?"
You can lift a freeze in minutes, 24/7, from any internet

connection. Most financial emergencies aren't so urgent that you can't take five minutes to unfreeze your credit first.

"Don't I need to tell my bank about this?

No. Freezes only affect new account applications, your existing credit cards, bank accounts, and loans keep working normally.

"Is this the same as credit monitoring?"

Completely different. Monitoring tells you when someone has stolen your identity. Freezing prevents them from stealing it in the first place.

SITREP: Threat Assessment

- Over 1 million cases of identity theft were reported in the U.S. last year
- New-account fraud remains one of the most common forms, driven by stolen SSNs sold in bulk on dark-web "identity kits"
- The going rate for a complete identity package, SSN, date of birth, and address, is less than $20

Your SITREP is blunt: A credit freeze is the single most effective step you can take to deny thieves the ability to weaponize your identity.

RED TEAM INSIGHT

In one simulation, we tested the ease of opening a credit card using stolen data. With nothing but an SSN and address, applications sailed through in hours. The only barrier that stopped the fraud cold was the credit freeze. The lesson was unmistakable: stronger passwords or "watchdog services" couldn't help here. The only defense was shutting down the credit pull itself.

When the System Doesn't Cooperate

Sometimes the freeze process hits snags. How to handle the most common problems:

"The website won't accept my information."

This usually means there's a mismatch between what you're entering and what's in their system.

- Use your exact legal name as it appears on government ID
- Try address variations: "Street" vs "St.", "Apartment" vs "Apt."
- Clear your browser cache and try again.
- Use a different browser if the first one doesn't work.

"I can't answer the security questions correctly."

These questions come from your actual credit history, so they can be surprisingly tricky.

- Think about old addresses, previous jobs, and former loans.
- "None of the above" is often the correct answer if nothing seems to fit.
- Some sites offer photo ID upload as an alternative to questions.

"I forgot my PIN already."

This is why we save everything in password managers immediately.

- Log into the bureau's website.
- Use "Forgot PIN" or "Reset PIN" option.
- Update your password manager with the new PIN.

"I need to apply for credit, but I forgot how to lift the freeze"

Each bureau's website has clear instructions for temporary lifts. Log in, look for "Lift freeze" or "Thaw credit," choose your timeframe, and you're done.

Emergency procedures: If you can't access your password manager, most bureaus offer phone support for freeze management. Keep their customer service numbers written down separately. Have a backup plan for accessing your accounts if your primary method fails.

Chapter 3: Freeze Your Credit in 15 Minutes

The Quarterly Maintenance Check

Set a calendar reminder every three months to verify your freezes are still active. This takes about five minutes:

The checklist:

- Log into each bureau to confirm freeze status.
- Update contact information if you've moved.
- Test your password manager access to all three accounts.
- Verify you can still access your PINs/credentials.

Why quarterly? Because these companies sometimes have "system updates" that affect freeze status. Better to catch problems when you're not in a hurry to apply for credit.

Family Maintenance Day

Every January, I help my family members check their freeze status. Sarah, my son, my wife, and even my brother Mike. We spend one Saturday morning making sure everyone's protection is still active.

Last year, we discovered that Experian had "upgraded" their system and disabled some older freezes. Good thing we checked. We re-enabled everything and updated password managers with new credentials.

It takes about an hour for the whole family, and then we go out for lunch. Small price for peace of mind.

Success Metrics: You'll Know It's Working

Immediate results:

- Three confirmation emails in your inbox.
- All bureau websites show "frozen" or "locked" status.
- Credit applications get rejected until you lift the freeze.

Medium-term verification:

- Credit monitoring services can't access your files
- Pre-approved credit offers stop coming in the mail
- You successfully lift and re-freeze for legitimate applications

Long-term protection:

- No unauthorized accounts appear on credit reports
- Your credit score remains stable and under your control
- Family members ask you to help them set up freezes too

Checkpoint: Can you log into all three bureaus and see "frozen" status? Can you temporarily lift a freeze and restore it? If yes, you've just built a financial fortress that stops the vast majority of identity theft attempts.

Chapter 3: Freeze Your Credit in 15 Minutes

Why This Matters More Than Technical Security

I spent three decades protecting systems that could end civilization if compromised. But you know what keeps me awake at night? Watching good people like Sarah get hurt by criminals who are basically checking if doors are locked.

Credit freezes are the equivalent of locking your front door. Simple, effective, and free. The fact that most Americans are unaware of them (or think they're too complicated) is a failure of education, not intelligence.

You've just fixed that failure for yourself and anyone you teach this to.

Sarah's credit was fully recovered within six months. More importantly, she now helps her friends set up freezes during their freshman orientation week. Last count, she's protected about fifteen classmates from the same experience she had.

The criminals who target college students? They're looking for easy victims with unlocked credit files. Sarah and her friends are no longer easy victims.

Neither are you.

Mission Complete

By the end of this chapter, you should:

- Recognize that a credit freeze is your legal right, free of charge, and federally backed
- Understand the difference between freezes, fraud alerts, locks, and monitoring
- Know what to expect when living with a freeze, including temporary lifts
- Have all three credit bureaus frozen with secure access management

- Be convinced that freezing your credit at all three bureaus is non-negotiable

Call to Action

Use free tools to form your Fortress, protect everything with one password, and hold the line with a shield wall no thief can cross.

Reference Materials: Keep the Oh-No Playbook handy for identity theft response procedures and emergency contact information.

Next up: Chapter 4 shows you the daily habits that keep your entire Fortress Shield strong with just seconds of effort.

Chief Palmer's daughter, Sarah, graduated summa cum laude and now works as a forensic accountant, helping investigate financial crimes. She credits her experience with identity theft for sparking her interest in financial security. "Dad always says the best security comes from understanding how the bad guys think," she notes.

Chapter 4: Daily Habits That Take Seconds

🕐 10 minutes setup + ongoing alerts | Essential

CALL SIGN: CLOAK. HIDE IN PLAIN SIGHT. WHAT THEY CAN'T SEE, THEY CAN'T SELL.

My brother-in-law Mike called me last winter, and I could tell he was embarrassed before he said a word.

"Alan, I think I messed up. Bad."

Mike's the kind of guy who rebuilds truck engines in his garage and can fix anything with moving parts. But he'd clicked on a link in an email that looked like it came from his bank, entered his login credentials on a fake website, and handed criminals the keys to his business account.

"The weird thing is," he said, "I knew it might be fake. Something felt off about the email. But I was rushing between job sites, it was on my phone, and I just... clicked."

That's when I realized something important: even smart, careful people make mistakes when they're tired, distracted, or in a hurry. The strongest password in the world doesn't help if you hand it to criminals yourself.

The solution isn't being perfect all the time. The solution is building habits that protect you even when you're not at your best.

Why This Step Matters

If Chapter 3 built your shield wall, this chapter puts on your cloak and teaches you to move with operational discipline.

The modern battlefield isn't just hackers and thieves, it's data brokers. These companies collect your personal details, build profiles on your habits, and sell them to the highest bidder. Unlike criminals, they operate legally, quietly harvesting data from public records, online purchases, social media, and app activity.

The result? Your phone number, address, relatives, income bracket, and buying preferences can all be bought by anyone willing to pay. Marketers use it to target you. Scammers use it to impersonate your bank or employer. Attackers use it to craft spear-phishing messages so convincing you might not spot the trap.

Cloaking your personal data makes you a harder target. You won't stop all data collection, that's impossible, but you can deny brokers the easy wins. Think of it as taking your name off the street signs so strangers can't find your door.

Combined with daily security habits that work automatically, you create a defense that operates even when you're not thinking about security.

⚠ THREAT ALERT

Your data is a commodity, and it's for sale legally.

Data brokers buy and sell your personal information the way supermarkets stock products. Anyone can purchase it. Awareness is your first defense.

Why Perfect People Get Hacked

After thirty years of watching security failures, I've learned that the biggest breaches almost never happen because of sophisticated attacks. They happen because someone skipped a basic step they knew they should take.

I've seen multi-million-dollar security systems compromised because someone disabled automatic updates to avoid restart notifications. I've watched experienced professionals fall for phishing emails that would have fooled nobody if they'd just slowed down for two seconds.

Mike isn't careless. But he was trying to manage his business from a phone while driving between work sites. In that moment, the part of his brain that evaluates links wasn't fully engaged.

That's human nature, and there's no point fighting it. Instead, we build systems that work even when we're running on autopilot.

The Day My Nephew Learned About Automatic Defense

My nephew Jake is a college sophomore, computer science major, knows more about programming than I ever will. Last summer, he came to visit with his laptop running so slowly he could barely check email.

"What happened to this thing?" I asked.

"I don't know. It's been getting worse for months. I think it's just old."

I ran a malware scan. Found seventeen different infections, some dating back almost a year. His antivirus was six months out of date, his operating system hadn't been updated since he bought the laptop, and his browser was running extensions he didn't remember installing.

"Jake, when's the last time you updated anything?"

"I kept getting those annoying pop-ups asking me to restart for updates. I always clicked 'remind me later' because I was in the middle of something."

That's when I explained something that changed how he thinks about computer security: the best defenses are the ones that work automatically, even when you're not thinking about security at all.

Chapter 4: Daily Habits That Take Seconds

Step 1: Automate Your Fortress (5 minutes setup)

In military operations, we never relied on people remembering to do critical tasks. Important stuff happened automatically, with manual oversight only for exceptional situations.

Your digital security should work the same way.

Turn On Auto-Updates Everywhere

Every software update closes security holes that criminals are actively exploiting. When you delay updates, you're essentially leaving known vulnerabilities open for attackers to use.

On your phone:

- **iPhone:** Settings → App Store → "App Updates" (ON)
- **Android:** Play Store → Profile → Settings → "Auto-update apps" (ON)

On your computer:

- **Windows:** Settings → "Windows Update" → enable automatic updates
- **Mac:** System Settings → "Software Update" → enable automatic updates

In your browser:

- Chrome, Firefox, Safari all update automatically by default
- Check: Menu → Help → "About [Browser]" should show "up to date"

Critical point: Don't click "remind me later" forever. These aren't suggestions, they're security patches for known vulnerabilities.

65

Backup consideration: Auto-updates can occasionally break something. Set your computer to create automatic restore points (Windows) or Time Machine backups (Mac) so you can roll back if needed. Set active hours to prevent updates during work time.

Install an Ad Blocker (2 minutes)

You know what the most common attack vector is these days? Malicious advertisements on legitimate websites. Criminals buy ad space on popular sites and use it to distribute malware or redirect visitors to phishing pages.

Ad blockers don't just improve your browsing experience, they're security tools.

For Chrome/Firefox: Install uBlock Origin from the official extension store
For Safari: Enable built-in content blockers in Settings → Safari → Extensions
For mobile: Use Brave browser (built-in blocking) or install a content blocker app

Look for the uBlock Origin icon in your toolbar. When it's working, you'll see dramatically fewer ads and much faster page loading.

Fallback plan: Keep a second browser without ad blocking for sites that absolutely require ads to function. Most legitimate sites work fine with blockers, but you want options if needed.

Jake's Transformation

After we cleaned up Jake's laptop and automated his defenses, I asked him to check back in three months.

"How's your computer running?"

"Perfect. And I haven't thought about updates once. They just happen."

Chapter 4: Daily Habits That Take Seconds

That's the goal, security that works while you're focused on more important things.

Step 2: Develop Your Digital Reflexes (Immediate)

Military training is really about building reflexes, automatic responses to dangerous situations that happen faster than conscious thought. You need the same thing for digital threats.

The Two-Second Rule

Before clicking any link (email, text, social media, anywhere), pause for two seconds and ask:

1. Was I expecting this message?
2. Does the sender make sense?
3. Does the urgency feel manufactured?

On desktop: Hover over links to see the real destination in the bottom-left corner
On mobile: Long-press links to see a preview popup

This tiny pause prevents the vast majority of successful phishing attacks.

Building the habit: Practice deliberately on legitimate emails first. Make the pause automatic before it matters for suspicious ones. If you have family members who can help, ask them to quiz you occasionally on suspicious versus legitimate messages.

Mike's New Habit

After Mike's close call with the fake bank email, I taught him the two-second rule. He was skeptical.

"Alan, I get hundreds of emails a day. I can't analyze every single link."

"You don't analyze them. You just pause. Most phishing emails fall apart under two seconds of attention."

67

Six months later, Mike texted me a screenshot of an obvious phishing email. "Two-second rule just saved me again. This one was pretending to be from my insurance company, but the link went to some random website in Russia."

The pause had become automatic. He wasn't consciously analyzing threats anymore, his brain was just taking a moment to process what it was seeing.

Step 3: Disappearing from Data Broker Radar

Remember Janet from Chapter 2 with scammers who knew too much about her? Data brokers are the source of that information, companies that collect and sell personal details legally.

Think of them as legal intelligence-gathering operations that sell to anyone: advertisers, marketers, and unfortunately, criminals.

The Legal Backstory: Why Cloaking Matters

Unlike your right to freeze your credit, there's no single federal law that forces data brokers to delete your information on request. That's the loophole they profit from.

Federal law: The U.S. has no overarching privacy law like Europe's GDPR. Instead, there's a patchwork, HIPAA for health records, GLBA for financial institutions, COPPA for children, but nothing broad enough to cover everyday consumer data.

State-level rights: In recent years, states like California, Virginia, Colorado, Connecticut, Utah, Oregon, Texas, and Delaware have passed laws requiring brokers to honor deletion or opt-out requests. If you live in one of those states, the law is on your side. If you don't, many brokers still comply voluntarily to avoid lawsuits.

Industry pressure: FTC fines and lawsuits have pushed brokers into offering opt-outs nationwide, even if the law doesn't force them.

Your SITREP: Cloaking isn't just defense; it's part of a larger consumer-rights movement pushing back against surveillance capitalism.

The Shadow Industry

Data brokers maintain massive databases where your life is reduced to a file, bundled into lists like:

- "Homeowners over 60 with pets"
- "Parents with teenage drivers"
- "Frequent online shoppers in ZIP code 37809"

It sounds harmless until you realize the same lists are used for fraud. Criminals buy "fresh" data on households with good credit, then launch targeted scams.

Henry's Story: When Broker Data Fuels a Scam

Henry was a retired Air Force mechanic living quietly in Florida. One afternoon he answered a call from a man who seemed to know him well. The caller addressed Henry by his full name, confirmed his home address, and even mentioned the names of his wife and granddaughter.

Then came the hook: "Your granddaughter's been in an accident. She's unconscious. The hospital needs a credit card immediately to authorize treatment."

Panicked, Henry nearly gave up his card number. What stopped him was a neighbor arriving at the door, breaking the trance of fear. Later, he discovered his granddaughter was safe at school. The scammer had pieced together enough of Henry's life, phone, relatives, address, from a data broker profile to craft a convincing emergency.

The information was legal to buy. The scam was not. But the damage was almost done.

Had Henry's information been cloaked, had his address and relatives been scrubbed from broker sites, the scammer's pitch would have lacked the credibility that nearly convinced him.

🔒 FORTIFY PROTOCOL'

Opt-out is your cloak.

Search for yourself on major people-search and broker sites

File opt-out requests at each site

Use automation services (see below) to handle bulk removals

Re-check quarterly, brokers repopulate data over time

The Big Four Targets

Start with these, they're the major suppliers that feed smaller brokers:

- Whitepages.com
- Spokeo.com
- BeenVerified.com
- PeopleFinder.com

The removal process:

1. Search for yourself on each site (prepare to be disturbed by what they know)
2. Find their opt-out page (usually buried in the privacy policy)
3. Fill out the removal request (they'll want email verification)
4. Wait 48 hours and verify you're gone

5. Mark your calendar to repeat quarterly (they get new data constantly)

Time investment: About 30 minutes the first time, 15 minutes every three months after that.

Pro tip from helping my family: Use an email alias for the verification process. Don't give them your real email address just to remove your real email address from their database.

Janet's Results

After Janet completed her first round of removals, the scammer calls dropped dramatically. Not completely gone (some information had already been sold to criminal organizations before she opted out), but the change was remarkable.

Six months later, she told me, "I can actually answer my phone again without wondering if it's someone trying to steal from me."

The Automation Option - Optional but High-Value

Doing removals yourself is always free, but it takes time. If you'd rather spend your Saturday living life instead of clicking opt-out forms, there are paid services that will do it for you.

Optery - Transparency First

- Free tier shows you where your info is exposed
- Paid "Autopilot" tier automatically files and re-files removals
- Unique value: they also publish free DIY guides, so you know what's being done on your behalf

Incogni - Budget-Friendly

- Created by the team behind Surfshark VPN
- Automates requests under laws like CCPA and GDPR, even if you don't live in those jurisdictions
- Easy dashboard, good entry point for non-technical users

DeleteMe - Veteran Service

- One of the oldest removal services
- Provides quarterly reports showing what was found and removed
- More expensive than newer competitors, but well established

Other players include Kanary and OneRep, both automate removals and offer family plans.

Cost: Most of these run about $7-12/month. For some readers, that's a small price to avoid the time and frustration of DIY.

🚨 MISSION CRITICAL

Remove your home address and phone number from public broker sites immediately.

Even partial removal makes you significantly harder to impersonate. Paid services can accelerate this, but don't skip the step entirely.

Practical Lessons: Living Under the Cloak

This isn't one-and-done. Data brokers repopulate data constantly.

- Opt-outs vary. Some are simple; others are buried in fine print
- Automation saves time. Paid services handle repetition, but you still need quarterly checks
- Partial removal is powerful. Even scrubbing just the top 20 broker sites makes impersonation far harder

Step 4: Use Aliases Like Operational Security (3 minutes setup)

You know what we never did in sensitive environments? Use our real names and contact information when we didn't have to. Same principle applies to your online life.

When to use your real information:

- Banking, healthcare, government services
- Work-related accounts
- Legal documents and contracts
- Family communications

When to use aliases:

- Online shopping and retail accounts
- Newsletter subscriptions and promotional emails
- Social media accounts (where allowed)
- Free trials and one-time signups
- Any service you don't completely trust

Email Alias Strategy

Think of aliases like having different business cards for different situations:

- **Your real email:** Banking, healthcare, government, work, family
- **Shopping alias:** Online purchases, retail accounts, delivery services
- **Social alias:** Social media, forums, gaming accounts
- **Newsletter alias:** Subscriptions, promotional emails
- **Testing alias:** Free trials, one-time signups, anything suspicious

Setting Up Email Aliases (5 minutes)

Proton Pass users:

- Generate aliases directly in your password manager
- Format: random@pass.proton.me
- Track which alias goes with which service

DuckDuckGo Email Protection:

- Go to duckduckgo.com/email
- Get unlimited aliases like yourname@duck.com
- They strip tracking from forwarded emails

Firefox Relay:

- Visit relay.firefox.com
- Get up to 5 free aliases
- Format: randomname@mozmail.com

All of these forward to your real email, but you can disable any alias that starts getting spam.

Redundancy planning: Set up aliases with multiple providers so you're not dependent on one service. Document which alias serves which purpose in your password manager so you can maintain the system consistently.

Phone Number Alias

Google Voice gives you a free second phone number:

1. Go to voice.google.com
2. Choose a number in your area code
3. Link it to your real phone
4. Use this number for online shopping, public listings, services you don't fully trust

Calls and texts forward to your real phone, but you can block spam numbers permanently without affecting your real number.

Backup consideration: Google Voice requires a real phone number to set up. If you lose access to your Google account, you might lose the Voice number too. Keep your most important services on your real number.

My Sister-in-Law's Email Strategy

Janet (remember her from earlier?) now uses four different email addresses:

- **Real email:** Banking, healthcare, family, work
- **Shopping email:** All retail purchases and delivery services
- **Newsletter email:** Subscriptions, promotions, marketing
- **Burner email:** Free trials, one-time signups, anything suspicious

When her shopping email started getting spam, she just switched to a new alias and updated her important retail accounts. Her real email stayed clean.

"It's like having different phone numbers for different purposes," she told me. "When one gets too much junk, I just get a new one."

Step 5: Stopping Spam and Scams at the Source

Your phone and email already have defensive systems; most people don't know how to activate them.

Phone Protection (2 minutes setup)

iPhone users: Settings → Phone → "Silence Unknown Callers" (ON)

This sends unknown numbers straight to voicemail. Your contacts, recent calls, and Siri suggestions still ring through.

Android users: Phone app → Settings → "Filter spam calls" (ON)

All carriers offer free basic protection:

- Verizon: Text "BLOCK" to 7726
- AT&T: Download "ActiveArmor" app
- T-Mobile: "Scam Shield" app

Email Protection (1 minute setup)

iPhone: Settings → Messages → "Filter Unknown Senders" (ON)

Android: Messages app → Settings → "Spam protection" (ON)

For spam texts: Forward them to 7726 (SPAM). This helps carriers improve their filters for everyone.

Step 6: Recognizing Scam Patterns

After helping family members deal with various scams, I've noticed the same patterns:

Phone call red flags:

- Urgent threats about account closure or arrest
- Requests for passwords, SSN, or verification codes
- Pressure to pay with gift cards or wire transfers
- Claims to be from "the fraud department," but they called you

Email/text red flags:

- Generic greetings ("Dear Customer")
- Suspicious links that don't match the claimed company
- Urgent action required with tight deadlines
- Too-good-to-be-true offers or prizes

The universal rule: When in doubt, verify through a separate channel. Hang up and call the official number. Go directly to the website instead of clicking links.

Your Monthly Intelligence Brief

Set a calendar reminder for the first of each month: 15 minutes to maintain your early warning systems:

Automation check (3 minutes):

- Verify auto-updates are still working.
- Check ad blocker is active.
- Update browser extensions if needed.

Data broker removal (5 minutes):

- Remove yourself from 2-3 major broker sites.
- Verify that previous removals are still effective.
- Document any new broker sites you discover.

Alias management (3 minutes):

- Review alias performance (any getting too much spam?).
- Disable problematic aliases and create replacements.
- Update your password manager notes with new alias assignments.

System check (4 minutes):

- Verify your two-second pause is becoming automatic.
- Check spam filter effectiveness.
- Test that aliases are still forwarding properly.

This routine keeps you ahead of the vast majority of internet users. Most people are reactive, they deal with problems after they happen. You're being proactive.

When Things Go Wrong (And How to Fix Them)

"Auto-updates are disrupting my work."

Set "active hours" in Windows or Mac to prevent updates during your work schedule. Updates will happen overnight when you're not using the computer.

"My ad blocker is breaking websites I need."

Temporarily disable it for specific problematic sites or add those sites to your whitelist. Most website breakage from ad blockers is temporary, try refreshing the page.

"I keep forgetting to use aliases."

Start with just one category (shopping) and use aliases only for retail purchases. Once that becomes habit, expand to other categories.

Chapter 4: Daily Habits That Take Seconds

"The monthly routine takes too long."
Break it into smaller pieces. Do automation checks one week, data broker removal the next. The important thing is consistency, not doing everything at once.

"Family members won't follow these habits."
Focus on the automated protections first (auto-updates and ad blockers). These work without requiring behavior change. Add the manual habits gradually.

Recovery planning: Document your habit-based systems so family members can help maintain them if you're unable to. Include instructions for accessing your monitoring services and alias management systems.

SITREP: Threat Assessment

- Hundreds of active data brokers operate in the U.S.
- Profiles often include addresses, phone numbers, relatives, and purchase history
- Opt-out rights exist in some states, but compliance elsewhere is voluntary
- Paid services aren't mandatory, but they can save hours and improve consistency

RED TEAM INSIGHT

In a phishing simulation, we built messages using nothing but broker data. The scam emails looked like they came from a target's real bank, referencing their spouse by name. Nearly half clicked. When broker data was scrubbed, the success rate dropped by more than 60%. Cloaking directly reduces attack success, whether you do it yourself or hire a service to help.

Success Milestones

Week 1:

- Auto-updates enabled and working without disrupting workflow.
- Ad blocker installed and reducing page load times.
- You catch yourself pausing before clicking suspicious links.
- First round of data broker removals completed.

Month 1:

- Aliases become your default for new signups.
- Monthly security routine feels manageable and productive.
- You recognize and ignore obvious scam attempts automatically.
- Data broker search results show less of your information.

Quarter 1:

- Security habits feel natural rather than forced.
- You help family members improve their digital safety.
- Attempted scams bounce off your defenses without causing stress.
- Your cloak is maintained with quarterly re-checks.

Checkpoint: Are your devices updating automatically, do you pause before clicking suspicious links, and have you removed yourself from major data broker sites? If yes, your

Chapter 4: Daily Habits That Take Seconds

security habits are now working for you instead of against you.

Why Habits Matter More Than Knowledge

I've trained thousands of people in security procedures over the years. The ones who stayed secure weren't necessarily the smartest or most technically knowledgeable. They were the ones who built good habits and stuck to them.

Mike didn't become a cybersecurity expert after his close call. He just developed the habit of pausing before clicking links. That habit has saved him multiple times since then.

Jake didn't learn to analyze malware or understand network security. He just automated his defenses and developed basic caution about unexpected messages.

Henry's near-miss taught him to verify emergency calls through separate channels, and to understand that the personal information scammers use comes from data brokers he can opt out from.

These aren't complex skills. They're simple habits that become automatic with practice.

Mission Complete

At the end of this chapter, you should:

- Understand what data brokers are and how they profit from your personal life
- Recognize the uneven legal protections, strong in some states, weak at the federal level
- See the real danger through Henry's story: how a scammer weaponized broker data against him
- Know your options: DIY for free, or paid services for convenience and consistency

- Have automated your core defenses (updates, ad blocking)
- Developed the two-second pause reflex
- Be using aliases to protect your real contact information
- Be ready to maintain your cloak with periodic re-checks

Your digital life is now protected by systems that work even when you're tired, distracted, or in a hurry. The criminals who count on people making careless mistakes? You're no longer one of their potential victims.

Call to Action

Use free tools to form your Fortress, protect everything with one password, and vanish from the easy target lists of data brokers.

Reference Materials: Use the Monthly Maintenance Routine to keep your automated systems running smoothly and your habits sharp.

Next up: Chapter 5 covers what's new in 2026, updated tools, emerging threats, and how to keep your shield sharp as the digital landscape evolves.

Chief Palmer notes that the best security advice he ever received came from an old sergeant who told him: "You can't be alert 100% of the time, but you can build systems that are alert 100% of the time." This principle has guided his approach to both military and civilian cybersecurity for over thirty years.

Chapter 5: Stay Current with 2026 Updates

⏱ 20 minutes to update your shield | Recommended

CALL SIGN: VIGIL, STAY READY FOR THE NEXT ATTACK BY STAYING UP TO DATE.

My nephew Jake called me from his dorm room last semester, frustrated and a little embarrassed.

"Uncle Alan, remember that cybersecurity stuff you taught me? I need an update."

Jake had been following everything we'd set up, password manager, credit freezes, the works. But he'd just gotten a text message that looked exactly like it came from his bank, complete with his actual account balance and recent transaction details.

"The crazy part is," he said, "it knew I'd bought coffee at that place on campus this morning. How could a scammer know that?"

That's when I realized something that's been keeping me busy since I retired: the threat landscape changes faster than most people can adapt to it. The basics we covered, strong passwords, credit freezes, good habits, those are timeless. But the specific tactics criminals use evolves constantly.

Jake wasn't dealing with the clumsy, typo-filled scam emails I used to show people as examples. He was facing AI-generated attacks that could pull real information from data breaches and weave it into convincing scenarios.

The fundamentals of defense haven't changed. But the execution needs regular updates.

Why 2026 Is Different (And Why It Matters)

When I started my career, threats moved slowly. A new attack technique might take months or years to spread. Security professionals had time to analyze threats, develop countermeasures, and train people on new defensive practices.

Now? Criminal organizations use the same AI tools that power customer service chatbots to generate thousands of personalized phishing emails daily. They scrape social media for personal details and incorporate them into voice clones that sound like your relatives asking for emergency money.

But what hasn't changed: criminals still target the path of least resistance. They're not trying to break into Fort Knox; they're checking if your front door is unlocked.

The people who stay protected are the ones who adapt their tactics while maintaining their core defensive principles.

The Morning My Sister Got Catfished by AI

My sister Linda, who's probably the most cautious person in our family when it comes to technology, got a voicemail last

Chapter 5: Stay Current with 2026 Updates

month that sounded exactly like her grandson asking for bail money.

"Grandma, I'm in jail in Denver. I was in a car accident and they're saying it's my fault. Please don't tell Mom and Dad, they'll kill me. Can you wire $2,500 to this account number?"

The voice was perfect. The stress and embarrassment sounded completely authentic. Even the slight rasp he gets when he's been crying.

Linda was halfway to the bank before she thought to call me.

"Alan, something feels wrong about this, but it sounds exactly like Tyler. What should I do?"

"Call Tyler directly," I said. "Right now."

Tyler answered on the second ring. He was in his apartment in Fort Collins, studying for finals. No jail, no accident, no idea anyone was impersonating him.

Someone had scraped audio of Tyler's voice from social media videos, fed it into an AI voice cloning program, and created a convincing emergency scenario designed to bypass Linda's natural caution.

Five years ago, this technology required a Hollywood sound studio. Now it's available to anyone with a smartphone and a few dollars.

What's Actually New in 2026

Passkeys Go Mainstream

The technology industry finally got its act together on passwordless authentication.

When I first started discussing passkeys two years ago, they were supported on only a dozen major websites. Now they're

85

everywhere: banks, government services, social media platforms, even my local credit union.

Where passkeys work in 2026:

- All major banks (Chase, Bank of America, Wells Fargo, credit unions)
- Government services (IRS, Social Security, state DMV offices)
- Workplace systems (Microsoft 365, Google Workspace, most corporate email)
- Shopping platforms (Amazon, eBay, major retailers)
- Social media (Facebook, Instagram, LinkedIn, Twitter, TikTok)

Why this matters: Passkeys can't be phished, stolen in data breaches, or guessed by criminals. When you see the option to enable them, do it immediately.

My brother Mike, who's not exactly an early adopter of technology, now uses passkeys for his bank account. "I just put my thumb on my phone, and I'm logged in," he told me. "It's actually easier than passwords."

Critical backup strategy: Always set up passkeys on at least two devices (your phone and computer, or phone and tablet). If you lose your primary device, you need an alternative way to authenticate. Save backup codes in your password manager as a third option.

Breach Alerts Get Faster and More Comprehensive

The breach monitoring system you set up in Chapter 2 has become significantly better without you having to do anything.

Firefox Monitor now integrates with email aliases, so you get alerts even for masked email addresses. Google sends immediate alerts when breaches affect your Gmail account. Apple does the same for iCloud users.

Most importantly, password managers now cross-check against expanded breach databases in real-time, rather than waiting for weekly updates.

What this means for you: You'll know about breaches within hours instead of days, giving you more time to respond before criminals can exploit the stolen data.

Redundancy consideration: With faster alerts coming from multiple sources, you might get duplicate notifications. That's better than missing a breach entirely, but document which services are alerting you so you can adjust if it becomes overwhelming.

Data Broker Laws Actually Work

Remember the quarterly data broker removal routine we set up? It just got much more effective.

New regulations in several states require data brokers to process opt-out requests within seven days and send confirmation emails. More importantly, they face real penalties for ignoring removal requests or immediately re-adding your information.

The practical difference: Your opt-out requests are now confirmed via email within a week, and the removals tend to stay in place longer.

My sister-in-law Janet, who used to get fifteen scam calls per week, now gets maybe two per month. "I can actually answer my phone again," she told me.

Compliance monitoring: Save the confirmation emails you receive from data brokers. If they re-add your information without justification, you now have evidence of their non-compliance with privacy laws.

New Threats You Need to Know About

AI-Generated Everything

A human didn't write the text message Jake received. It was generated by AI that had been trained on thousands of legitimate bank communications and fed specific details about his account from a data breach.

What AI-powered attacks look like:

- Perfect grammar and spelling (no more obvious typos to catch scammers)
- Personalized details from data breaches woven seamlessly into messages
- Voice clones that sound like people you know
- Dynamic content that adapts based on your response

How to protect yourself:

- Trust your instincts even when communications look perfect
- Verify through separate channels instead of responding directly
- Be suspicious of unexpected urgency regardless of how professional it sounds
- Ask specific questions that only the real person would know

Verification protocols: Develop family code words or security questions that only real family members would know. When Linda gets emergency calls now, she asks specific questions about family history before taking any action.

Cross-Platform Attacks

Criminals no longer just use email. They're operating across WhatsApp, Instagram, LinkedIn, dating apps, gaming platforms, and other communication channels.

Chapter 5: Stay Current with 2026 Updates

My daughter Sarah was contacted on three different platforms by someone claiming to be a photography scout. The same scam, perpetrated by the same person, approached her through Instagram DMs, LinkedIn messages, and even Discord.

Protection strategy:

- Apply the same caution everywhere you communicate online
- Verify unexpected opportunities through official channels
- Be suspicious of unsolicited contact on any platform
- Don't click links from strangers regardless of which app they use

Cross-reference suspicious contacts: If someone contacts you on multiple platforms, that's often a red flag. Legitimate businesses usually have established communication channels they use consistently.

Smishing Becomes the Primary Attack Vector

Traditional email filters have gotten good enough that criminals are shifting to SMS and messaging apps.

Common 2026 smishing tactics:

- Package delivery notifications requiring you to "reschedule"
- Account security alerts demanding immediate verification
- Prize notifications for contests you didn't enter
- Payment failure notifications requiring billing updates

My nephew's new habit: Jake now treats unexpected text messages the same way he treats suspicious emails. Two-second pause, verify the sender, check links before clicking.

SMS backup verification: Keep the customer service numbers for your bank, major retailers, and service providers saved in a separate location. When you get suspicious texts, call these official numbers directly rather than using any contact information from the suspicious message.

What to Retire in 2026

SMS-Based Two-Factor Authentication (2FA)

Text message codes were a good intermediate step, but they're no longer secure enough for primary protection.

Why SMS 2FA is obsolete: SIM-swapping attacks and SMS interception have made text-based codes too vulnerable. Criminals can convince phone companies to transfer your number to their device, giving them access to all your SMS codes.

What to use instead:

- Authenticator apps (Microsoft Authenticator, Google Authenticator, Authy)
- Passkeys where available
- Hardware keys for highest-value accounts

Migration strategy: Start with your most important accounts (banking, email, password manager). Look for "app-based authentication" in security settings, scan the QR code with your authenticator app, test it, then disable SMS.

Keep SMS as a backup method only, not your primary protection.

Transition planning: Don't disable SMS 2FA until you've confirmed the new method works reliably. Test your

Chapter 5: Stay Current with 2026 Updates

authenticator apps on multiple devices and save backup codes before removing SMS as an option.

Paid Credit Monitoring Services

With free credit freezes now widely available and working effectively, paid monitoring services that only alert you after fraud occurs provide minimal additional value.

What to cancel:

- Basic credit monitoring that duplicates free annual credit reports
- Identity theft protection that only monitors without preventing
- Single-bureau monitoring when you can freeze all three for free

Exceptions: Services that include meaningful identity theft insurance or cover multiple family members cost-effectively might still be worth keeping.

One-Time Privacy Cleanup Services

Companies promising to remove you from data brokers "permanently" for a one-time fee don't work because brokers refresh their databases constantly.

The quarterly removal process we set up in Chapter 4 is more effective than expensive one-time cleanup services, especially with the new regulations making removal requests more reliable.

Your 2026 Action Plan

This Week (20 minutes)

Enable passkeys everywhere possible:

- Check all your essential accounts for passkey options
- Enable them on banking, email, and password manager first
- Test that they work before relying on them completely
- Set up passkeys on at least two devices

Switch critical accounts from SMS to app-based 2FA:

- Start with email, banking, and password manager
- Download an authenticator app if you don't have one
- Scan QR codes and save backup codes in your password manager
- Test new method before disabling SMS

Update your browser extensions:

- Remove any extensions you don't actively use
- Update ad blockers and password manager extensions
- Check that all remaining extensions are from trusted developers

This Month (30 minutes)

Test your enhanced monitoring:

- Verify you're getting faster breach alerts from multiple sources
- Check that password manager breach detection is working
- Confirm data broker opt-out requests are getting confirmed

Audit family members' security:

- Help elderly relatives recognize AI-generated scams
- Update family group chat about new threat patterns
- Share successful passkey experiences to encourage adoption

Cancel redundant services:

- Review credit monitoring subscriptions for unnecessary overlap
- Evaluate whether paid services provide value beyond free alternatives

Recovery preparation: Document your updated security setup so family members can assist if needed. Include information on which devices have passkeys, where backup codes are stored, and how to access your authenticator apps in an emergency.

Quarterly Updates

Stay current with emerging threats:

- Check for new passkey support on accounts you use regularly
- Review and update scam recognition patterns
- Share new threat awareness with family and friends

Maintain your defenses:

- Continue quarterly data broker removal routine
- Update email aliases that are getting too much spam
- Verify credit freezes are still active

Staying Informed Beyond 2026

After thirty years of tracking threats professionally, I rely on these sources for civilian threat intelligence:

Privacy Guides (privacyguides.org) - Regularly updated tool recommendations from security professionals

Krebs on Security (krebsonsecurity.com) - Brian Krebs covers threats that actually affect regular people

Have I Been Pwned (@troyhunt on Twitter) - Troy Hunt announces major breaches as they're discovered

Chapter 5: Stay Current with 2026 Updates

Annual review process:

- **January:** Assess how well your defenses worked the previous year
- **April:** Review and update all security tools and services
- **July:** Check for new privacy laws that affect your rights
- **October:** Prepare for holiday shopping season security risks

Information verification: Cross-reference threat intelligence from multiple sources before making significant changes to your security setup. Even security experts sometimes make mistakes, so look for consensus among trusted sources.

The Threat Assessment Reality

What's getting worse:

- AI makes scams more convincing and harder to detect
- Cross-platform attacks coordinate across multiple communication channels
- Voice and video deepfakes enable sophisticated impersonation
- Mobile-focused attacks target phones more than computers

What's getting better:

- Passkey adoption eliminates password-based vulnerabilities
- Legal protections for privacy have real enforcement mechanisms
- Free tools continue improving and becoming more accessible

- User awareness of basic security principles is growing

Bottom line: The defensive improvements are keeping pace with offensive advances. The key is staying current and not falling behind on updates.

Family Success Stories

Jake's Evolution

My nephew Jake, who started as the college kid with the malware-infected laptop, is now the one his friends ask for security advice.

Last month, he helped his roommate recognize a scholarship scam that was using AI-generated recommendation letters from fake professors. The scam was sophisticated enough to fool financial aid counselors, but Jake caught it because he's developed good verification habits.

"The letter sounded perfect," Jake told me, "but when we called the professor's office, he'd never heard of the scholarship program."

Linda's Confidence

My sister Linda, who almost fell for the AI voice clone scam, now questions everything unexpected, in a good way.

When she got a legitimate call from her doctor's office about a changed appointment, she said, "I'll call you back to confirm." The receptionist understood completely.

"Better safe than sorry," Linda told me. "And if it's really them, they won't mind me verifying."

Sarah's Professional Edge

My daughter Sarah now uses her cybersecurity awareness professionally. As a forensic accountant, she's seeing more cases involving AI-generated fake documentation and sophisticated social engineering.

"Dad, the stuff you taught me about questioning unexpected communications? That's literally my job now. Companies hire me to figure out how they got fooled by criminals using the same tactics you warned us about."

Success Metrics for 2026

This month:

- Passkeys enabled on your most important accounts
- You recognize that professional appearance doesn't guarantee legitimacy
- App-based 2FA has replaced SMS codes for critical accounts
- Breach alerts reach you from multiple sources quickly

This quarter:

- Data broker opt-out requests receive prompt confirmations
- Your security habits adapt naturally to new threat patterns
- Family members ask for your updated security guidance
- You spot cross-platform scam attempts across different apps

This year:

- Your Fortress Shield evolves smoothly with the threat landscape
- You help others update their outdated security practices

- New tools integrate seamlessly into your existing defensive systems
- You feel confident navigating emerging digital threats

Checkpoint: Are you using 2026's best practices instead of outdated methods? If yes, your shield stays sharp as threats continue to evolve.

Mission Complete

The core principles we've built your Fortress Shield on, strong authentication, early warning systems, financial protection, and good habits, never change. But the specific tactics require regular updates to remain effective against evolving threats.

Jake's not dealing with the same scams I showed him examples of two years ago. Linda faces threats that didn't exist when I first started helping her. Sarah investigates crimes using techniques that were science fiction when I was learning cybersecurity.

But they're all prepared because they understand the fundamentals and know how to adapt when new challenges arise.

You're now equipped with the latest defenses of 2026 and the framework to keep adapting as the digital landscape continues to evolve. The criminals who count on people using outdated protection? You're no longer one of their potential victims.

Call to Action

Use free tools to form your Fortress, protect everything with one password, and stay vigilant as the threat landscape evolves.

Reference Materials: Use the Monthly Maintenance Routine to stay current with evolving threats and refer to the Oh-No Playbook for responding to new types of attacks.

Next up: Chapter 6 shows you how to secure your home network, the gateway through which all your devices connect to the internet.

Chief Palmer notes that staying current with threats is similar to staying current in any professional field, it requires ongoing education and adaptation. "The day you stop learning is the day you start becoming vulnerable," he often tells the veteran cybersecurity groups he speaks to.

Chapter 6: Secure Your Home Network

⏱ 20 minutes setup | Recommended

CALL SIGN: LOCKDOWN, CONTROL THE PERIMETER.

IF THE GATE IS OPEN, NOTHING ELSE MATTERS.

My neighbor Dave called me one Saturday morning, and I could hear the confusion in his voice.

"Alan, my internet provider just sent me a threatening letter. They claim I've been downloading pirated movies and running an illegal file-sharing operation. They're threatening to shut off my service and report me to the police."

Dave's a retired postal worker who barely knows how to attach a photo to an email. The idea of him running a piracy operation was absurd.

"When did this start?" I asked.

"They say it's been going on for three months. But Alan, I swear I haven't downloaded anything illegal. I barely use the internet except for email and watching the news."

I walked over to Dave's house with my laptop. Took me about five minutes to figure out what happened. Dave was still using the default Wi-Fi password that came printed on a sticker on the bottom of his router: "Linksys12345."

Someone, probably one of his neighbors, had been using his internet connection for months. All that illegal activity? It was happening through Dave's network, but it wasn't Dave doing it.

The internet provider didn't care. As far as they were concerned, the activity came from Dave's address, so Dave was responsible.

That's when I realized most people have no idea their home network is the digital equivalent of leaving their front door wide open with a sign saying, "Come on in."

Why This Step Matters

In military operations, the first rule of base security is straightforward: secure the perimeter. If the wire is cut and the gates are left open, the enemy doesn't need clever tricks; they simply walk in.

Your home network is the perimeter of your digital life. Every device in your house, laptops, phones, tablets, smart TVs, even doorbell cameras, connects through your router. If that router is exposed, attackers can spy on your traffic, hijack devices, or launch attacks using your connection.

Most households never change the factory defaults. Many leave weak Wi-Fi passwords in place or never update router firmware. That's like leaving the gate unguarded with the keys hanging on a hook. LOCKDOWN is about sealing the gate.

Chapter 6: Secure Your Home Network

⚠ THREAT ALERT

Your home Wi-Fi is the front gate to everything you do online.

Default passwords, weak encryption, or outdated routers are open invitations to attackers.

The Backstory: Why This Became a Battlefield

In the early 2000s, most people's home Wi-Fi wasn't even encrypted. Drive-by hackers could sit in a car outside and join networks freely. I remember helping my brother Mike set up his first wireless router back then. The instruction manual actually said encryption was "optional" and might "slow down your connection."

Even as encryption improved, the problem shifted: manufacturers continued to ship routers with default logins like admin/password. Attackers compiled lists of those defaults and built "wardriving" maps of unsecured homes. They'd drive through neighborhoods with laptops, mapping every vulnerable network, then sell the lists to other criminals.

Today, attackers continue to seek out easy targets. Automated tools scan entire neighborhoods for open or outdated routers. Criminal groups even compromise weak home routers in bulk and rent them out as "proxy networks", so another criminal can hide behind your connection while committing crimes. That means your IP address shows up on law enforcement logs, not theirs.

The law has evolved, the FTC has fined router manufacturers for selling products with known security flaws. But the reality is that the burden of securing your home network still rests with you.

The Intelligence War at Your Front Door

I've spent three decades protecting military networks, and the principle is always the same: the perimeter is everything. You can have the most sophisticated internal security in the world, but if someone can walk in through an unlocked door, none of it matters.

Your router is that door. Every device in your home, your laptop where you do your banking, your phone with your two-factor authentication codes, your smart TV that might have a camera and microphone, all connect through that one device.

When Dave's neighbor was using his Wi-Fi, they could see every device on his network. They could attempt to connect to his printer, file shares, even his security cameras if he had them. They were inside his perimeter, and Dave didn't even know they were there.

Henry's Neighbor: The Router Left Unlocked

During a neighborhood security audit I did for my HOA, we found one home where the Wi-Fi was still using the default password printed on the back of the router. A teenager down the street had been piggybacking for months, streaming movies and running game cheats through the connection. The homeowner had no idea until their internet provider flagged their account for suspicious traffic.

The homeowner thought, "It's just Wi-Fi, what harm could it do?" In reality, anyone connected could see devices inside, attempt to log in, or use that connection as cover.

Chapter 6: Secure Your Home Network

The fix took 15 minutes: changing the admin password, setting strong WPA3 Wi-Fi encryption, and updating the router firmware. LOCKDOWN engaged, gate closed.

The teenager? His parents were mortified. It turned out he'd been doing this to several neighbors, not realizing the legal liability he was creating for them. One angry conversation with his father about "theft of services" and "criminal liability" later, and the problem stopped.

The Day My Sister's Security Cameras Started Talking

My sister Linda called me at 11 PM on a Tuesday, and she was genuinely frightened.

"Alan, someone's watching us. They're talking through the baby monitor in Emma's room."

Linda's daughter Emma was six years old at the time. She'd woken up crying because she heard a stranger's voice coming from the monitor, saying her name and telling her to wake up her parents.

I drove to Linda's house immediately. While Linda comforted Emma, I looked at the baby monitor. It was one of those internet-connected models with a camera and two-way audio. Great for checking on kids from work. Also great for attackers if your network isn't secure.

Linda's router was still using the password her internet provider had set up: "Welcome123." Her Wi-Fi encryption was set to WEP, an outdated standard that can be cracked in minutes. The baby monitor had a default password that was listed in the manual, which was also available online.

Whoever did this had connected to Linda's Wi-Fi, found the camera on the network, logged in with the default credentials, and decided to terrorize a six-year-old for fun.

We filed a police report, but the chances of finding the person were slim. What we could do was lock down Linda's network so it never happened again.

🔒 FORTIFY PROTOCOL

Your lockdown checklist:

Change the default admin password on your router

Use WPA3 encryption (or WPA2 if WPA3 isn't available)

Create a strong Wi-Fi password stored in your password manager

Update your router's firmware, set automatic updates if available

Create a guest network for visitors and smart home devices

Turn off remote administration unless you explicitly need it

Step-by-Step: Locking Down Your Network

You don't need to be a network engineer to do this. If you can log into your email, you can secure your router.

Step 1: Find Your Router's Login Page (3 minutes)

Your router's settings live on a web page that you access from any device connected to your network.

Find your router's address:

1. **Windows:** Open Command Prompt, type ipconfig, look for "Default Gateway"

2. **Mac:** System Settings → Network → Your connection → Details, look for "Router"
3. **Common defaults:** Try 192.168.1.1 or 192.168.0.1 in your browser

Or use your phone:

- Most modern routers have apps (Netgear, TP-Link, ASUS, Linksys, Google Nest)
- Download your router manufacturer's app for easier setup

What you'll see: A login page asking for username and password.

Default credentials to try:

- admin / admin
- admin / password
- admin / (blank)
- Check the sticker on your router for defaults

Save this information: Once you're logged in, you'll change these defaults. Save the new credentials in your password manager immediately.

Step 2: Change the Admin Password (2 minutes)

This is the password that controls your router settings, not your Wi-Fi password. They're different.

Find the setting:

- Look for "Administration," "Management," or "System"
- Find "Change Password" or "Admin Password"

107

Create a strong password:

- Generate one with your password manager
- Make it 20+ characters
- Save it immediately, you'll need it to access router settings later

Test it: Log out and back in with the new password to make sure it works.

When Dave changed his admin password, I had him write it on a piece of paper and put it in his file cabinet with his important documents. "Only until you memorize it," I told him. He never did memorize it, but at least it wasn't the default anymore and he knew where to find it.

Step 3: Update Your Wi-Fi Encryption (3 minutes)

This controls who can connect to your network and whether the connection is encrypted.

Find the setting:

- Look for "Wireless," "Wi-Fi," or "Network"
- Find "Security" or "Encryption"

Choose the strongest option available:

- **Best:** WPA3 Personal
- **Good:** WPA2 Personal (AES)
- **Never use:** WEP, WPA, or "Open" network

Why this matters: WEP encryption can be cracked in under five minutes by someone sitting in a car outside your house. WPA2 is much stronger. WPA3 is even better and can't be cracked with current technology.

Linda's router supported WPA2 but was set to WEP. One setting change made her network exponentially more secure.

Chapter 6: Secure Your Home Network

Step 4: Change Your Wi-Fi Password (3 minutes)

This is the password people use to connect to your network. It's different from your admin password.

Find the setting:

- Same "Wireless" or "Wi-Fi" section
- Look for "Passphrase," "Network Key," or "Password"

Create a strong password:

- 16+ characters
- Mix of letters, numbers, symbols
- NOT your address, family names, or birthdates
- Generate with password manager and save it

Update all your devices: After making this change, you'll need to reconnect each device in your house using the new password.

Pro tip from my family: Create a QR code for your Wi-Fi password. Many phones can scan it to connect automatically. Print it and keep it somewhere accessible for guests, but out of sight from outside.

Step 5: Update Router Firmware (5 minutes)

Router firmware is like Windows or iOS updates, it patches security vulnerabilities that criminals actively exploit.

Find the setting:

- Look for "Administration," "Advanced," or "System"
- Find "Firmware Update" or "Router Update"

109

Check for updates:

- Click "Check for updates"
- If available, download and install
- **Don't interrupt the update**, let it finish completely

Enable automatic updates:

- If your router offers this option, turn it on
- Modern routers from major manufacturers usually update overnight

Warning: The update process can take 5-10 minutes and will disconnect your internet. Don't panic, it's normal. Don't unplug the router during updates.

When I helped Dave update his router firmware, it hadn't been updated in four years. Four years of known security vulnerabilities left unpatched. The update took eight minutes and fixed dozens of security holes.

Step 6: Create a Guest Network (4 minutes)

A guest network is a separate Wi-Fi network that allows internet access but prevents users from seeing or connecting to your other devices.

Why this matters: Remember Linda's baby monitor? If that monitor had been on a guest network, an attacker who'd cracked the Wi-Fi wouldn't have been able to reach it.

Find the setting:

- Look for "Guest Network" or "Guest Wi-Fi"
- Enable it and give it a name (like "Smith Family Guest")

Set a different password:

- Don't use the same password as your main network
- Give this password to guests

What goes on the guest network:

- Visiting friends' devices
- Smart TVs, streaming devices
- IoT devices (cameras, thermostats, smart speakers)
- Anything that doesn't need to access your computers or phones

My personal setup: My main network has my laptop, phone, and tablet. My guest network has my Roku, my smart thermostat, and the old tablet I use as a kitchen display. If someone hacks my Roku, they won't be able to access my banking laptop.

Step 7: Disable Remote Administration (1 minute)

Remote administration lets you access your router settings from outside your home network. Unless you specifically need this feature, disable it.

Find the setting:

- Look for "Remote Management" or "Remote Administration"
- Turn it OFF

Why this matters: This feature is often exploited to compromise routers. Attackers scan the internet for routers with remote administration enabled, then attempt to use default passwords.

When you might need it: Rarely. Even IT professionals rarely need this. If you're not sure, turn it off.

Free Tools That Help With Lockdown

You don't have to be a tech wizard to do this. Modern tools make network security accessible to everyone.

Router Manufacturer Apps (Free)

Netgear Nighthawk, TP-Link Tether, ASUS Router, Linksys, Google Home, Eero

These apps walk you through every step visually:

- Change admin password with guided prompts
- Enable WPA3 with one tap
- Create guest network with simple interface
- Push firmware updates automatically

My father-in-law Frank, who struggles with technology, successfully secured his router using the TP-Link app on his phone. "It asked me questions in plain English, and I just answered them," he told me. Much easier than the old web interface.

Fing - Home Network Scanner (Free)

What it does: Shows every device connected to your network

Why you need it:

- Spot unauthorized devices (like Dave's neighbor)
- Identify what each device is (phone, laptop, smart TV)
- Get alerts when new devices join

How to use:

1. Download Fing app on your phone
2. Connect to your Wi-Fi
3. Scan your network
4. Review the list, recognize everything?

When I ran Fing on Dave's network, it showed seven devices. Dave only had four devices in his house. Those extra three? Two belonged to his neighbor, and one was someone who drove by and took advantage of the opportunity.

WiFiman or NetSpot - Signal Analyzers (Free)

What they do: Show your Wi-Fi signal strength and encryption type

Why you need them:

- Verify encryption is actually enabled (WPA2/WPA3)
- Check if your signal is leaking far beyond your property
- Identify interference from neighbor networks

My neighborhood test: I walked around my block with WiFiman running. I could see 23 different Wi-Fi networks from the street. Six of them were using WEP or no encryption at all. Those six homes were wide open to anyone walking by.

The Nanny Cam Breach: Linda's Full Story

After securing Linda's router and changing all the default passwords on her smart devices, I sat down with her and explained what had happened.

"Someone found your Wi-Fi network," I told her. "Your router was using a default password that's published online. They connected, scanned your network for devices, found the baby monitor, and logged in with its default password."

Linda was shaken. "So, they could see into Emma's room?"

"Yes. And they could listen, talk through the speaker, even move the camera if your model has that feature."

We went through every internet-connected device in Linda's house:

- Baby monitor: Changed password, enabled two-factor authentication
- Smart TV: Moved to guest network
- Thermostat: Moved to guest network, changed password
- Smart doorbell: Moved to guest network, updated firmware

The complete security review took about an hour, but when we were finished, Linda's network was properly locked down. Emma hasn't heard strange voices since, and Linda can sleep knowing her home's private spaces are actually private.

Six months later, Linda helped her sister secure her network using the same process. "Once you know what to look for, it's not that complicated," she told me. "It's just that nobody teaches you this stuff."

SITREP: Threat Assessment

- Default credentials remain one of the top causes of home network breaches
- Outdated firmware leaves known vulnerabilities unpatched, attackers actively exploit them
- Compromised routers are rented out as criminal "proxy networks," leaving victims blamed for crimes they didn't commit

Chapter 6: Secure Your Home Network

- Smart home devices (cameras, speakers, thermostats) often lack strong security; isolating them on a guest network is proven defense

▨ RED TEAM INSIGHT

In one red-team test, we breached a corporate executive's home by first compromising his smart thermostat, connected to the same Wi-Fi as his laptop. From there, we mapped his traffic, captured logins, and escalated into his work VPN. The weakest link wasn't the corporate firewall; it was his living room.

Common Mistakes That Keep Me Awake

After helping family and neighbors secure their networks, I see the same errors repeatedly:

Using Wi-Fi passwords you can't remember: This leads people back to weak passwords like "Family2023" that are easy to guess. Use your password manager and copy-paste complex passwords.

Never checking what's connected: Run Fing every few months. If you see unknown devices, someone's on your network.

Assuming new routers are secure: Manufacturers ship with decent defaults now, but you still need to change the admin password and update firmware.

Putting everything on the main network: Your laptop and your smart TV don't need to talk to each other. Use the guest network for IoT devices.

Ignoring firmware updates: Your router is a computer. It needs security patches just like your phone or laptop.

When Things Don't Go According to Plan

"I can't log into my router"

Try the default credentials from the sticker or manual. If those don't work, you may need to reset the router to factory defaults (hold the reset button for 10 seconds). This erases all settings, so you'll start from scratch.

"The firmware update failed and now nothing works"

Unplug the router, wait 30 seconds, plug it back in. Most routers have recovery modes that automatically fix failed updates. Check your manufacturer's support site for specific instructions.

"My devices won't connect after changing the Wi-Fi password"

You need to "forget" the network on each device and reconnect with the new password. On phones, go to Wi-Fi settings, tap your network, select "Forget," then reconnect.

"I can't find my router's settings in the app"

Not all routers have apps, especially older models. Use the web interface instead, type the router's IP address into your browser.

"My internet is slower after enabling WPA3"

Some older devices don't support WPA3. Your router should fall back to WPA2 for those devices, but if problems persist, you can use WPA2/WPA3 mixed mode.

Chapter 6: Secure Your Home Network

Practical Lessons: Living in Lockdown

One password rules all: Save your Wi-Fi and router credentials in your password manager. Don't rely on memory or sticky notes.

Guest network = firebreak: Isolating smart TVs, speakers, and IoT devices prevents a breach in one device from spreading.

Updates matter: Routers are computers, firmware updates patch the same vulnerabilities as Windows or iOS.

Remote access is rarely needed: If you're unsure why you'd need it, turn it off.

Quarterly checks: Set a calendar reminder to check who's connected to your network. Run Fing, review the device list, and update firmware.

My Family's Network Audit

Every six months, I help family members check their network security. We spend about 30 minutes per household:

1. Log into the router, verify settings haven't changed
2. Run Fing to check connected devices
3. Update firmware if available
4. Review the guest network, is it being used correctly?
5. Check any new smart devices added since last audit

During our last audit, we found that my brother Mike had installed a smart garage door opener and connected it to his main network. Took five minutes to move it to the guest network, where it belonged.

My nephew Jake now runs his own audits without my help. "It's kind of satisfying," he told me. "Knowing everything is buttoned up properly."

Success Metrics: Your Armor Is Working

Month 1:

- Credit frozen at all three bureaus
- Freeze status verification completed
- Free monitoring tools set up
- First four-month credit report reviewed

Quarter 1:

- Quarterly freeze status check completed successfully
- No unauthorized accounts discovered
- Second four-month credit report pulled and reviewed
- Emergency drill practiced and documented

Year 1:

- Four credit reports reviewed (one from each bureau, plus one repeat)
- Zero successful fraud attempts
- Family members asking for help with their credit armor
- You understand the dispute process without needing to use it

Long-term:

- Credit monitoring becomes routine, not stressful
- You catch and correct errors before they become problems

Chapter 6: Secure Your Home Network

- Your credit score is stable and reflects only your actual activity
- Peace of mind about your financial identity

Checkpoint: Can you log into your router with your new admin password? Does Fing show only your devices? Is everything on the appropriate network? If yes, your perimeter is secured.

Why This Matters Beyond the Numbers

I spent three decades protecting networks that couldn't fail. But you know what? The principles are the same whether you're protecting nuclear weapon systems or protecting your family's baby monitor.

The difference is that military networks have dedicated security teams monitoring them 24/7. Your home network has you.

Dave's internet piracy problem was resolved with a single call to his provider, explaining the situation and demonstrating that he'd secured his network. They gave him a warning instead of terminating his service.

Linda's daughter Emma is now 12. She doesn't remember the nanny cam incident, but Linda never forgot it. "That was the moment I realized technology wasn't just convenient gadgets," she told me. "It was a window into my home that needed to be secured."

Henry's neighbor learned an expensive lesson when his parents had to hire a lawyer to respond to the internet provider's legal threats. Turns out "borrowing" someone's Wi-Fi is considered theft of services in most states.

The good news? Securing your home network isn't complicated. It's just a few settings most people never touch because nobody taught them to.

You've just learned. Your perimeter is no longer open. The criminals who scan neighborhoods for weak networks? Yours isn't one of them anymore.

Mission Complete

By the end of this chapter, you should:

- Understand why your home network is the perimeter of your Fortress
- Know that free apps exist to make LOCKDOWN realistic for anyone
- Recognize how insecure Wi-Fi can directly impact your family's safety
- Have changed your router's admin password and Wi-Fi password
- Be using WPA2 or WPA3 encryption
- Have a guest network for IoT devices
- Have disabled remote administration
- Know how to check who's on your network

Call to Action

Use free tools to form your Fortress, protect everything with one password, and lock down the gate of your home network.

Reference Materials: Use the Quarterly Network Audit Checklist to maintain your perimeter defenses and identify potential problems before they escalate into breaches.

Next up: Chapter 7 explores when paid services might actually make sense and how to evaluate them honestly against your proven free stack.

Chief Palmer notes that the same perimeter security principles that protect Air Force bases apply to home networks. "The only difference is scale," he says. "The fundamentals remain the same: control access, update defenses, and monitor for intrusions."

Fortress Shield - 2026 Edition

Chapter 7: When Paid Services Make Sense

⏱ Decision framework | Optional

CALL SIGN EVALUATOR – "SPEND WHEN IT ADDS ARMOR, NOT DECORATION.

My 78-year-old father-in-law called me last spring, and I could hear the frustration in his voice.

"Alan, I've been trying to do that password thing you showed me, but I keep getting locked out of everything. Yesterday I spent two hours on the phone with my bank because I couldn't remember which password went where."

Frank is a retired engineer. Built bridges for forty years, sharp as a tack when it comes to anything mechanical. But the password manager that works perfectly for my tech-savvy nephew Jake was causing Frank more stress than the problems it was supposed to solve.

"I know you mean well," Frank said, "but this is making my life harder, not easier. Isn't there some company that just handles all this computer security stuff, so I don't have to think about it?"

That conversation made me realize something important: the free Fortress Shield we've built works great for people who are willing and able to learn new systems. But not everyone fits that description, and that doesn't make them lazy or stupid.

Sometimes the best security solution is the one people will actually use consistently, even if it costs money.

The Honest Truth About Paid Services

After thirty years of watching people make security decisions, I've learned that the "best" solution on paper isn't always the best solution in practice. The most sophisticated defense system in the world is useless if people can't or won't use it properly.

About paid cybersecurity services: they're not magic, they don't eliminate all risks, and they often provide the same protection you can get for free. But for some people, in some situations, they solve real problems that the free alternatives don't address.

The key is understanding what you're actually buying versus what the marketing promises.

Chapter 7: When Paid Services Make Sense

⚠ THREAT ALERT

Marketing fear sells more subscriptions than actual protection.

Companies profit from anxiety. Before paying for any service, understand exactly what you're buying and whether free alternatives provide the same protection.

What Frank Actually Needed

After talking with Frank about his specific situation, I realized his problem wasn't technical. It was operational. He needed:

- Someone else to manage the complexity so he could focus on his life
- Phone support when things go wrong
- A system that worked without requiring him to learn new habits
- Peace of mind that someone was watching out for his digital safety

Those are legitimate needs that free tools don't always address, especially for people who didn't grow up with computers.

We ended up setting Frank up with a reputable all-in-one service that costs about $15 per month. Six months later, he told me it was the best money he'd ever spent on technology.

"I sleep better knowing professionals are handling this stuff," he said. "And when I have problems, I call a real person who speaks English and actually helps me."

125

What You're Actually Buying (The Real Story)

Let me break down what companies like Aura, LifeLock, and Identity Guard actually deliver versus what their marketing claims:

The Marketing Promises vs. Reality

Promise: "Complete digital protection"

Reality: They use many of the same free tools you've learned about, just packaged in a single interface

Promise: "Advanced dark web monitoring"
Reality: Mostly the same breach databases as Have I Been Pwned, sometimes with additional forums

Promise: "Automated data broker removal"
Reality: They submit the same opt-out forms you can fill out yourself, just systematically

Promise: "24/7 monitoring and alerts"
Reality: Automated systems that scan databases, plus human support during business hours

Promise: "Identity theft insurance"
Reality: Coverage for specific expenses related to identity recovery, not reimbursement for stolen money

What They Actually Do Well

Dashboard convenience: Managing everything in one place is genuinely easier than juggling multiple free services

Consistent execution: They don't forget to check for breaches or skip monthly data broker removals

Customer support: When things go wrong, you can call someone for help instead of troubleshooting alone

Family coverage: Protecting multiple people under one service can be more cost-effective than individual setups

Simplicity: They handle the complexity, so you don't have to learn multiple systems

🔒 FORTIFY PROTOCOL

Your decision framework:

Assess your risk level honestly (not based on fear)

Calculate true costs: time, opportunity, and complexity

Test services with free trials before committing

Evaluate results every 6 months (are you using what you're paying for?)

Choose consciously, use consistently, review periodically

When Paid Services Actually Make Sense

Scenario 1: Supporting Elderly Family Members

My mother-in-law Dorothy is 82, lives independently, and has been targeted by scammers repeatedly. She's smart enough to be suspicious, but not technically comfortable enough to manage password managers and breach monitoring.

The challenge with DIY approaches:

- Learning new technology feels overwhelming
- Remembering to do monthly maintenance is inconsistent
- When problems arise, she needs human help immediately
- The stress of managing security affects her quality of life

How paid services help:

- Everything runs automatically in the background
- One phone number for all security-related problems
- Professional monitoring that catches threats she might miss
- Family members can get status updates without managing the system themselves

Dorothy's been using a paid service for two years now. The scam calls have dropped dramatically, and she feels confident that someone is watching out for her digital safety.

Cost-benefit for elderly users: About $180 per year for peace of mind and professional management versus hours of family time trying to teach and support complex systems.

Service evaluation criteria: Look for companies that offer genuine human customer support, don't require annual contracts, and provide clear monthly reports. Avoid services that use high-pressure sales tactics or make unrealistic promises about "complete protection."

Scenario 2: High-Risk Individuals

My daughter Sarah, the forensic accountant, occasionally consults for executives and public figures who face enhanced threats.

Chapter 7: When Paid Services Make Sense

Who qualifies as high-risk:

- Public figures (politicians, activists, journalists)
- Business executives with access to sensitive information
- High-net-worth individuals
- People in domestic violence situations
- Anyone who's been specifically targeted before

Why they need more than the basic stack:

- Criminals research them specifically instead of using generic attacks
- Personal information exposure can lead to physical safety risks
- Professional reputation damage from breaches has higher stakes
- They're targets for sophisticated social engineering

What enhanced services provide:

- More comprehensive monitoring across additional databases
- Faster response times when threats are detected
- Legal support for privacy violations
- Integration with physical security measures
- Threat assessment and personalized risk management

Sarah worked with one client who was being stalked. The enhanced monitoring service detected when the stalker was searching for the client's information on people-search websites and helped coordinate with law enforcement.

129

Due diligence requirements: High-risk individuals should verify that paid services have appropriate security certifications, experienced staff, and established relationships with law enforcement. Request references and case studies before committing.

Scenario 3: Time-Poor Professionals

My neighbor Dave runs a small construction company. He's on job sites ten hours a day, managing crews, dealing with clients, and handling paperwork in the evenings.

Dave's reality:

- No consistent time for monthly security maintenance
- Travels frequently between job sites with unreliable internet
- Can't afford security breaches that might compromise client information
- Values his time at $75+ per hour for business activities

The math that convinced him:

- DIY approach: 6 hours per year of personal time equals $450 in opportunity cost
- Paid service: $200 per year with no time investment
- The paid service actually saves him money while providing equal protection

Dave's been using a business-focused security service for three years. It handles everything automatically, and he gets monthly reports showing what was detected and resolved.

"Best $200 I spend every year," he told me. "I don't think about cybersecurity anymore except to read the monthly report they send."

Chapter 7: When Paid Services Make Sense

Business consideration: Paid services for professionals should include business liability coverage, compliance assistance for industry regulations, and integration with existing business systems. Document the service relationship for tax and compliance purposes.

MISSION CRITICAL

Don't pay for security theater.

If a service can't explain specifically what protection it provides beyond what free tools offer, you're paying for marketing, not security. Demand transparency.

Advanced Tools Worth Paying For

Some security tools genuinely provide capabilities that free alternatives can't match. These aren't about convenience. They're about enhanced protection for specific use cases.

VPN Services for Real Privacy Needs

Free VPNs are usually terrible (they sell your data or have severe limitations). But paid VPNs provide legitimate value for specific situations:

When VPNs make sense:
- Frequent travel with public Wi-Fi use
- Accessing geo-restricted content while abroad
- ISP privacy concerns in countries with weak privacy laws
- High-risk activities like journalism or activism

Services worth paying for:

- **Mullvad:** Anonymous signup, strong privacy focus (€5/month)
- **ProtonVPN:** Swiss privacy laws, excellent free tier with paid upgrades
- **IVPN:** Independent audits, no-logs policy verified

My nephew Jake uses ProtonVPN when he's studying abroad. "I don't trust the Wi-Fi in hostels," he says, "and this lets me access my streaming services from home."

Service verification: Research VPN providers' privacy policies, logging practices, and jurisdiction before subscribing. Avoid services with unrealistic speed claims or prices that seem too good to be true.

Encrypted Email for Sensitive Communications

Standard email is like sending postcards. Anyone handling it can read the content. Encrypted email provides genuine confidentiality for sensitive communications.

When encrypted email is worth paying for:

- Healthcare communications requiring HIPAA compliance
- Legal communications protected by attorney-client privilege
- Business negotiations involving confidential information
- Personal situations involving safety or privacy concerns

Recommended services:

- **ProtonMail:** Swiss-based, excellent free tier, paid plans add features

- **Tutanota:** German privacy laws, affordable paid plans, good mobile apps

Sarah uses encrypted email for her forensic accounting work. "When I'm investigating financial crimes, the last thing I want is for the criminals to read my communications with law enforcement," she explains.

Migration planning: Test encrypted email services with non-critical communications first. Make sure all parties you communicate with can handle encrypted messages before switching important correspondence.

Hardware Security Keys for Ultimate Protection

For your most valuable accounts (banking, password manager, work email), hardware keys provide unphishable authentication.

Cost-benefit analysis:

- **Cost:** $25 to 60 per key, one-time purchase
- **Benefit:** Eliminates account takeover risk even with compromised passwords
- **ROI:** Prevents potentially thousands in fraud losses
- **Convenience:** Faster than typing codes after initial setup

I use hardware keys for my most sensitive accounts. My wife was skeptical until I showed her how it works: plug in the key, touch the button, instant login.

"It's actually easier than remembering passwords," she admitted.

Redundancy requirements: Buy at least two identical keys, set them both up on critical accounts, store one in a secure location as backup. Test both keys periodically to ensure they're working properly.

Red Flags to Avoid

After helping family members evaluate various security services, I've learned to recognize companies that are more interested in fear-mongering than actual protection.

Marketing Red Flags

Scare tactics: "Hackers are targeting you right now!" or "Your identity is being sold on the dark web!"

Impossible claims: "Complete protection" or "100% secure" (no security solution provides this)

Urgency pressure: "Limited time offer" for ongoing security services

Vague benefits: Companies that can't explain specifically what they provide beyond marketing buzzwords

Service Quality Red Flags

Poor customer support: Long wait times, offshore call centers with scripted responses, unhelpful resolution

Frequent outages: Security services that aren't available when you need them

Privacy concerns: Companies with poor privacy practices themselves

No transparency: Won't explain how their services actually work or where their data comes from

Contract Red Flags

Required annual contracts: Basic security services should be month-to-month

Auto-renewal traps: Difficult cancellation processes or hidden renewal terms

Hidden fees: Setup costs, cancellation fees, or charges for premium features

Chapter 7: When Paid Services Make Sense

Data ownership claims: Services that claim rights to your personal information

RED TEAM INSIGHT

In security assessments, we've seen companies pay hundreds monthly for "comprehensive protection" that consisted entirely of repackaged free tools. When we tested response times, the paid service detected breaches no faster than Have I Been Pwned. The only real benefit was consolidated reporting. That's worth something, but not $30/month.

SITREP: The Paid Services Landscape

What's improved:

- More companies offer genuine month-to-month plans
- Customer support quality has gotten better
- Identity theft insurance coverage has expanded
- Family plans provide better value than individual plans

What remains problematic:

- Marketing still relies heavily on fear tactics
- Many services provide minimal value over free alternatives
- Contract terms can be predatory
- "Dark web monitoring" is often oversold

Bottom line: Paid services can solve real problems for specific people, but most users get excellent protection from the free Fortress Shield we've built throughout this book.

The Decision Framework

Step 1: Honest Self-Assessment

Ask yourself these questions:

- **Risk level:** What would actually happen if my digital security was compromised?
- **Time availability:** Can I realistically maintain DIY security systems long-term?
- **Technical comfort:** Am I willing to learn and troubleshoot security tools?
- **Budget reality:** What can I afford monthly without financial stress?
- **Family situation:** Am I protecting just myself or multiple people with different needs?

Step 2: Calculate True Costs

DIY approach costs:

- Your time valued at your hourly rate (6 hours/year times your hourly value)
- Opportunity cost of time spent on security instead of other priorities
- Risk cost if you make mistakes or skip maintenance

Paid service costs:

- Monthly/annual subscription fees
- Setup time and learning curve
- Dependency on the service provider

Frank's calculation: He values his retirement time highly and finds technology stressful. For him, $180/year to eliminate security-related stress was an easy decision.

Chapter 7: When Paid Services Make Sense

My calculation: I enjoy learning about security tools and have the technical background to troubleshoot problems. The free approach works great for my situation.

Step 3: Test Before Committing

Most reputable services offer:

- 30-day free trials with full feature access
- Money-back guarantees if you're not satisfied
- Month-to-month billing so you can cancel anytime

Start small: Begin with one service for one specific need rather than comprehensive coverage

Set evaluation criteria: Decide in advance what would make the service worth keeping

Documentation requirements: Keep records of your evaluation process, including what worked well and what didn't. This information helps with future decisions and can be valuable for family members making similar choices.

The Hybrid Approach (Best of Both Worlds)

You don't have to choose between "all free" and "all paid." Many people use a hybrid approach that combines free foundations with strategic paid additions.

Keep the Free Foundation

What works great for free:

- Password managers (Bitwarden, Proton Pass)
- Credit freezes (legally required to be free)
- Breach monitoring (Have I Been Pwned, Firefox Monitor)
- Basic habits (auto-updates, ad blocking, link awareness)

137

Add Strategic Paid Services

Where paid services add value:

- VPN for travel and public Wi-Fi protection
- Hardware keys for highest-value accounts
- Comprehensive service for elderly family members
- Professional services for high-risk individuals

Regular Evaluation

Review your setup every six months:

- Are you actually using the paid services you're paying for?
- Have free alternatives improved enough to replace paid services?
- Has your risk profile or life situation changed?

My brother Mike uses this approach. He handles his own password management and credit monitoring but pays for a VPN because he travels frequently for work.

"I'm comfortable managing passwords," he says, "but I don't want to research VPN providers or worry about whether free ones are actually protecting my privacy."

Success Stories from Both Approaches

DIY Success: My Nephew Jake

Jake (the college student who started with a malware-infected laptop) now manages comprehensive security for himself using entirely free tools. He's become the cybersecurity expert for his friend group and helps roommates set up their own protection.

Total annual cost: $0
Time investment: About 4 hours per year

Chapter 7: When Paid Services Make Sense

Satisfaction level: High. He enjoys understanding and controlling his security

Paid Service Success: Frank

My father-in-law Frank uses a comprehensive paid service and couldn't be happier. His security is actually better than most people using DIY approaches because the paid service does everything consistently.

Total annual cost: $180
Time investment: 30 minutes per year reading monthly reports
Satisfaction level: High. He has peace of mind without complexity

Hybrid Success: My Family

My wife and I use free tools for most things but pay for a family VPN and hardware keys for our most sensitive accounts. Our adult children manage their own security using the free stack we taught them.

Total annual cost: About $100 for services that provide clear value
Time investment: 2 to 3 hours per year maintaining free tools
Satisfaction level: High. We get the best of both approaches

The Bottom Line

The free Fortress Shield we've built throughout this book provides excellent protection for most people in most situations. You don't need paid services to stay secure.

But security isn't one-size-fits-all. Some people genuinely benefit from paid services because of their specific circumstances, risk levels, or preferences.

The key is making informed decisions based on your actual needs rather than marketing pressure or ideological positions about free versus paid.

Choose DIY if:

- You have time for quarterly maintenance
- You enjoy learning about security tools
- Budget is a primary concern
- You want maximum control over your protection

Consider paid services if:

- You have limited time for security maintenance
- You're protecting elderly family members
- You face higher than normal risks
- You prioritize convenience over cost
- You want professional support when problems arise

Go hybrid if:

- You want control over some aspects but convenience for others
- You have specific high-value needs (travel, sensitive communications)
- You're comfortable with complexity in some areas but not others

Whatever approach you choose, the most important thing is that you choose consciously, use consistently, and evaluate periodically.

Mission Complete

By the end of this chapter, you should:

- Understand what paid services actually provide versus marketing promises
- Know when paid services solve real problems versus security theater

Chapter 7: When Paid Services Make Sense

- Recognize red flags in marketing, service quality, and contracts
- Have a framework for making informed decisions
- See examples of DIY, paid, and hybrid approaches working well
- Feel confident evaluating services based on your actual needs

Call to Action

Use free tools to form your Fortress, protect everything with one password, and make informed decisions about when paid services genuinely add value.

Reference Materials: Use the decision framework and evaluation criteria to assess paid services objectively and avoid common marketing traps.

Next up: Chapter 8 dives deep into password management, your one key to the entire Fortress.

Chief Palmer notes that the best security solution is the one people actually use consistently. "I've seen billion-dollar security systems fail because people found ways around them," he says. "Sometimes the 80% solution that people follow religiously is better than the 100% solution they ignore."

Chapter 8: Password Command - Your One Key to the Fortress

⏱ 20 minutes setup + ongoing practice | Essential

CALL SIGN: COMMAND, CONTROL THE KEYS, CONTROL THE FORTRESS.

My niece Emma called me from her apartment one evening, and I could hear the exhaustion in her voice.

"Uncle Alan, I give up. I'm trying to follow the advice you gave me about passwords, but I have literally eighty-three accounts. I counted them. I can't make eighty-three different complicated passwords and remember them all. It's impossible."

She'd been sitting at her computer for two hours, trying to change all her passwords after a breach alert. She'd gotten through eleven accounts before hitting a wall.

"I made a spreadsheet," she continued. "But then I realized I'm keeping all my passwords in an unencrypted Excel file, which seems stupid. So I tried to memorize them instead, but now I can't remember which random string corresponds to which account. I'm locked out of three sites already."

Emma's a smart person. She graduated summa cum laude in accounting. She manages complex financial data for her job. But here she was, defeated by basic password security.

That's when I explained something that changed her entire approach: "Emma, you're not supposed to remember eighty-three passwords. That's not how this works."

Why This Step Matters

Every fortress has keys: gates, armories, bunkers. If those keys are scattered, unguarded, or duplicated without control, the entire defense falls.

Passwords are the keys to your digital fortress. But the problem is that most people have dozens, sometimes hundreds, of accounts. From banking to social media, healthcare to utilities, each one demands a password. Nobody can remember them all. That's why people reuse weak passwords, write them down on sticky notes, or save them in browsers without a second thought.

This isn't stupidity. It's human nature. Our brains are wired to conserve energy, form routines, and rely on shortcuts. It's why we take the same route to work, eat the same breakfast, or type the same password everywhere. We crave simplicity because complexity slows us down.

Attackers know this. They exploit it. But with planning and the right tools, you can flip that psychology on its head. You can have simplicity and security. The answer is a single, strong master password that unlocks a password manager, and from there, everything runs automatically.

Chapter 8: Password Command - Your One Key to the Fortress

⚠ THREAT ALERT

Your habits can be weaponized against you.

The instinct to "keep it simple" often leads to password reuse, which gives attackers the master key to your life.

The Psychology of Passwords: Why We Slip

After thirty years of watching people struggle with security, I've learned that password problems aren't technical problems. They're psychological problems.

Cognitive Load: The average person has 80 to 120 accounts. Nobody can memorize 120 unique 20-character passwords. Your brain cheats and reuses them.

Routine and Muscle Memory: People reuse passwords because it makes logging in feel automatic. That's why "petname123" keeps showing up on breach lists.

Illusion of Control: Writing passwords on sticky notes feels safe because you can see them. In reality, it's one of the riskiest behaviors.

Overconfidence in Passphrases: "But mine is clever and 20 characters long." Clever doesn't matter if you type it into a fake login page.

The bottom line: people aren't bad at passwords because they're lazy. They're bad at passwords because they're human.

My Brother Mike's Password System

Mike kept all his passwords in a notebook in his desk drawer. Not random ones, he had a "system." He'd take a base password like "Broncos" and add the name of the service: "BroncosAmazon," "BroncosBanking," "BroncosNetflix."

"It's easy to remember," he told me proudly. "I just take my favorite team and add where I'm logging in."

"Mike," I said, "that's not security. That's a pattern. Once someone figures out your system, they can guess every password you have."

"But how would they figure out my system?" he asked.

I showed him. One data breach at a retail site exposed "BroncosTarget." I wrote down on a piece of paper: "BroncosBanking," "BroncosAmazon," "BroncosEmail."

Mike's face went pale. "Oh."

That conversation happened six years ago. Mike's been using a password manager ever since, and he's never looked back.

How Attackers Peel the Shield

Bad actors don't always need to guess your password. Sometimes, they don't even need to "know" it in the traditional sense.

What actually happens:

1. You click a login link in an email or fill out a web form
2. Malicious code captures what you typed or submitted
3. The attacker doesn't "crack" it; they copy it

Chapter 8: Password Command - Your One Key to the Fortress

4. That captured email plus password is fed into bots that test it across dozens of other sites in seconds

If you reused that password, the shield peels away like a boiled egg. What began as one crack turns into full exposure across banking, shopping, healthcare, and work accounts.

This is why long passphrases alone are no longer enough. Math doesn't stop phishing. Routine doesn't stop reuse. Only strategy, Command, does.

Maria's Story: The Recycled Password Trap

Maria ran a small online boutique selling handmade jewelry. She was meticulous about her business, tracking inventory, managing customer relationships, and keeping detailed financial records. She was anything but careless.

But Maria used the same passphrase for her online store account and her personal email: "Sunset&Mountains2019!" It was 21 characters long, had uppercase, lowercase, numbers, and symbols. By most standards, it was a strong password.

When her e-commerce platform was breached in early 2023, the criminals obtained her credentials, as well as those of thousands of other merchants. The platform notified users about the breach three weeks later, standard procedure while they investigated.

In those three weeks, the criminals had already moved. They didn't try to crack Maria's password. They didn't need to. They already had it.

They logged into her email using the same credentials. Once in her email, they searched for "bank," "account," "statement." They found her banking information and used her email to reset her bank password, then initiated wire transfers totaling $8,400.

Maria discovered the theft when her automatic rent payment bounced. By then, the money was gone, laundered through cryptocurrency exchanges and international transfers.

I met Maria through a mutual friend who knew I helped people recover from identity theft. We spent three weeks working with her bank, the FBI's IC3 division, and her email provider. She eventually recovered most of the money, but the process was exhausting.

"I didn't do this because I was careless," Maria told me afterward. "I did it because I was overwhelmed and wanted simplicity. I thought a long, complicated password was enough."

"It would have been," I said, "if you'd only used it in one place. The criminals understood your psychology. They knew people reuse passwords, even strong ones."

A password manager would have broken that chain. Each account would have had a unique password. Even if the boutique were breached, her email would have remained secure.

Maria now uses Bitwarden, and every password is different. "It's actually simpler than my old system," she told me. "I don't have to remember anything except one password. Everything else just works."

Password Command: Make Security Automatic

A password manager is the antidote to human nature. Instead of fighting your instincts for routine, it uses them.

1. You create one master password, just one, and commit it to memory
2. The password manager generates long, random, unbreakable keys for every account

3. Logins become easier, not harder, and auto-fill makes them feel like muscle memory
4. Your brain is freed from clutter. Routine stays simple. Security stays strong

This is Command: one key to rule them all, one vault to guard the rest.

🔒 FORTIFY PROTOCOL

Password Command checklist:

Choose a trusted password manager (Bitwarden, KeePass, or Proton Pass for free; 1Password or Dashlane if you want polish)

Memorize one master password (14+ characters, mix of words + symbols)

Let the manager generate unique random passwords for every account

Use autofill; it doubles as a spoof detector

Back up your master recovery code and store it securely

Step-by-Step: Establishing Command

Step 1: Choose Your Password Manager (5 minutes)

We covered this in Chapter 1, but it bears repeating here in the context of Command.

Free options that work excellently:

Bitwarden - Open source, security audited, trusted by professionals.

- Free tier includes unlimited passwords and devices
- Browser extensions, mobile apps, desktop apps
- Generate passwords up to 128 characters

Proton Pass - Swiss privacy laws, made by the Proton Mail team

- Includes email aliasing built in
- Strong focus on privacy and encryption
- Newer than Bitwarden but rapidly improving

KeePass - Offline password manager for maximum control

- You store the database file yourself
- No cloud sync (which some consider more secure)
- Steeper learning curve but unmatched control

Paid options if you want premium features:

1Password - Polished interface, excellent family sharing

- Travel mode (hide vaults when crossing borders)
- Watchtower alerts for breaches
- About $3/month individual, $5/month family

Dashlane - Built-in VPN, dark web monitoring

- User-friendly interface
- Good for less technical users
- About $5/month

My recommendation: Start with Bitwarden. It's free, powerful, and trusted. You can always upgrade or switch later if you need features it doesn't offer.

Step 2: Create Your Master Password (10 minutes)

This is the most important password decision you'll ever make. This one password protects everything else.

Requirements:

- Minimum 14 characters (longer is better)
- Mix of words, numbers, and symbols
- Memorable but not guessable

- Never used anywhere else
- Never shared with anyone

Method 1: Passphrase with modifications

Take 4 to 5 unrelated words that mean something to you, add numbers and symbols:

"Coffee-Mountain-Sunset-Guitar-77!"
"Pizza@Denver!Hockey#Springer"
"River&Fishing*Camping!2019"

Method 2: Sentence with substitutions

Take a sentence, use first letters, add substitutions:

"My daughter graduated from Colorado State in 2019" becomes "MdgfCS!n2019"
"I adopted my dog Luna in March of 2020" becomes "IamdL!Mo2020"

Method 3: Memorable phrase with modifications

"The quick brown fox jumps 27 times!"
"Sunsets in Colorado are brighter than city lights 77"

Practice it: Type your master password 20 times. Seriously. Right now. Muscle memory is crucial.

Write it down temporarily: Use paper (not digital) and store it securely. Once you've memorized it completely and can type it blindfolded, destroy the paper.

Critical backup: Set up emergency access or recovery codes BEFORE you rely on the manager completely.

When Emma finally created her master password, I made her practice typing it while we talked. By the end of our conversation, her fingers knew it automatically.

"It feels weird to have just one password to remember," she said.

"That's the point," I told her. "Your brain isn't a database. Stop trying to use it like one."

Step 3: Import Existing Passwords (5 minutes)

Most password managers can import from your browser's saved passwords.

From Chrome/Edge:

1. Settings → Passwords → three dots → Export passwords
2. Save the CSV file
3. In your password manager, Import → Chrome CSV
4. Delete the CSV file immediately after import

From Firefox:

1. about:logins → three dots → Export Logins
2. Save the CSV file
3. Import into password manager
4. Delete the CSV file

From Safari:

1. Keychain Access → Passwords → Select All → Export
2. Import into password manager
3. Delete the export file

Security note: That CSV file contains all your passwords in plain text. Delete it as soon as you're done importing. Empty your trash too.

Step 4: Generate Strong Passwords for Critical Accounts (15 minutes)

Start with your most important accounts and upgrade them to unique, manager-generated passwords.

Priority order:

1. Email (this protects everything else)
2. Banking and financial accounts
3. Password manager itself
4. Work accounts
5. Healthcare portals
6. Shopping accounts with saved payment methods

For each account:

1. Log in one last time with your old password
2. Navigate to security settings
3. Select "Change password"
4. Use your password manager to generate a new password (20+ characters)
5. Save it in your vault with the account name and URL
6. Test by logging out and back in

Generation settings:

- Length: 20 to 32 characters (use maximum allowed by site)
- Include uppercase, lowercase, numbers, symbols
- Avoid ambiguous characters if you might need to type it manually

Emma spent one Saturday afternoon updating her top 20 accounts. "It was tedious," she told me, "but now I feel like I actually have control instead of just hoping nothing bad happens."

Tom's Story: The Phishing Trap

Tom was a retired Air Force veteran, sharp as they come. He'd spent his career in logistics, managing supply chains for critical operations. He understood operational security.

Chapter 8: Password Command - Your One Key to the Fortress

Tom was proud of his password: "Falcon!AFB&Colorado@1989", eighteen characters, mixing his first duty station with symbols and numbers. He'd created it following advice from an IT security briefing in 2018, and he used variations of it across his most important accounts.

One Tuesday morning, Tom received an email from "USAA Security Department" warning of suspicious login attempts on his account. The email looked perfect, with the right logo, correct formatting, and official-sounding language. It even referenced his membership number.

The link opened a login page that looked identical to the real USAA site. Tom, trusting his eyes and the email's authenticity, typed in his password.

Nothing happened. The page said "System error, please try again later." Tom shrugged and closed the tab.

Fifteen minutes later, criminals were in his account. They'd captured his password when he typed it on the fake page. They immediately initiated wire transfers to external accounts, requested cash advances on his credit card, and attempted to open new loans.

Tom discovered the breach when his phone rang, USAA's actual fraud department calling about suspicious activity. By then, $12,000 had been transferred out.

Tom called me that afternoon, shaken. "Alan, I don't understand. My password was strong. Eighteen characters. How did they get it?"

"They didn't crack it, Tom. You gave it to them."

I walked him through what happened. The email was a phishing attempt. The website was a perfect clone, hosted on a domain that appeared legitimate: usaa-security-verify.com, instead of usaa.com. When Tom typed his password, it was sent directly to the criminals.

"But how could I have known?" Tom asked. "It looked exactly like the real site."

"If you'd been using a password manager with auto-fill," I explained, "it wouldn't have filled in the password on that fake page. The URL didn't match. That one signal would have saved you."

We spent the next two weeks helping Tom recover his accounts, file fraud reports, and rebuild his security. USAA reversed most of the fraudulent transactions, but the stress took a toll.

Tom now uses Bitwarden with hardware key authentication. "I learned a hard lesson," he told me. "Technical security isn't enough. You need system security. The password manager is the system."

🚨 MISSION CRITICAL

Stop trying to memorize dozens of passwords.

Your brain is not a database. Simplify your life: one master password, one command center, auto-fill for everything else.

The Auto-Fill Security Feature

Most people don't realize: password manager autofill isn't just convenient. It's a security feature.

How it works:

- Your password manager stores the exact URL for each login
- When you visit a website, it checks if the URL matches
- If it matches, auto-fill is available

Chapter 8: Password Command - Your One Key to the Fortress

- If it doesn't match, auto-fill stays locked

Why this matters:

- Phishing sites use URLs that look similar but aren't exact matches
- phishing-amazon.com is not equal to amazon.com
- secure-bankofamerica-login.net is not equal to bankofamerica.com
- Even perfect-looking clone sites fail the URL test

Your brain sees: A perfect-looking login page
Your password manager sees: Wrong URL = possible phishing = no auto-fill

When auto-fill doesn't work, that's your alarm bell. Stop. Verify the URL manually. Don't override the security check by typing the password anyway.

My nephew Jake uses this as his primary phishing detector. "If my password manager doesn't fill it in, I don't trust it," he says. "Saved me three times last semester."

Reinforcement: The Role of MFA

Password Command is strongest when paired with Multi-Factor Authentication (MFA). Think of it as a double-lock system:

- **Something you know:** your master password
- **Something you have:** your phone or authenticator app
- **Something you are:** your fingerprint or Face ID

We covered MFA in Chapter 1, but let's reinforce why it's particularly critical for Password Command.

The layers work together:

Layer 1: Password Manager - Unique password for every account

Layer 2: MFA - Second verification even if password is compromised

Layer 3: Auto-fill - Phishing detector built into your workflow

MFA: Don't Trust SMS Codes

SMS codes can be intercepted through SIM-swapping or message redirection. I've seen it happen to three people I know personally.

Use instead:

- Authenticator apps (Google Authenticator, Microsoft Authenticator, Authy, Duo)
- Hardware security keys (YubiKey, Titan Security Key)
- Passkeys (the newest and strongest option)

If a service only offers SMS:

- Enable it as a stopgap, it's better than nothing
- Upgrade the moment stronger MFA becomes available
- Consider whether you really need that account

With MFA from an authenticator app or hardware key, even if attackers capture your password, they're stopped cold at the second gate.

▨ RED TEAM INSIGHT

In a phishing test, employees using password managers had a 70% lower failure rate. Auto-fill refused to engage on spoofed sites, tipping them off. Those relying on memorized passphrases failed far more often, human instinct overrode training.

Emergency Drill: If You Suspect Capture

Speed is your shield. The faster you respond, the less damage attackers can do.

If you think a password was compromised:

Immediate (within 5 minutes):

1. Open your password manager
2. Generate a new password for the affected account
3. Log into the real site directly (don't use any links from suspicious emails)
4. Change the password immediately
5. Log out all other sessions/devices

Within 1 hour:

1. Enable MFA if not already active
2. Check account activity logs for unauthorized access
3. Review recovery options (email, phone) and secure them
4. Update security questions if they might have been exposed

Within 24 hours:

1. Check password manager for reuse, did you use that password anywhere else?
2. Rotate any shared passwords immediately
3. If financial accounts involved, alert your bank/issuer
4. Review connected accounts (OAuth, linked services)
5. Document what happened for future reference

Chapter 8: Password Command - Your One Key to the Fortress

My neighbor Dave's drill response:

Dave got a phishing email and almost fell for it. He caught himself at the last second, closed the tab, and called me.

"Did you type anything in?" I asked.

"I typed my username but stopped before entering my password."

"Good. Change that password anyway, just in case. Better safe than sorry."

We ran through the drill together. Changed password, enabled MFA, checked activity logs. Total time: twelve minutes. Zero damage.

"That was actually kind of satisfying," Dave said. "Having a plan to follow instead of just panicking."

Practice this drill once with a low-stakes account. The muscle memory will be there when you need it for real.

SITREP: Threat Assessment

- Billions of credentials are already exposed in dark web dumps
- Attackers capture credentials through phishing, form skimming, or malware, no brute force needed
- Credential stuffing bots spread one stolen password across dozens of accounts instantly
- Passphrases remain mathematically strong, but practically weak if reused or phished
- Password managers flip human psychology into strength: simplicity plus automation plus redundancy

Common Mistakes That Keep Me Awake

Using weak master passwords because they're "easier to remember." Your master password is the ONE password worth memorizing perfectly. Make it count. Practice typing it until it's muscle memory.

Sharing master passwords with family members. Use the password manager's sharing features instead. Most managers let you share specific passwords without revealing your master password.

Not setting up recovery options. If you forget your master password and have no recovery method, you lose everything. Set up emergency access or recovery codes immediately.

Storing the master password digitally. Paper only, until it's memorized. Then destroy the paper. Never save it in a note on your phone or computer.

Ignoring auto-fill warnings. If autofill doesn't work, don't manually type passwords on pages where autofill fails.

Reusing the master password anywhere else. This password unlocks everything. It should NEVER be used for any other purpose. Ever.

When Things Don't Go According to Plan

"I forgot my master password."
This is why emergency access and recovery codes are critical. If you set them up:

- Use your recovery codes to regain access
- Reset your master password immediately
- Update your emergency access contacts

Chapter 8: Password Command - Your One Key to the Fortress

If you didn't set them up:

- Contact your password manager's support (they can't recover your password, but may have options)
- You might need to start fresh with a new account
- This is a hard lesson about backup procedures

"My password manager isn't auto-filling."

Could be legitimate (wrong URL, possible phishing) or technical:

- Refresh the page and try again
- Check that the browser extension is enabled
- Verify you're logged into your password manager
- Update the extension if it's outdated
- Try manually copying the password from your vault

"I can't access my password manager on a new device."

You need your master password and potentially MFA:

- Install the app or extension
- Log in with master password
- Verify with MFA (authenticator app or hardware key)
- Sync should happen automatically
- If sync fails, check your internet connection

163

"A website rejected the generated password."

Some sites have weird password requirements:

- Adjust the generation settings (shorter length, no special characters)
- Try removing ambiguous characters
- Some sites foolishly limit password length, use the maximum they allow
- Save whatever works in your password manager

Practical Lessons: Commanding the Keys

One master password: Treat it like your military ID, essential, irreplaceable

Everything else is random: Don't even try to memorize them. That's the point.

Auto-fill equals alarm system: If it doesn't fill, assume the site is fake until proven otherwise

Family Command: Share a secure vault with spouses or kids for emergencies. Most password managers support this.

Emergency drills: Know what to do if capture happens. Routine beats panic.

Quarterly audits: Check your password manager's security report. Change any weak or reused passwords.

Export backups: Quarterly, export an encrypted backup and store it securely offline

Chapter 8: Password Command - Your One Key to the Fortress

My Family's Password Command

My wife and I share a family vault in Bitwarden. It contains:

- Shared accounts (streaming services, utilities)
- Emergency contacts
- Important document locations
- Safe combination and security codes

Our kids each have their own vaults, plus access to the family vault. When Sarah needed our insurance information from college, she could access it without calling us.

Every six months, we run a security report together. Last check, we found three passwords that had been in breaches. Changed them in about ten minutes.

"This feels like a family fire drill," my son said.

"Exactly right," I told him. "We practice so when it matters, we're ready."

Success Metrics: You'll Know Command Is Working

Week 1:

- Master password committed to memory
- Top 10 accounts using unique, manager-generated passwords
- Auto-fill working smoothly on main devices
- MFA enabled on critical accounts

Month 1:

- All important accounts using unique passwords
- Auto-fill feels natural, not annoying
- You catch yourself using auto-fill as a phishing detector
- Password manager syncing across all devices

Quarter 1:

- Old password habits have been completely replaced
- Security report shows no weak or reused passwords
- You help family members set up their own password managers
- Emergency drill practiced and ready

Year 1:

- Password security is automatic, not a chore
- You can't remember most of your passwords (and that's good)

- Phishing attempts fail because auto-fill doesn't engage
- Your digital security is better than most companies'

Checkpoint: Can you log into your three most important accounts using only your password manager and MFA? Do you trust auto-fill to warn you about suspicious sites? If yes, you've established Command.

Why This Matters More Than Technical Security

I've spent three decades protecting systems where one mistake could have catastrophic consequences. But you know what? The principles are the same whether you're protecting nuclear weapons or protecting your grandmother's email account.

The difference is that military systems have dedicated security teams, mandatory protocols, and consequences for non-compliance. Your personal security has you.

Maria recovered her money, but the three-week recovery process cost her business momentum and countless hours of stress. "I thought I was being secure," she told me. "I just didn't realize that even strong passwords need to be unique."

Tom's fraud was mostly reversed by USAA, but the experience shook his confidence. "I felt stupid for falling for it," he admitted. "But I've seen dozens of people fall for the same thing. The criminals are good at this."

Emma finally has her security under control. All eighty-three accounts (now ninety-one, she found more) have unique passwords. "I don't stress about it anymore," she said. "When I get a breach alert, I just change that one password. Takes thirty seconds."

The best part? She's helping her coworkers at the accounting firm set up password managers. Last count, she's secured nine people who were all struggling with the same problems she had.

Your brain isn't designed to be a password database. Stop fighting your psychology. Use it instead.

Mission Complete

By the end of this chapter you should:

- Recognize that weak passwords aren't a failing, they're a predictable human habit
- Understand why passphrases alone are no longer sufficient
- Know how attackers capture and reuse credentials at scale
- Have chosen and set up a password manager
- Created a strong master password you've practiced typing
- Upgraded your critical accounts to unique, generated passwords
- Understand how auto-fill serves as a phishing detector
- Be prepared to run an emergency drill if a capture happens
- Know how to pair Password Command with MFA for maximum security

Call to Action

Use free tools to form your Fortress, protect everything with one password, and put every key under Command.

Reference Materials: Use the Emergency Response Drill to practice your breach response until it becomes automatic.

Next up: Chapter 9 builds your ALERT system for early warning when threats emerge.

Chief Palmer notes that password security is where psychology meets technology. "The best technical solutions fail if they don't account for how humans actually behave," he says. "Password managers succeed because they work with human nature instead of against it."

Chapter 9: ALERT - Early Warning Systems

⏱ 15 minutes setup + ongoing monitoring | Essential

Call Sign: ALERT, Know first, act fast.

My sister-in-law Janet called me on a Thursday afternoon, and her voice had that edge that told me something was very wrong.

"Alan, I just got off the phone with my bank. Someone tried to wire $15,000 out of my account this morning. They say it's my fault for having a weak password, but I didn't even know my information was out there."

"When did you change your bank password last?" I asked.

"I... I don't know. Years ago? Why would I change it if nothing was wrong?"

That's when I had to explain something that surprised her: her email address had been sitting in a publicly available breach database for eight months. Anyone with an internet connection could search for it and see that her credentials from an old shopping site had been exposed. Criminals had been testing those credentials across banking sites for months, and Janet's bank was one of the sites where the password still worked.

"Why didn't anyone tell me?" she asked.

"Someone tried to," I said. "The company that got breached probably sent you an email notification. Did you read it?"

Long pause. "I get so many emails. I probably deleted it thinking it was spam."

Janet wasn't careless. She was overwhelmed. And she had no system in place to cut through the noise and alert her when something actually mattered.

That conversation happened three years ago. Janet now has early warning systems that would have caught that breach within hours instead of months. She's never had another close call.

Why This Step Matters

No fortress is perfect. Even with the strongest locks, a breach can happen. In military terms, this is why bases use perimeter alarms, radar, and watchtowers: not because they expect failure, but because early warning gives them time to respond.

The same principle applies to digital security. If your email, password, or personal details are leaked in a breach, time is everything. The difference between a near miss and financial ruin often comes down to whether you find out first, or whether the attacker does.

That's the job of ALERT: putting early warning systems in place so cracks are spotted before they spread.

Note: We covered basic breach monitoring setup in Chapter 2. This chapter goes deeper into the emergency response procedures, the psychology of breach fatigue, and when paid monitoring services actually make sense.

Chapter 9: ALERT - Early Warning Systems

🔬 SITREP Reminder: Regulation Shifts

As outlined in Chapter 2, federal consumer protection enforcement has become inconsistent. The FCC has reclaimed some authority over ISPs, but agencies like the CFPB and FTC have scaled back. This means:

- *Government Alerts Lag. You may not hear from regulators until long after your data is already circulating*
- *State Attorneys General Step Up. Some states enforce aggressively; others don't*
- *Personal ALERT Systems Close the Gap. Free tools like Have I Been Pwned and Firefox Monitor, paired with breach alerts from your password manager, ensure you hear about exposures first*

The Backstory: The Rise of the Breach Economy

In 2013, Yahoo suffered the largest breach in history, over 3 billion accounts compromised. Adobe, LinkedIn, Marriott, Equifax, and countless others have followed. Each breach adds more fuel to the underground market: usernames, passwords, security questions, and even passport numbers.

This has created a "breach economy" on the dark web. Criminals don't need to hack you, they just buy a database dump and test the logins.

I remember when the Equifax breach happened in 2017. I spent that entire weekend helping family members freeze their credit and change passwords. My phone didn't stop ringing. Everyone was panicked, asking the same questions: "Am I affected? What do I do? How did this happen?"

The frustrating part? Most of them had been affected by smaller breaches for years without knowing it. Equifax made headlines because it was massive and involved a credit bureau. But the principle was the same as dozens of breaches that never made the news.

The FTC has fined companies for failing to protect consumer data, but the damage to individuals is rarely reversed. That means detection is your responsibility.

The Intelligence Failure That Cost Carla Everything

Carla was a nurse in Ohio, working twelve-hour shifts in the ICU. She was meticulous about patient care, double-checked medications, followed protocols perfectly, never cut corners. But she had no idea her personal email had been exposed in a breach at a hospital vendor that managed scheduling software.

The breach happened in March. The vendor sent notification emails in April. Carla's email provider, overwhelmed with promotional messages and spam, filtered the notification to her spam folder. She never saw it.

By May, criminals had her email address and the password she'd used for the scheduling software. They tested that password against common sites: Gmail, Yahoo, Outlook. It worked on her personal Gmail account, she'd reused the password.

Once in her email, they searched for "bank," "account," and "statement." Found her banking information. Used the "forgot password" feature to reset her bank password, the reset link went to her email, which they controlled.

They initiated wire transfers. Changed her mailing address. Opened credit cards. Applied for personal loans.

Carla discovered the breach when she went to pay rent and found her checking account empty. $8,400 gone. Her credit score had dropped 180 points from new accounts she'd never opened.

I met Carla through a veterans' support group, her husband was former Army. We spent three weeks helping her recover: filing police reports, working with banks, disputing fraudulent accounts, freezing her credit.

"I keep thinking about the timeline," Carla told me. "March to May. Two months. If I'd known in March, I could have changed my password and none of this would have happened."

"That's exactly right," I said. "You needed an early warning system. Something that cuts through the noise and tells you immediately when your information is exposed."

We set up her ALERT systems together. Within a week, she got her first notification, a different breach from 2019 she'd never known about. Changed that password immediately.

"This feels like having a smoke detector in every room," she said. "I don't live in fear anymore. I just know I'll be warned if there's smoke."

Fortress Shield - 2026 Edition

🔒 FORTIFY PROTOCOL

Your ALERT checklist:

Register your primary email addresses with a breach notification service

Set up dark web monitoring for critical accounts (email, phone, SSN if offered)

Respond instantly to alerts: rotate passwords, enable MFA, review account recovery

Schedule quarterly checks, breaches are ongoing, not one-time

---

Building Your ALERT Network (Detailed Setup)

We covered the basics in Chapter 2. Now let's build a comprehensive, redundant system that ensures you're always the first to know.

Layer 1: Have I Been Pwned (Primary Alert System)

What it does: Monitors a database of billions of compromised accounts from known breaches

Cost: Free

Coverage: Email addresses and passwords

Setup (5 minutes):

1. Go to haveibeenpwned.com
2. Enter your primary email address
3. Review current breaches (don't panic, most people have several)
4. Click "notify me of pwnages" at the top

Chapter 9: ALERT - Early Warning Systems

5. Enter your email and confirm via the link
6. Repeat for ALL your email addresses:
   o Work email
   o Personal email
   o Old emails you barely use anymore
   o That Hotmail account from 2005

What happens next: You'll get an email within hours of your address appearing in a newly discovered breach

My family's experience: When I set this up for my extended family, we found that every single person had at least one email in a breach database. My father-in-law had seven breaches he knew nothing about. We spent one Saturday afternoon changing passwords and enabling MFA.

Layer 2: Password Manager Health Check (Continuous Monitoring)

What it does: Scans your saved passwords against breach databases automatically

Cost: Free (built into most password managers)

Coverage: All passwords saved in your vault

Setup in Bitwarden (3 minutes):

1. Log into Bitwarden
2. Go to Tools → Reports
3. Select "Data Breach Report"
4. Review any flagged passwords
5. Enable continuous monitoring in Settings

177

Setup in Proton Pass (2 minutes):

1. Open Proton Pass
2. Go to Settings → Security
3. Toggle "Dark Web Monitoring" to ON
4. Review the security dashboard

What happens next: You'll see immediate alerts in your password manager when saved credentials appear in breaches

The advantage: This catches breaches even if you didn't notice the email notification. It's your backup alarm.

Layer 3: Firefox Monitor (Secondary Verification)

What it does: Provides breach monitoring powered by Have I Been Pwned with a cleaner interface

Cost: Free

Coverage: Email addresses

Setup (3 minutes):

1. Go to monitor.firefox.com
2. Enter your email address
3. Click "Sign Up for Alerts"
4. Confirm via email
5. Repeat for all email addresses

Why add this if you have HIBP: Redundancy. Sometimes one service catches a breach before another. Sometimes emails get filtered to spam. Multiple alerts increase your chances of getting the warning in time.

My neighbor Dave's story: He had HIBP set up, but the notification email went to spam. Firefox Monitor sent a browser notification that he saw immediately. That redundancy saved him from a credential stuffing attack.

Layer 4: Credit Bureau Monitoring (Financial Focus)

What it does: Alerts you to new credit inquiries, accounts, or changes to your credit file

Cost: Free basic monitoring from all three bureaus; paid tiers offer more features

Setup (covered in Chapter 3):

If you froze your credit in Chapter 3, you already have accounts with Equifax, Experian, and TransUnion. Enable the free monitoring features:

1. Log into each bureau
2. Look for "Credit Monitoring" or "Alerts"
3. Enable notifications for:
   - New credit inquiries
   - New accounts opened
   - Changes to personal information
   - Public records (bankruptcies, liens)

What happens next: You'll be alerted if someone tries to open credit in your name despite the freeze, or if there are inquiries you don't recognize

🚨 MISSION CRITICAL

Don't wait for your bank or the FTC to call you.

Your ALERT system is your radar, and it's free.

Free vs. Paid ALERT Services: The Honest Assessment

After helping dozens of people set up monitoring, I've learned when paid services make sense and when they're unnecessary.

Free Services Cover the Essentials

What you get for free:

- Breach notifications (HIBP, Firefox Monitor)
- Password health checks (Bitwarden, Proton Pass)
- Credit monitoring basics (all three bureaus)
- Dark web email monitoring (some password managers)

For most people, this is enough. The free stack catches the vast majority of threats in time to respond effectively.

Chapter 9: ALERT - Early Warning Systems

Paid Services Add Convenience and Coverage

Premium features worth considering:

Aura / Identity Guard / LifeLock ($8-25/month):

- Monitor email, phone, SSN, bank accounts
- Alerts for fraudulent applications (loans, credit cards)
- Identity theft insurance (coverage for recovery costs)
- White-glove restoration support
- Family plans covering multiple people

Credit Bureau Paid Tiers ($10-30/month):

- More frequent credit report updates
- 3-bureau monitoring (free versions often cover one bureau)
- Credit score tracking
- Identity theft insurance
- Lock/unlock features for credit

Specialized Dark Web Monitoring ($5-15/month):

- Deeper scanning of dark web forums
- SSN and financial data monitoring
- Passport and driver's license number monitoring
- Family member monitoring

Who Should Consider Paid Services

Good candidates for paid monitoring:

Elderly family members who need simplicity: One service, one bill, comprehensive coverage, phone support when alerts arrive

Business owners with significant assets: The cost is trivial compared to potential losses; insurance coverage adds value

High-profile individuals: Public figures, executives, activists who face elevated targeting

Families with children: Family plans can cover multiple people cost-effectively; monitoring children's SSNs before they have credit files

People recovering from identity theft: Extra monitoring provides peace of mind during the recovery period

Who should stick with free services:

Tech-comfortable individuals: If you can manage multiple free tools, you don't need to pay for consolidation

Budget-conscious families: Free services provide excellent coverage for $0

People who follow the Fortress Shield: If you've implemented everything in this book, paid monitoring adds relatively little additional security

My personal setup: I use only free services. My wife and I are comfortable managing multiple alerts, and we've implemented all the Fortress Shield defenses. The free tools catch everything we need.

My father-in-law Frank's setup: He uses a paid service ($12/month). Frank doesn't want to manage multiple tools or worry about technical details. He gets monthly reports showing what was checked, and he can call someone if he gets an alert. For him, that's worth the cost.

Both approaches work. Choose based on your comfort level, not fear.

Chapter 9: ALERT - Early Warning Systems

SITREP: Threat Assessment

- Breaches are constant: thousands of companies are compromised each year
- Data sold on the dark web fuels credential stuffing, phishing, and identity theft
- Free tools like HIBP provide early warnings, but only if you set them up
- Paid monitoring can extend coverage, but the basics are free
- The average time between breach and notification is 3-6 months, your early warning systems close this gap

RED TEAM INSIGHT

In a simulation, we purchased a breached database on the dark web for $20. Within hours, 40% of the logins still worked because users hadn't changed their passwords. Of those, half used the same password on at least one other account. ALERT isn't just nice to have, it's the tripwire that prevents disaster.

Emergency Drill: When ALERT Sounds

Speed determines outcome. Practice this drill until it's automatic.

183

Phase 1: Initial Assessment (First 5 minutes)

When you get an alert:

Read the alert carefully

- Which service was breached?
- What data was exposed? (Email? Password? Security questions? Payment info?)
- When did the breach occur?

Don't panic

- Alerts don't always mean active compromise
- You're getting this notification so you can prevent damage
- Take a breath and follow the procedure

Open your password manager

- Search for the breached service
- Check if you have an account there
- See what password you were using

My nephew Jake's first alert: He got a breach notification for a gaming site he'd used once in 2019. "Uncle Alan, am I hacked?"

"No," I told him. "You're being warned. Now you act before the hackers do."

Phase 2: Immediate Response (Next 15 minutes)

Action checklist:

Change the password immediately

- Go directly to the real website (don't click links in the alert email)
- Log in with your current credentials

- Generate a new password with your password manager
- Save and test the new password

Enable MFA if not already active

- This adds a second layer even if the password is compromised
- Use authenticator app, not SMS
- Save backup codes in your password manager

Check for password reuse

- Did you use that password anywhere else?
- Password manager health check shows this
- Change it everywhere it appears

Review account activity

- Look at login history
- Check for unauthorized access
- Review account settings for changes
- Examine recent transactions if it's a financial account

Carla's drill response now: When she got her first alert after we set up her systems, she followed this procedure and had everything secured within twenty minutes. "I felt in control instead of panicked," she told me.

Phase 3: Extended Security (Next 24 hours)

Additional steps:

Update security questions

- If the breach included security question answers
- Use false answers stored in your password manager

185

- "Mother's maiden name" can be "Purple!Elephant77"

Review connected accounts

- OAuth authorizations
- Third-party app access
- Linked payment methods

Check email forwarding rules

- If the breach was your email account
- Attackers sometimes set up forwarding to monitor you
- Settings → Forwarding (look for rules you didn't create)

Monitor financial accounts

- If the breach included payment information
- Check for unauthorized charges
- Consider placing fraud alerts

Document the incident

- Keep a log: what was breached, when you were notified, what actions you took
- Save the notification email
- This helps if you need to prove you responded promptly

Phase 4: Ongoing Vigilance (Next 90 days)

Sustained monitoring:

Watch for phishing attempts

- Criminals often follow breaches with targeted phishing
- Be extra cautious about emails from the breached company

Chapter 9: ALERT - Early Warning Systems

- Verify everything through official channels

Monitor credit if SSN or financial data was exposed

- Check credit reports monthly (free at annualcreditreport.com)
- Look for new accounts or inquiries
- Consider placing fraud alerts if the breach was severe

Review account statements carefully

- Banking, credit cards, investment accounts
- Look for small unauthorized charges (criminals test with tiny amounts)

My family's breach log: We keep a shared document tracking every breach notification anyone in the family receives. Dates, services, actions taken. It's become a useful reference for seeing patterns and staying organized.

The Psychology of Alert Fatigue

Here's something I've noticed: when people first set up ALERT systems, they often get overwhelmed by the sheer number of breaches they're already in.

My sister Linda set up HIBP and discovered she was in 11 breaches. "Alan, this is terrifying. How can I possibly be in eleven breaches?"

"You've been using the internet for twenty years," I reminded her. "You have accounts at dozens of sites. Some of those sites got hacked. This isn't your fault."

187

Managing breach fatigue:

Prioritize by severity:

- Email breach = highest priority
- Banking breach = highest priority
- Obscure forum from 2012 = lower priority

Batch process when possible:

- Set aside one hour to address all historical breaches
- Focus on accounts you still use
- Close accounts you don't need anymore

Accept that breaches are normal:

- They happen to everyone
- Having ALERT systems means you're prepared
- Most breaches can be addressed without lasting damage

Focus on forward motion:

- Each password you change makes you more secure
- Each MFA you enable adds protection
- Progress beats perfection

After Linda worked through her breach list over two weekends, she told me: "I actually feel better now. Before, I had no idea what was out there. Now I know, and I've dealt with it."

Common Mistakes That Keep Me Awake

Ignoring alerts because "I'll deal with it later"

Later becomes never. Set a two-hour deadline: if you get an alert, you respond within two hours. No exceptions.

Changing only the breached password
If you reused that password, change it everywhere. The breach notification is your early warning, use it.

Not enabling MFA after a breach
This is your opportunity to add a second layer. Don't waste it.

Assuming paid services are better than free services
The free tools are excellent. Paid services add convenience, not fundamentally better security for most people.

Setting up alerts and then never checking email
ALERT systems only work if you see the notifications. Check your email daily or enable push notifications.

Not practicing the emergency drill
When a real alert comes, you'll be stressed. Having practiced the procedure makes you faster and more effective.

When Things Don't Go According to Plan

"I'm getting too many breach alerts"
This usually means you have many old accounts. Focus on accounts you actively use. For abandoned accounts, either secure them or delete them entirely.

"The breach notification email looks like spam"
Legitimate breach notifications often do look suspicious. Always verify by going directly to haveibeenpwned.com or your password manager, never by clicking links in alert emails.

"I can't remember if I had an account at the breached service"
Check your password manager. Search your email for messages from that company. When in doubt, assume you

might have an account and change any passwords that could have been used there.

"The breach included my SSN. What do I do?"

This is more serious. Freeze your credit immediately if you haven't already (Chapter 3). Place fraud alerts with all three credit bureaus. Monitor credit reports monthly. Consider paid monitoring for the next year.

"I'm overwhelmed and don't know where to start"

Start with email and banking. Those two categories protect the most important things. You can address other breaches gradually.

Success Metrics: You'll Know ALERT Is Working

Week 1:

- All email addresses registered with HIBP
- Password manager health check enabled
- Firefox Monitor set up as backup
- Credit bureau monitoring activated

Month 1:

- First breach alert received and handled within two hours
- Emergency drill feels familiar, not scary
- You catch yourself checking breach status periodically
- Family members ask you for help setting up their ALERT systems

Chapter 9: ALERT - Early Warning Systems

Quarter 1:

- All historical breaches addressed
- New breach alerts handled routinely
- You help others interpret their breach notifications
- No successful attacks despite several breach exposures

Year 1:

- ALERT has caught at least 2-3 breaches you wouldn't have known about
- Emergency response is automatic, not stressful
- You've successfully prevented credential stuffing attacks
- Your data is still out there (unavoidable), but it's not actively harming you

Checkpoint: Do you have multiple ALERT systems set up? Can you respond to a breach notification within two hours? Have you practiced the emergency drill? If yes, you're protected by early warning.

Why This Matters More Than You Think

I spent thirty years in environments where early warning systems were the difference between mission success and catastrophic failure. Radar detects incoming threats. Perimeter sensors spot infiltration. Intelligence networks provide advance notice.

Your personal digital life deserves the same level of vigilance.

Janet's near-miss with the $15,000 wire transfer ended well because her bank's fraud detection caught it. But she got lucky. Many people aren't so lucky.

Carla's breach recovery took three weeks of her life. She missed work. She lost sleep. She questioned whether she could trust online banking anymore. An ALERT system would have prevented all of it.

My nephew Jake gets breach notifications every few months. Each time, he follows the drill: assess, respond, document. Total time: usually under 20 minutes. He's never had a successful attack.

The criminals who buy breach databases and run credential stuffing attacks are counting on people like Janet, people who don't know their information is exposed until it's too late.

You're no longer one of those people. You have radar. You know first. You act fast.

Mission Complete

By the end of this chapter, you should:

- Understand the breach economy and why your data is valuable
- See how attackers weaponize exposed credentials silently before victims notice
- Have set up multiple free ALERT systems for redundant warnings
- Recognize when paid services add value versus when free tools are sufficient
- Know the emergency drill by heart: assess, respond, monitor, document
- Understand breach fatigue and how to manage it without becoming complacent

Chapter 9: ALERT - Early Warning Systems

Call to Action

Use free tools to form your Fortress, protect everything with one password, and install ALERT as your radar.

Reference Materials: Use the Emergency Breach Response Checklist (page reference) to guide your actions when alerts arrive.

Next: Your Fortress Shield is nearly complete. Continue maintaining these systems and staying vigilant.

Chief Palmer notes that early warning systems saved countless missions during his career. "The side that knows first usually wins," he says. "In cybersecurity, being warned first means you can prevent the attack entirely. That's always better than recovering from one."

Chapter 10: Credit Armor - Fortifying Your Financial Identity

⏱ 30 minutes setup + ongoing monitoring | Essential

CALL SIGN: ARMOR, SEAL THE GATES, MONITOR THE WALLS.

My daughter Sarah called me from her apartment one evening, two years after we'd cleaned up her identity theft mess from college. Her voice had that careful, controlled tone that told me she was trying not to panic.

"Dad, I just got a letter from a collections agency. They say I owe $4,200 on a medical bill from a hospital in Phoenix. I've never even been to Arizona."

We'd frozen Sarah's credit after her BMW incident in Chapter 3. Her credit had been locked down tight for over a year. How was someone able to open medical accounts in her name?

"Did you lift your freeze recently?" I asked.

"Yes, when I applied for that apartment last month. I unfroze all three bureaus for a week, like you showed me. Then I refroze them."

That was the problem. That one-week window. Someone had been monitoring Sarah's credit, waiting for an opportunity. The moment the freeze lifted, they pounced. Medical identity theft doesn't always trigger the same alarms as credit card or loan fraud, and it often slips through.

This conversation taught me something important: freezing your credit is essential, but it's not complete armor. You need monitoring systems that watch for moments when your shield is down, and you need to understand the entire landscape of financial identity protection.

Why This Step Matters

Your Social Security number is the skeleton key to your financial life. With it, a criminal can open loans, credit cards, utilities, or even file fraudulent tax returns. Unlike a stolen credit card, which can be canceled in minutes, a stolen SSN can shadow you for years.

Credit Armor is about building a strong shield around your financial identity. At its core are two powerful rights under U.S. law: the right to freeze your credit for free, and the right to monitor your credit file. When combined, these measures act as armor. The freeze keeps the enemy from breaching the walls. Monitoring tells you if they're probing the defenses.

We covered the basics of credit freezes in Chapter 3. This chapter delves deeper into the monitoring ecosystem, regulatory landscape, and advanced protection strategies for maintaining your armor in the long term.

⚠ THREAT ALERT

Credit freezes are backed by federal law.

Every U.S. citizen has the legal right to place or lift a freeze at no cost. This was solidified by the Economic Growth, Regulatory Relief, and Consumer Protection Act of 2018, following the Equifax breach. Use this right.

The Backstory: The Equifax Breach

In 2017, credit bureau Equifax disclosed a catastrophic breach. Hackers stole sensitive information for 147 million Americans. Social Security numbers, birth dates, addresses. That's nearly half the country.

I remember that September as if it were yesterday. My phone didn't stop ringing for weeks. Every family member, every friend, everyone I'd ever helped with technology wanted to know: "Am I affected? What do I do?"

The breach happened because Equifax failed to patch a known vulnerability in its web application. Security researchers had identified the flaw months earlier. Equifax knew about it. And they didn't fix it fast enough.

Hackers exploited that vulnerability for months before anyone noticed. By the time Equifax discovered the intrusion, attackers had already copied complete identity profiles on nearly half of all American adults.

Equifax failed in its most fundamental duty: protecting the data it was entrusted to safeguard. The fallout was historic. Congressional hearings, fines, and lawsuits followed. Public outrage forced a change in federal law. Credit freezes, once costly, were made free for all consumers.

But the sobering truth: while Equifax paid settlements, the stolen data didn't vanish. It still circulates in underground markets. The law gave us a tool (the freeze) but using it is up to us.

Lisa's Story: The Teacher Who Learned Too Late

Lisa taught fifth-grade students in North Carolina. She was organized, conscientious, beloved by her students and their parents. She read the news about the Equifax breach, felt a vague sense of concern, and then did nothing.

"I thought someone would tell me if I needed to do something," Lisa explained later. "I figured the government or the credit bureau or my bank would contact me if I were affected."

Eight months after the breach, Lisa applied for a car loan. She needed reliable transportation; her old sedan was on its last legs, and she had a 45-minute commute to school. The dealer came back from the finance office looking uncomfortable.

"Ma'am, I'm sorry, but your application was denied. Your credit score shows as 512."

Lisa was confused. "That can't be right. I've never missed a payment on anything."

They pulled her credit report together. Three credit cards she'd never opened. A personal loan she'd never applied for. A cell phone contract in her name at an address she'd never lived at. Total fraudulent debt: $18,400.

Someone had used her information from the Equifax breach to build an entire fake financial life. They'd been careful, making minimum payments, keeping the accounts barely active, flying under the radar until they maxed everything out and disappeared.

Lisa spent the next four months of her life fighting this. Police reports. Fraud affidavits. Certified letters to credit bureaus. Calls with creditors who initially didn't believe her. Attorney fees when some creditors refused to remove the fraudulent accounts.

She missed school because of court dates. She cried in her classroom after the students left. She couldn't sleep, running through endless scenarios of what else might be out there in her name.

"I thought protecting my identity was someone else's job," Lisa told me when a mutual friend connected us. "I didn't know I was supposed to freeze my credit. Nobody told me that was even an option."

We froze Lisa's credit during our first conversation. It took fifteen minutes. That fifteen-minute action, done eight months earlier, would have prevented everything.

Lisa now teaches identity theft prevention to her fellow teachers during professional development days. "I don't want anyone to learn this lesson the way I did," she says.

🔒 FORTIFY PROTOCOL

Credit Armor is layers, not a single action.

Freeze your credit at all three bureaus

Check freeze status quarterly

Rotate free credit reports every four months

Enable free monitoring from your bank or credit card

Know how to respond when fraud is detected

Building Complete Credit Armor

If you completed Chapter 3, you already have your credit frozen at all three bureaus. That's your primary armor. Now let's add the monitoring systems that watch for threats even when your armor is in place.

The Quarterly Check-In

Every three months, I spend about fifteen minutes verifying that my family's credit freezes are still active. It sounds paranoid until you hear what happened to my father-in-law Frank last year.

Frank had frozen his credit right after the Equifax breach. Did everything correctly, saved his PINs in his password manager, thought he was set for life. Then during a routine quarterly check, he discovered that Experian had "upgraded" his account. His freeze was now shown as "temporary" with an expiration date three weeks away.

He hadn't done anything. The system had changed. Five minutes to re-enable the permanent freeze, but if he hadn't checked, his credit would have been wide open within weeks.

Chapter 10: Credit Armor - Fortifying Your Financial Identity

That's why the quarterly check matters. Systems glitch. Bureaus "upgrade" their interfaces. Sometimes freeze status changes without your knowledge. I've seen it happen to three family members over the years.

The check is simple. Log into each bureau, verify the freeze shows as active, make sure your contact information is current, update your password manager if any credentials have changed, and document the check in your security log. Set a calendar reminder for the first of every third month. Takes fifteen minutes total.

The Credit Report Rotation

You're entitled to one free credit report per year from each bureau. Most people pull all three at once in January, then have no free monitoring for the rest of the year. That's a wasted opportunity.

Instead, stagger them every four months for continuous monitoring. Pull Experian in January, Equifax in May, TransUnion in September, then repeat with Experian in January. This gives you visibility every four months instead of once a year.

When you pull the report, review every single line carefully. Look for accounts you don't recognize, inquiries you didn't authorize, addresses you've never lived at, employment you've never had, public records that aren't yours. Save a PDF copy for your records and set a calendar reminder for four months from now.

My nephew Jake uses this rotation method. Last spring, his May report showed a credit inquiry from a car dealership he'd never visited. Turned out to be a case of mistaken identity (someone with a similar name), but Jake caught it and had it corrected before it could cause problems. He only caught it because he was checking regularly, not waiting a full year between reports.

The Free Monitoring Your Bank Already Offers

Most major credit cards and banks now offer free credit score monitoring as a customer benefit. Monthly score updates, alerts for significant changes, notifications when new accounts appear. Some even offer full credit report access.

The setup takes about ten minutes. Log into your credit card account, look for "Credit Score" or "Credit Monitoring," enable all available alerts, verify how you'll be notified (email, app notification, SMS), and test it to make sure it works.

You don't need all your cards doing this. One or two provide good coverage. Chase, Discover, Capital One, American Express, Bank of America, any major issuer will work fine.

Jake uses his Chase card for monitoring. Gets monthly score updates without thinking about it. Last year it alerted him to a new inquiry he didn't recognize. Turned out a landlord had run his credit without permission. Jake disputed it and had it removed. The whole thing happened because the free monitoring caught it.

When You Need a Fraud Alert

Fraud alerts are different from freezes. A freeze blocks access completely. A fraud alert warns creditors to verify your identity before approving credit, but doesn't stop them from checking your file.

There are three types, and understanding when to use each one matters.

The initial fraud alert lasts one year and requires no proof. You just suspect identity theft, maybe you got a breach notification that included your SSN, maybe you lost your wallet with your SSN card, maybe you're going through a contentious divorce and your ex has access to all your financial information. You place the alert as a precaution.

My sister Linda used this during her divorce. Her ex-husband had access to all her financial information from their years together. She placed a fraud alert as insurance. Three months later, someone tried to open a credit card in her name. Turns out it was her ex trying to run up debt before the settlement. The fraud alert triggered a verification call to Linda, and she blocked the application. That alert bought her time to freeze her credit completely.

The extended fraud alert lasts seven years and requires an FTC Identity Theft Report. This is for confirmed victims. It adds stronger verification requirements and automatically removes you from pre-approved credit offer lists. Lisa used this after her identity theft recovery. She wanted every possible layer of protection.

The active-duty alert is for military personnel deploying. It protects your credit while you're unable to monitor it. One year duration, specifically designed for service members.

To place any fraud alert, you only need to contact one bureau. They're required to notify the other two. Fill out the request form, provide contact information for creditor verification, and save the confirmation. The whole process takes about ten minutes.

🚨 MISSION CRITICAL

Don't confuse credit monitoring with credit freezing.

Monitoring tells you after the fact. Freezing prevents the breach in the first place. You need both: freeze as prevention, monitoring as backup detection.

Fortress Shield - 2026 Edition

SITREP: The Regulatory Landscape

The Equifax breach spurred Congress to strengthen your rights. But the regulatory landscape has shifted since then, and understanding these changes helps you protect yourself more effectively.

The good news: free credit freezes are now federal law. The Economic Growth, Regulatory Relief, and Consumer Protection Act of 2018 guarantees your right to freeze and unfreeze without fees. Extended fraud alerts are available at no cost if you're a victim of identity theft. Many state attorneys general aggressively pursue credit fraud cases, sometimes with more urgency than federal agencies. And during the pandemic, AnnualCreditReport.com began offering weekly access to your reports, a feature that's been extended beyond the original temporary period.

The challenging news: the Consumer Financial Protection Bureau has scaled back enforcement, limiting oversight of lenders and credit bureaus. Federal agencies often react months or years after breaches, long after your data is already being exploited. And your protections may depend more on your state than on federal oversight, creating a patchwork of remedies.

What this means for you: use your freeze rights aggressively because they're strong and enforceable. Don't rely on regulators to notify you; use the ALERT tools from Chapter 9 to detect breaches early. Report fraud to your state attorney general as well as the FTC because your state may act faster. And take advantage of weekly credit report access while it lasts.

The bottom line is that the law gave you powerful tools, but the responsibility to use them rests with you, not with government agencies that may or may not act in time.

Chapter 10: Credit Armor - Fortifying Your Financial Identity

Free vs. Paid Credit Monitoring

After helping family members evaluate monitoring options, I've learned when paid services make sense and when they're unnecessary.

The free options cover the essentials remarkably well. AnnualCreditReport.com gives you access to your full reports from all three bureaus. Your credit cards and bank accounts offer free score monitoring with alerts for new accounts and inquiries. Credit Karma provides free scores from two bureaus with weekly updates. Between these free tools, you get excellent coverage for zero cost.

Paid services offer convenience and additional features. Bureau services like Experian Identity Works, Equifax Complete, and TransUnion Credit Monitoring provide more frequent updates, three-bureau coverage, score tracking, and sometimes identity theft insurance. Third-party services like Aura, LifeLock, and Identity Guard bundle credit monitoring with dark web scanning, SSN monitoring, identity theft insurance ranging from $25,000 to $1,000,000, white-glove restoration support, and family plans. The cost runs from $8 to $35 per month, which translates to $96 to $420 per year.

The question is whether that cost provides value beyond what the free tools offer. For most people following the Fortress Shield we've built throughout this book, the answer is no. The free stack provides excellent protection.

But some people genuinely benefit from paid services. Confirmed identity theft victims during recovery and for a year or two afterward. Elderly family members who need simplicity (one service, one bill, phone support). Business owners with significant assets where the cost is trivial relative to potential losses. Families with young children who want to monitor their kids' SSNs before they have credit files. High-net-worth individuals for whom the cost is meaningless.

Tech-comfortable individuals who can manage multiple free tools don't need paid services. Budget-conscious families get excellent coverage for free. People who've implemented everything in this book already have strong protection.

My personal approach: I use only free monitoring. Credit frozen at all three bureaus, rotating free credit reports every four months, alerts from my credit cards. Cost: $0. Effectiveness: excellent.

Lisa's approach after her incident: she pays for monitoring ($15/month) for the peace of mind and the identity theft insurance. "After what I went through, it's worth it," she says.

Both approaches work. Choose based on your actual needs, not on fear.

RED TEAM INSIGHT

During penetration testing, we found that credit freezes stopped 100% of new credit account fraud attempts. However, medical identity theft, utility fraud, and tax fraud can still occur because these types of fraud don't always trigger credit checks. Complete protection requires both freezing and monitoring.

When Fraud Strikes: The Emergency Response

Speed and documentation determine your recovery success. Let me walk you through what Lisa went through so you understand the process before you ever need it.

Chapter 10: Credit Armor - Fortifying Your Financial Identity

The First Hour

When Lisa discovered the fraud, she was panicked. Understandable. But panic wastes time. The first hour is about containment and documentation.

She contacted all three bureaus immediately. Verified her freeze status (she didn't have one yet, which was the problem). Placed fraud alerts on all three files. This stops additional damage while you're working on recovery.

Then she pulled credit reports from all three bureaus using AnnualCreditReport.com. Documented everything fraudulent. Took screenshots, saved PDFs. Created a fraud documentation folder, both digital and physical, because she knew it would fill up quickly. Organization is crucial for recovery.

Sarah had her credit reports pulled, and fraud alerts placed within 45 minutes when we discovered her Phoenix medical fraud. That immediate action prevented any additional fraud attempts while we worked on recovery.

The First Day

Within 24 hours, you need to file official reports. These become your legal evidence.

Lisa went to IdentityTheft.gov and completed the online questionnaire. Got her official FTC Identity Theft Report. This is legal documentation that shifts the burden of proof to creditors. She printed and saved multiple copies.

Then she filed a police report with her local department. Brought her FTC report and all her documentation. Got a case number. Requested copies of the police report because some creditors require it.

She also filed a complaint with her state attorney general. Many states have better enforcement than federal agencies.

This provided additional legal documentation and potentially triggered a state-level investigation.

The documentation to bring government-issued ID, proof of address, all fraudulent account statements, credit reports with fraud highlighted, and a timeline of discovery.

The First Week

For each fraudulent account, you need to contact the creditor directly and dispute with the credit bureaus.

Lisa called each creditor's fraud department. Followed up in writing using certified mail with return receipt. Included her FTC Identity Theft Report and police report. Requested account closure and debt removal.

Then she filed disputes with all three bureaus. Each bureau has online dispute systems. She attached her FTC and police reports, requested full investigation, and got confirmation numbers for everything.

She created a dispute tracking log. Date contacted, method used (phone, mail, online), name of representative, case and reference numbers, follow-up due dates. This log became her lifeline during the recovery process.

The sample dispute letter is straightforward. Date it, address it to the credit bureau fraud department, state clearly that you're a victim of identity theft, list the fraudulent accounts with account numbers and dates opened, reference the enclosed FTC report and police report, request immediate investigation and removal under the Fair Credit Reporting Act, ask for confirmation and expected resolution timeline, sign it.

The First 90 Days

Recovery requires sustained vigilance. Lisa checked her credit weekly using the free weekly reports available during recovery. Watched for new fraudulent accounts. Verified disputed items were being removed.

She monitored her financial accounts daily. Bank accounts, credit cards, investment accounts. Looked for small unauthorized charges because criminals often test with tiny amounts.

She watched her mail carefully. Collection letters, new credit card offers, court documents. Anything unusual got documented.

The bureaus must investigate within 30 days. Creditors must respond to disputes. Lisa tracked all deadlines rigorously and followed up on any missed deadlines.

Recovery timelines vary. Simple cases take one to three months. Complex cases take six to twelve months. Some elements may take years to resolve fully. Extended fraud alerts help during the recovery period.

Lisa's recovery took four months for the main accounts, but a small medical bill kept appearing for two years. Each time she disputed it, had it removed, then it would reappear when the hospital sold the debt to a new collector. Finally, her attorney sent a letter citing federal law, and it stopped. Persistence matters.

Protecting Children's Credit

My neighbor discovered his daughter was denied a student loan at age 19. Someone had been using her SSN since she was 12, racking up utility bills and small loans. Seven years of fraud, undetected because nobody checks children's credit files.

Children's SSNs are valuable to criminals because fraud can go undetected for years. The child doesn't apply for credit, so they don't discover the problem until they try to get their first credit card or student loan at 18 or 19.

To check, request a credit report for your child from each bureau. Most children should have no credit file at all. If a file exists, it may indicate fraud.

To freeze a child's credit, each bureau has specific procedures for minor freezes. You'll need proof of identity for both parent and child. Birth certificate, SSN card, parents' ID. The freeze remains until the child turns 16 to 18, depending on state law.

After discovering his daughter's situation, my neighbor immediately froze his younger son's credit. Preventive action based on a hard lesson learned.

Protecting Deceased Family Members

Criminals monitor obituaries and death records. Deceased individuals' SSNs are often used for fraud because the fraud can continue for months or years before anyone notices.

Contact all three bureaus within days of the death, before the obituary is published. Request a "Deceased Alert" on the credit file. Provide a death certificate. This prevents new accounts from being opened in the deceased's name.

My uncle passed away two years ago. My aunt contacted the bureaus within 48 hours. Three weeks later, someone tried to

Chapter 10: Credit Armor - Fortifying Your Financial Identity

open a credit card in his name. The deceased alert blocked it. Without that alert, the fraud might have succeeded, and my aunt would have spent months dealing with collections agencies and fraudulent debt.

For Survivors of Domestic Violence

If you're escaping domestic violence, credit protection takes on additional urgency. Your abuser may have access to all your financial information and may try to sabotage your credit as a form of control or revenge.

Special considerations include placing a credit freeze with different contact information so your abuser can't access it. Fraud alerts requiring specific verification. Address confidentiality programs in many states that hide your new address from public records. Court-ordered credit monitoring in some jurisdictions.

Resources that can help: the National Domestic Violence Hotline at 1-800-799-7233, state victim services that can assist with credit protection, and address confidentiality programs that many states offer to protect survivors.

Common Mistakes I Keep Seeing

The biggest mistake is freezing credit but never monitoring it. Freezes can be circumvented or bypassed in some situations. You still need to check quarterly that everything is clean.

Another common error is lifting the freeze at all three bureaus when only one is needed. When applying for credit, ask which bureau the lender uses. Only lift that one. Keep the others frozen for additional protection. Sarah learned this lesson. Now when she needs to apply for credit, she asks first, lifts only what's necessary, and refreezes immediately after.

Some people use a credit lock instead of a credit freeze. Locks are products sold by bureaus. Freezes are legal rights backed by federal law. Always choose the freeze because it's stronger and you control it completely.

Not documenting the freeze is another mistake. Save confirmation emails, take screenshots of freeze status, note the dates in your calendar. You may need proof years later if there's a dispute about when you froze your credit.

People forget about credit-reporting alternatives. Specialty agencies like ChexSystems for checking accounts or LexisNexis for insurance aren't covered by the big three bureaus. Research your specific industry to understand all the agencies that might have information about you.

And perhaps the most dangerous assumption: that frozen credit means total immunity. Credit freezes stop new credit accounts, but determined criminals can still commit medical fraud, tax fraud, or employment fraud with your SSN. The freeze is powerful but not absolute. That's why monitoring remains essential even with a freeze in place.

When Things Go Wrong

If you can't lift your freeze because you forgot your PIN, each bureau has recovery procedures. You'll need to verify your identity, often with personal questions or document upload. This can take several days, so don't wait until the last minute when applying for credit.

If a freeze didn't stop a fraudulent account, understand that some creditors don't check credit at all. Utilities, medical providers, some retail accounts proceed without credit checks. File fraud reports immediately. Credit freezes stop credit-based accounts, but not all types of accounts.

If a creditor says you're lying about identity theft, this is why you file FTC and police reports immediately. These are legal

Chapter 10: Credit Armor - Fortifying Your Financial Identity

documents that shift the burden of proof to the creditor. If they continue to claim you're responsible, consult an attorney specializing in credit law. Many offer free consultations for identity theft cases.

If a fraudulent account was removed but keeps reappearing, this happens when debt is sold to collection agencies. Each time, re-file the dispute with full documentation. Eventually, send a cease-and-desist letter citing the Fair Credit Reporting Act. Consider legal consultation if it persists beyond multiple disputes.

If you were denied credit despite properly lifting the freeze, sometimes there's a delay between lifting and the creditor seeing the unfrozen file. Wait 15 minutes after lifting before applying. If denial persists, contact the creditor directly; they may need to retry the credit pull.

Why This Matters More Than Technical Security

I spent three decades protecting systems where failure meant catastrophic consequences. But you know what haunts me? It's not the sophisticated attacks or complex breaches.

It's Lisa, sitting in her classroom, crying after her students left because she didn't know she could have prevented everything with fifteen minutes of action.

It's Sarah, having to explain to her new landlord why there's a collection account in her name, hoping it doesn't cost her the apartment.

It's the families I've helped who spent months fighting fraud instead of living their lives, all because nobody told them that credit freezes existed, were free, and were their legal right.

The Equifax breach exposed nearly half of America's adults. That data is still out there. It will be out there for decades, circulating in underground markets, being bought and sold by criminals who view identity theft as a business.

But you have armor now. Legal rights backed by federal law. Free tools that actually work. Knowledge of how to respond when threats appear.

The criminals who buy SSN databases and test them against credit applications are looking for unlocked doors. Yours isn't unlocked anymore.

Mission Complete

By the end of this chapter, you should understand your legal right to a free credit freeze and how it evolved from the Equifax breach. You should know how to maintain credit armor with quarterly checks and rotating credit reports. You should recognize the difference between freeze (preventive) and monitoring (detective). You should understand when paid monitoring adds value versus when free tools are sufficient. You should be prepared to execute an emergency fraud response with documentation and timelines. You should know advanced strategies for protecting children, estates, and vulnerable family members. And you should know how to use both federal and state resources to enforce your rights.

Call to Action

Use free tools to form your Fortress, freeze your credit, monitor the walls, and live under Credit ARMOR.

Reference Materials: Use the Credit Fraud Response Kit with dispute letter templates, timeline checklists, and documentation logs.

Next: Your Fortress Shield is complete. Continue maintaining these integrated systems for lifetime protection.

Chief Palmer notes that credit protection is where your legal rights meet practical action. "The law gave you tools after Equifax," he says. "But tools only work if you use them. Your financial identity is too important to leave unprotected."

Chapter 11: Community - Building Collective Defense

⏱ Ongoing commitment | Essential

CALL SIGN: COMMUNITY, NO ONE FIGHTS ALONE.

My brother Mike called me on a Saturday morning, and his voice had that edge that told me he was trying not to be angry.

"Alan, someone hacked Mom's email and sent messages to everyone in her address book asking for money. I got three calls from relatives asking if Mom was okay. Aunt Susan actually sent $500 to some Western Union account before we figured out it was fake."

"Is Mom okay?" I asked.

"She's fine. She's at home, has no idea her email was hacked. But Alan, here's the thing. I've been doing everything you taught me: using a password manager, MFA, and having my credit frozen. I'm locked down tight. But Mom still uses 'password123' for everything. And because her email has my contact info, the scammers now have my email, my phone number, everyone in our family."

That conversation happened three years ago, and it taught me something I should have understood earlier: individual security doesn't work when you're part of a network of people who trust each other.

You can build the strongest fortress in the world, but if the people around you have unlocked doors, attackers will use those doors to get to you.

Why This Step Matters

Cybercriminals don't just target individuals; they target groups. Families, workplaces, congregations, veterans' networks, and seniors' communities are all prime hunting grounds because one weak link opens the door to many.

In the military, defense is never isolated. Bases rely on overlapping security perimeters, patrols, and shared intelligence. The same principle applies here: your Fortress becomes exponentially stronger when your circle adopts the same protocols.

⚠ THREAT ALERT

Attackers love the weak link.

If your spouse, parent, or coworker reuses passwords or ignores alerts, the whole family, or even your workplace, can be compromised through them.

Chapter 11: Community - Building Collective Defense

The Human Nature of Trust

Attackers know that humans trust people they know. This is why social engineering is so powerful. One hacked email account can send malicious links to everyone in the address book, and most of those people will click, because they trust the sender.

This principle isn't new. In the military, it's well understood that soft targets, such as casual conversations in the chow hall, text messages between active-duty personnel and spouses, or even relaxed talk at the NCO club, can be exploited by adversaries. Whole units are trained to watch their words, because even small leaks can be pieced together into intelligence.

I saw this firsthand during my career. We'd spend millions on hardened communications systems, encrypted networks, and multi-factor authentication for classified systems. However, someone would then text their spouse about deployment dates using their personal phone. Or mention a project name in a Facebook message. Or discuss sensitive topics over lunch in a place where conversations could be overheard.

The most sophisticated technical security in the world doesn't matter if someone in your network is having unencrypted conversations about sensitive information. The chow hall, the NCO club, and the parking lot after work were always the soft targets that kept security officers awake at night.

It takes a village to maintain security, both at home and on base. Cybersecurity works the same way. An attacker doesn't always need to breach a bank's firewall. Sometimes, they only need a chat message, a relative's email, or a friend's Facebook login.

Your defenses can collapse if your community isn't trained to spot the same threats.

Grandpa Joe's Email: How One Compromise Spreads

Joe was 82 years old, a Korean War veteran, and a beloved grandfather of seven. He used email mainly to stay in touch with his kids and grandkids, share photos, and forward jokes to his buddies from the VFW.

One afternoon, Joe received an email that appeared to be from his bank. The message said there was suspicious activity on his account, and he needed to verify his information immediately. The link opened a page that looked exactly like his bank's website.

Joe typed in his email and password. Nothing happened. The page displayed "System Error" and instructed him to try again later. Joe shrugged and went about his day.

What Joe didn't know: he'd just handed his email credentials to criminals. Within minutes, they were inside his email account. They read through his messages, learned about his family, studied his writing style, and noted with whom he communicated most often.

Then they changed his password so Joe couldn't get back in. And they started sending messages.

"I'm traveling in Spain and my wallet was stolen. The embassy can help, but I need $2,500 wired to Western Union to get home. Please don't tell the kids. I'm embarrassed about this."

The message went to everyone in Joe's address book. His children, grandchildren, brother, church friends, and VFW buddies. All people who knew Joe trusted him and wanted to help.

His daughter, Susan, saw the message at work. She panicked. Her dad traveling alone at 82? His wallet was stolen. She

Chapter 11: Community - Building Collective Defense

immediately went to Western Union and wired $2,500 to the account listed in the email.

Joe's son, Mark, received the same email an hour later. He called Joe's home phone immediately. Joe answered on the second ring, confused about why Mark sounded so worried.

"Dad, are you in Spain?"

"Spain? No, I'm sitting in my living room watching TV. Why would I be in Spain?"

That's when they realized Joe's email account had been hacked. By then, Susan's $2,500 was gone. Two of Joe's church friends had also wired money before word spread.

But the damage didn't stop there. The criminals now had email addresses, phone numbers, and personal information about Joe's entire family. They'd read messages mentioning birthdays, anniversaries, medical appointments, and financial discussions.

They used that information to craft new attacks. Joe's granddaughter got a Facebook message from what appeared to be her cousin, asking for help with a "confidential family matter." Joe's son got a fake IRS call that referenced his mother's actual medical bills (mentioned in an email chain).

One compromised email account became the gateway to attacking an entire family network.

I met Joe through the VFW. We spent an afternoon helping him recover his email, setting up a password manager, enabling MFA, and most importantly, teaching his whole family about the attack patterns that criminals use.

"I feel so stupid," Joe said. "I gave them everything."

"Joe, you're not stupid. You're human. These criminals are professionals who know exactly how to exploit trust. But now your whole family knows what to watch for. That's how we turn one mistake into community strength."

🔒 FORTIFY PROTOCOL

Community Defense Checklist:

Family Command: Help spouses, kids, and parents set up password managers and MFA

Shared ALERT: Register family emails with Have I Been Pwned or password manager breach alerts

Credit Armor for All: Freeze the credit of vulnerable family members, especially children and the elderly

Emergency Signals: Agree on a "family code phrase" for emergencies so scams like "stranded abroad" calls don't work

Spread the Doctrine: Share this book, or at least the key drills, with your circle

Building Your Community Defense Network

Individual security is necessary but not sufficient. You need coordinated defense across your trusted networks.

Identify Your Security Perimeter

Who's in your immediate trust network? Spouse or partner. Children, including adult children. Parents. Siblings. Close friends who have your financial information. Anyone with your emergency contacts.

For each person, ask these questions. Do they use a password manager? Do they have MFA enabled on critical accounts? Is their credit frozen? Do they know what phishing looks like? Would they recognize a compromised account message?

Chapter 11: Community - Building Collective Defense

Document this assessment in your password manager notes. Who has strong security. Who needs help urgently. Who might resist making changes. Who could help train others.

My family's assessment results: When I did this three years ago, my wife had strong security and was helping others. My daughter, Sarah, had a strong sense of security after her experience with identity theft. My son had decent security but needed MFA improvements. My mother had weak security and didn't know what a password manager was. My father-in-law Frank had weak security and was resistant to technology. My brother, Mike, had medium security and was making improvements. My sister Linda had medium security and was willing to learn.

This honest assessment told me where to focus my efforts.

Priority Interventions

Start with high-risk family members. Elderly parents or grandparents are most vulnerable to scams, often use simple passwords, and may not recognize phishing attempts. Their compromise can affect the entire family. Young adults aged 18 to 25 have high online exposure, are a target demographic for student loans and credit, may not take security seriously yet, and are often first to get jobs requiring security. Anyone with your financial power of attorney can access your accounts, their compromise equals your compromise, and they need the strongest security possible.

Set up sessions of one to two hours with each person. Use Appendix A as your template but adapt it for each person's needs.

The session structure works like this. Explain why these matters use stories, not fear. Set up a password manager together. Enable MFA on critical accounts. Freeze credit if they haven't already. Practice recognizing phishing. Establish family code phrase.

My mother's setup session took two hours over coffee at her kitchen table. She was skeptical at first. "I don't do anything important online," until I showed her the breach database, which listed her email in five different compromises.

"Nobody told me this was happening," she said.

"That's why I'm here," I told her. "Now you'll know immediately when it happens."

🚨 MISSION CRITICAL

Don't keep Fortress Shield to yourself.

Your security depends on the people around you. Share the doctrine, practice the drills, and build collective defense.

Family Code Phrases

Why they work: Criminals can spoof emails, texts, and even voices (with AI). They can't read your mind.

How to create:

Choose a phrase that:

- Only family members know
- Isn't guessable (not your dog's name)
- Is easy to remember
- Can be used in conversation naturally

Examples:

"What was the name of that restaurant we loved in Denver?" (Answer: "The Blue Mesa" or whatever your actual shared experience was)

Chapter 11: Community - Building Collective Defense

"Remember what Grandma always said about winter?" (Answer: Some specific family saying)

Protocol:

If anyone contacts you asking for money or sensitive information:

- Use the code phrase to verify identity
- No code phrase = not really them, even if it sounds like them
- Never share the code phrase in writing

How it works in practice:

You get a text from your daughter: "Mom, I'm stranded in Miami, lost my wallet, need $1,000 wired urgently."

You respond: "Oh no! By the way, what restaurant did we go to for your graduation?"

Real daughter: Knows the answer immediately. Scammer: Either makes up an answer, doesn't respond, or tries to avoid the question.

My family's code phrases: We have three different ones for different security levels:

- Financial requests: Require code phrase + voice verification
- Password resets: Code phrase sufficient
- General family info: No code phrase needed, but suspicious requests get questioned

Community-Wide Defense Drills

Schedule regular family security check-ins:

What to cover (30 minutes quarterly):

1. **Breach review:** Did anyone get breach alerts this quarter?
2. **Near-miss sharing:** Did anyone almost fall for something?
3. **New threat awareness:** What new scams are circulating?
4. **Security updates:** Who needs help updating their defenses?
5. **Success stories:** Celebrate when someone catches a scam

Format options:

- Family dinner discussion
- Group video call
- Shared document everyone reviews
- Dedicated "security Sunday" quarterly meetup

Making it not awkward: Frame it like home maintenance. You check smoke detectors, you check security. No judgment, just preparation.

My family's quarterly drill: We do ours the first Sunday after New Year's, Easter, July 4th, and Thanksgiving. It takes about 30 minutes over coffee. Last quarter, my nephew Jake shared a new AI voice scam he'd encountered. Now everyone's aware and watching for it.

Chapter 11: Community - Building Collective Defense

SITREP: Regulation & Community

With federal enforcement scaled back, local communities are becoming more important. State attorneys general and local organizations often lead the way on scam awareness campaigns. A neighbor or coworker may be your first warning system if they see a new scam spreading.

Better Protections: Some states fund senior scam hotlines and publish alerts. Colorado, for instance, has excellent resources through the Attorney General's office.

Weaker Protections: Without consistent federal enforcement, the landscape is uneven. One town may be flooded with awareness posters, another left in the dark.

This makes you the intelligence officer for your family and network.

State-level resources to check:

- Your state Attorney General's consumer protection division
- Local Area Agency on Aging (often has scam awareness programs)
- AARP state chapters (free resources even for non-members)
- Local police department community outreach
- Credit unions and community banks (often host security workshops)

The Force Multiplier Effect

When you share Fortress Shield principles with even a handful of people, the protection multiplies. A family that uses password managers and MFA is almost impossible to compromise through a single weak link. A small business where employees understand ALERT drills will withstand phishing better than many Fortune 500 companies.

Think of it as a convoy. A single armored truck can be ambushed. A convoy with mutual support and radio communication can fight through.

The PTA Scam: When Community Protocol Fails

The Lincoln Elementary PTA in suburban Texas had 45 active members, all dedicated parents volunteering their time. The treasurer, Michelle, managed a budget of approximately $30,000 per year, comprising fundraisers, grants, and donations for school programs.

One Tuesday afternoon, the PTA president received an email from Michelle's address:

"Hi everyone! The book fair vendor needs payment today, or they'll cancel our order. Can you authorize a wire transfer for $4,200? Here's the account information. Thanks!"

The president thought it was odd that Michelle was asking for approval via email instead of at their regular meeting. But Michelle's email had been reliable before; the request seemed urgent, and the president trusted her.

She called the bank, authorized the wire transfer, and emailed Michelle back confirming it was done.

Two hours later, Michelle called the president, confused. "What wire transfer? I didn't send any email about the book fair."

The president's stomach dropped. She pulled up the email again. The sender address was michelle.ptatreasurer@gmail.com, not Michelle's actual email, michellej@outlook.com. Close enough that nobody had checked carefully.

Michelle's personal email had been compromised weeks earlier in a data breach. The attackers had been reading her emails, learning about the PTA, and studying the communication patterns. They'd created a spoofed account and timed their attack perfectly.

The $4,200 was gone. The bank was unable to reverse a wire transfer to an overseas account. The PTA's insurance didn't cover "authorized" transfers, even those that were fraudulent. The school programs that money would have funded were canceled.

The parents were devastated. Some blamed the president. Some blamed Michelle. Everyone felt violated and angry.

I got involved because the president's husband was a member of my VFW post. We spent an afternoon doing a security review and implementing protocols that would have prevented the attack:

New PTA protocols:

1. All financial requests require voice verification: Email is never sufficient for money movement
2. **Two-person authorization for transfers:** The President and treasurer must both approve
3. **24-hour waiting period:** No same-day wire transfers regardless of urgency
4. Code phrase for financial requests: Similar to family code phrases
5. **Regular security training:** Brief 15-minute discussion at each monthly meeting

What they learned:

This wasn't a failing of individuals, it was a failing of systems. Michelle had decent personal security, but nobody had thought about organizational security. The PTA had no protocols for verifying financial requests. Trust was assumed, not verified.

Within a year, two other PTAs in the district had similar attacks attempted. Both were stopped because they'd heard about Lincoln Elementary's experience and implemented identical protocols.

One weak link had taught an entire community how to defend itself.

Emergency Drill: Community Lockdown

When one person in your network is compromised, assume everyone is a potential target.

Phase 1: Immediate Alert (First 15 minutes)

When you discover a compromise:

1. Alert the network immediately
   - Call (don't email) other family members
   - "Mom's email was hacked. Don't trust any emails from her right now."
   - Use group chat or phone tree
   - Be specific about what was compromised

2. Identify the scope
- What accounts were compromised?
- What information was accessible?
  - Who else might be targeted?
  - What did the attacker learn about the family?
3. Issue specific warnings
- "They have access to all our addresses and phone numbers."
- "They've read emails about Dad's medical bills."
- "They know about Sarah's graduation trip."

A real-life example from my family: When my mom's email was compromised, I had the family on alert within 20 minutes. Mike called everyone on his contact list. Sarah posted in the family group chat. Dad called the relatives who don't use smartphones.

Phase 2: Help the Victim Recover (First 2 hours)

Don't leave them to figure it out alone:

1. Sit down with them (in person or video call)
- Physical presence reduces stress
- You can see what they're doing
- Faster than talking them through it

2. Follow the breach response drill from Chapter 13
   - Change all passwords using a password manager
   - Enable MFA on all accounts
   - Check account activity for unauthorized actions
   - Review recovery options and contact information
3. Check for lateral movement
   - Did they use that password anywhere else?
   - Are other accounts showing suspicious activity?
   - Have financial accounts been accessed?
4. Document what happened
   - Timeline of events
   - What was exposed
   - What actions were taken
   - What family members need to watch for

The victim needs support, not blame: Joe felt humiliated after his email hack. "I should have known better." What he needed was help and reassurance that this happens to everyone, and that the family was rallying to protect each other.

Phase 3: Network-Wide Defense Check (First 24 hours)

Everyone in the network should:

1. Review their own security
- Change passwords if any were shared
- Enable MFA if they haven't already
- Check recent account activity
- Review email forwarding rules

2. Watch for secondary attacks
- Phishing emails referencing the compromise
- Calls claiming to be "helping" with the hack
- Messages from the compromised account asking for help

3. Verify any unusual communications
- Use code phrases
- Call to verify before acting
- Question urgency and emotional manipulation

4. Report suspicious activity immediately
- Keep the family alert active
- Share new attack attempts
- Document patterns

Phase 4: Post-Incident Review (Within 1 week)

Learn and adapt as a community:

1. Debrief together
   - What happened and how?
   - What worked in the response?
   - What could be improved?
   - Are there new protocols needed?
2. Close security gaps
   - Help anyone who realized they're vulnerable
   - Update family code phrases if needed
   - Strengthen verification procedures
3. Document lessons learned
   - Add to family security procedures
   - Share with extended network if appropriate
   - Update emergency contact lists

After Mom's email hack, we implemented:

- Monthly check-ins instead of quarterly
- Mandatory MFA for everyone (no exceptions)
- Simplified password manager setup for less technical family members
- Family security champion rotation (someone different leads each check-in)

Chapter 11: Community - Building Collective Defense

Extending Defense to Workplaces and Communities

Small businesses:

Many small businesses have weaker security than households because they assume "we're too small to be targeted." They're wrong.

Basic workplace protocols:

- **Verify financial requests by phone:** Never approve payments via email alone
- **Separate personal and work accounts:** Use different passwords, different password managers
- **Regular security briefings:** 15 minutes monthly, just like family check-ins
- **Designated security officer:** Someone owns this responsibility
- **Incident response plan:** Know who to call and what to do

My brother Mike's plumbing business: After his own close calls, Mike implemented these protocols with his employees. Last year, an employee almost fell for a fake invoice scam. The phone verification protocol saved them $12,000.

Churches and community organizations:

These groups are prime targets because they involve trust and often handle money.

Recommended practices:

- **Two-person rule for finances:** Never one person approves transfers alone
- **Public awareness sharing:** Brief announcements about current scams
- **Designated tech-savvy members:** Volunteer helpers for less technical members
- **Regular credential updates:** Change shared passwords quarterly
- **Security workshop annually:** Bring in speakers or use resources like this book

Veterans' organizations:

Fellow veterans are often targeted with service-related scams (fake VA benefits, phony veteran charities).

Specific considerations:

- **Verify veteran status claims:** Not everyone claiming to be a vet is one
- **Cross-check benefits info:** Call the VA directly about anything unusual
- **Share scam alerts:** When one post hears about a new scam, all should know
- **Buddy system:** Pair tech-comfortable vets with those who need help

Common Mistakes in Community Defense

Assuming everyone will figure it out themselves.

They won't. People need explicit invitations to learn and specific help implementing security.

Making people feel stupid for past mistakes.

Shame doesn't motivate. Support does. "This happened to me too" works better than "How could you fall for that?"

Overwhelming people with too much at once.

Start with the essentials: password manager and MFA. Add other layers gradually.

Not practicing drills when things are calm.

The time to practice fire drills is not during a fire. Run family security checks when there's no crisis.

Keeping knowledge to yourself.

If you know how to defend yourself, that knowledge should spread to your circle.

Forgetting that security evolves.

New threats emerge constantly. What you taught someone two years ago may need updating.

When Family Members Resist

The "it won't happen to me" attitude:
Some people genuinely don't believe they're targets until it happens.

Approach:

- Share stories (Joe, the PTA, real examples)
- Show them their email in breach databases
- Don't argue, just offer to help when they're ready
- Protect yourself from their vulnerability

The "I'm too old to learn new technology" excuse:
My father-in-law Frank used this one for years.

Approach:

- Start with the absolute minimum (freeze credit)
- Offer to do the setup for them
- Show how it makes life easier, not harder
- Accept that some people will never fully engage

The "I don't have time" deflection:
Everyone has time, they just don't prioritize it.

Approach:

- Offer specific time blocks: "Let's do this Saturday at 10am"
- Make it social: "I'll bring coffee and we'll knock this out together"
- Show how much time identity theft recovery takes (months vs. hours for prevention)

The "I'll do it later" procrastination:

Later never comes.

Approach:

- Send calendar invitations for setup sessions
- Make it a family event (security day for everyone)
- Follow up persistently but kindly
- Do what you can with those who are willing

Success Metrics: Community Defense Working

Month 1:

- Immediate family members have basic security assessed
- At least 2-3 vulnerable people helped with setup
- Family code phrase established and tested
- First family security discussion completed

Quarter 1:

- All immediate family has password managers and MFA
- Credit frozen for vulnerable members
- First quarterly security check-in completed
- One "near miss" caught and shared as learning experience

Year 1:

- Extended network starting to ask for help
- Community (church, workplace, club) implementing some protocols
- Family security is normalized, not awkward
- Zero successful attacks against family members

Long-term:

- Security is part of family culture
- New family members get briefed automatically
- Your network becomes resource for others
- Collective defense is stronger than individual defense ever was

Why This Matters More Than Individual Security

You can be the most secure person in the world. Password manager, MFA everywhere, credit frozen, breach alerts active, hardware keys, the works.

But if your mother clicks a phishing link, the attackers get your contact information and family details they'll use to target you.

Chapter 11: Community - Building Collective Defense

If your coworker uses "password123" and gets compromised, the company database with your information might be exposed.

If your church treasurer doesn't verify wire transfers, the church loses money that could have helped people in need.

Individual security is necessary. Community security is sufficient.

After helping dozens of families and organizations implement collective defense, I've learned that the strongest protection comes from networks that look out for each other.

Joe's email compromise could have bankrupted multiple family members. Instead, it became a teaching moment that protected his entire extended family and friend network.

The PTA scam cost one school $4,200 but prevented hundreds of thousands in losses at other schools that learned from their experience.

My family's quarterly security check-ins have caught three attempted compromises before they caused damage. Not because any individual was perfect, but because we watch out for each other.

You've built your personal Fortress. Now help others build theirs. Because in the end, no one fights alone.

Mission Complete

By the end of this chapter, you should:

- Recognize that your security is linked to your family, coworkers, and community
- Understand why attackers exploit trust within networks, and how military soft targets teach this lesson
- Know how to assess and strengthen your family's security posture
- Have established family code phrases and verification protocols
- Be able to run a Community Lockdown Drill when someone is compromised
- Understand how to extend defense to workplaces and organizations
- Appreciate the multiplier effect: more shields create stronger collective defense

Call to Action

Use free tools to form your Fortress, but don't fight alone. Share the shield, multiply the defense, and lead your community.

Reference Materials: Use the Family Security Assessment Worksheet to evaluate your network's vulnerabilities and track improvement over time.

Next: Your Fortress Shield is complete. Chapter 12 shows you how to think like the enemy through Red Team operations, testing your defenses before attackers do.

Chief Palmer notes that the strongest bases aren't built on individual heroics; they're built on coordinated team defense. "In thirty years, I never saw a secure facility that relied on one person doing everything right," he says. "Security is a team sport. Always has been."

Chapter 12: Red Team - Thinking Like the Enemy

🕐 2-3 hours quarterly | Recommended

Call Sign: RED TEAM, To beat the enemy, you must learn to think like one.

My nephew Jake called me one Sunday afternoon with a question that told me he was finally thinking like a defender.

"Uncle Alan, I've done everything you taught me. Password manager, MFA, credit frozen, breach alerts. But how do I know it's actually working? Like, what if I missed something and didn't know it?"

"That's the right question," I told him. "You've built defenses. Now you need to test them like an attacker would. You need to be the Red Team yourself."

"What does that mean?"

"It means you deliberately try to find holes in your own security. You think like the enemy. You look for the things you forgot, the weak spots you didn't see, the family members who haven't locked down their defenses. Because if you can find those holes, so can criminals."

Jake was quiet for a moment. "That sounds... kind of paranoid?"

"No," I said. "Paranoia is worrying about threats that don't exist. Red Teaming involves systematically checking for threats that are definitely present. In the military, it was called an Operational Readiness Inspection. You don't wait until you're under attack to find out your defenses have gaps. You test them when things are calm."

Why This Step Matters

You've built your Fortress Shield through eleven chapters. You have strong passwords, breach monitoring, frozen credit, automated defenses, and community awareness. That's excellent.

However, here's what I've learned from thirty years in military cybersecurity: defenses tend to degrade over time. People get lazy. Passwords get reused. Settings get changed during software updates. Family members who had good security six months ago might have reverted to bad habits.

The only way to know your defenses are actually working is to test them like an attacker would.

Red Teaming is the discipline of systematically probing your own security to find weaknesses before criminals do. It's structured, repeatable, and produces clear action items for improvement.

Chapter 12: Red Team - Thinking Like the Enemy

⚠ THREAT ALERT

Defense without testing is hope, not security.

You can't assume your Fortress is secure just because you built it. You need to verify it stays safe as threats evolve and circumstances change.

Red Team = Your Personal ORI (Operational Readiness Inspection)

In the Air Force, we conducted Operational Readiness Inspections on a regular schedule. An ORI wasn't about catching people doing things wrong, it was about objectively measuring whether a unit was ready to perform its mission if called upon.

The inspection team would arrive unannounced, simulate various scenarios, test procedures, and document their findings. Everything was scored with a simple traffic light system. Green meant you met standards and were ready. Amber meant you had minor issues that needed addressing within a set timeframe. Red meant critical failures requiring immediate correction.

The ORI was stressful, but it was also essential. Because it's better to discover your backup generator doesn't work during an inspection than during an actual power failure.

Your personal Red Team process works the same way. You're inspecting your household's cyber defenses to find problems when they're easy to fix, not during an active attack.

Fortress Shield - 2026 Edition

The Day I ORIed My Own Family

Two years ago, I decided to run a formal Red Team assessment on my immediate family. Wife, two adult children, and me. I announced it at Sunday dinner.

"Next Saturday, we're doing a security inspection. Everyone will be assessed, including me. We're going to find problems and fix them together."

My daughter Sarah was immediately interested, after her identity theft experience, she takes security seriously. My son rolled his eyes but agreed. My wife sighed and said, "Do we have to?"

"Yes," I said. "Because if there are holes in our defenses, I want to find them now, not when some criminal is exploiting them."

The inspection took about three hours for all four of us. Here's what we found:

Sarah scored ninety-five percent, which earned her a green rating. All her primary defenses were in place and functioning properly. However, we discovered one weak password on an old gaming account she'd forgotten about. More concerning, a recent platform update had loosened her social media privacy settings without her knowledge. She'd set everything to private six months earlier, but Facebook had reset some of those settings during an interface update.

My son scored seventy-eight percent, landing him in the amber category. He had his password manager installed, which was good, but he wasn't using it consistently. He'd enabled MFA on his banking, but not on his email, which meant attackers could reset his bank password through his unprotected email account. His credit was frozen, but he hadn't checked the status in eight months to verify it was still active. Most troubling, he was using his work laptop for

Chapter 12: Red Team - Thinking Like the Enemy

personal banking, mixing security domains in a way that could expose both his employer and his personal accounts if either was compromised.

My wife scored eighty-two percent, also amber. Her core security was strong, but she was still using SMS for two-factor authentication instead of an authenticator app, making her vulnerable to SIM swapping attacks. She'd set up email aliases for online shopping but was still using her real email address for some purchases. Her router firmware hadn't been updated in over a year, leaving known vulnerabilities unpatched.

I scored eighty-eight percent, which earned me a green rating but wasn't perfect. During the technical scan, I discovered I was still logged into an old tablet I'd given to my son months earlier. Two of my IoT devices, a smart speaker and a security camera, were on my main network instead of the isolated guest network where they belonged. My password manager had flagged three accounts with weak passwords that I'd been meaning to address but kept putting off.

None of us scored one hundred percent. And that was the point. We all had gaps we didn't know about until we looked systematically.

We spent the rest of the day fixing everything. By Sunday evening, we'd closed every gap and scheduled our next inspection for three months later.

My son grudgingly admitted, "Okay, that was actually useful. I had no idea I was still using the same password for my email that I used in college."

🔒 FORTIFY PROTOCOL

Red Team ORI Framework:

- *The purpose is straightforward: verify that your personal and household defenses are effective, identify exploitable gaps, and force corrective action until you meet mission standards. The scope covers everything from online accounts and devices to IoT security, communications, social media exposure, credit posture, and family readiness.*

- *You need four roles to run an effective ORI. The Commander is the owner who authorizes the inspection and implements corrective actions. For personal inspections, that's you. For household inspections, it's typically the head of the household. The Inspector is the Red Teamer who runs reconnaissance, conducts simulations, and documents findings. This can be the owner doing self-inspection, or a trusted friend or tech-savvy family member. For community inspections, rotate who serves as inspector to get fresh perspectives. The Recorder maintains the audit log, tracks corrective actions, and verifies closure. You can combine this with the Commander role for solo inspections. The Control Officer ensures drills are conducted ethically and legally, particularly critical when inspecting family members or community groups.*

- *The cadence matters. Run a full ORI quarterly, covering all categories with complete documentation and scoring. Conduct monthly quick checks focused on high-risk items like recent financial statements, social media posts,*

Chapter 12: Red Team - Thinking Like the Enemy

new device additions, and password manager security reports. Complete an annual comprehensive review that includes pulling all three credit reports, verifying data broker removal, assessing family security posture, and updating procedures for new threats. Finally, run immediate ORIs when trigger events occur, whether personal events like moving or getting married, security events like breach notifications or phishing attempts, or technology events like new devices or major software updates.

My Brother Mike's First ORI

Mike wanted to run an ORI but felt overwhelmed by the structure. "Alan, I don't need roles and frameworks. I want to check if I'm secure."

I explained it differently: "Think of it like a home inspection before you buy a house. You can walk through and visually inspect things, or you can hire an inspector with a checklist who documents every issue. Which gives you confidence that the house is actually sound?"

Mike got it. He ran his first self-inspection using the framework, playing all the roles himself. It took him about two hours. He found three old email accounts he'd completely forgotten about. His smart thermostat was still using the default password that came from the factory. His son's gaming console was connected to the main network instead of the guest network, creating a potential entry point for attackers. His wife was using "Mike1965" as a password on multiple sites, making credential stuffing attacks trivially easy.

"I thought I was secure," he told me afterward. "Turns out I had a bunch of unlocked doors I didn't even know existed."

251

⚔ SITREP: The Red Team Reality

Cybersecurity isn't static. Every quarter brings new threats such as breaches expose credentials monthly, platform updates reset privacy settings, software vulnerabilities emerge constantly, criminals adapt to defensive measures, and family circumstances change with new devices, moves, and job changes.

Regular ORIs matter because defenses degrade without maintenance. New devices create new vulnerabilities. Security fatigue leads to shortcuts. Platform changes undermine previous settings. What worked last quarter may have gaps today.

The bottom line is this: a one-time security setup is essentially security theater. Regular inspection and correction are what keep you protected. Red Teaming turns security from a project into a practice.

When to Run Your Inspections

Your routine cadence should include quarterly full ORIs that take two to three hours and cover complete inspections with full documentation, scoring, and corrective action plans. Monthly quick checks take fifteen to thirty minutes and focus on recent financial statements, social media posts particularly around travel, new device additions, and password manager security reports. Annual comprehensive reviews take half a day and include pulling all three credit reports, verifying data broker removal, assessing family security posture, and updating procedures for new threats.

Certain events trigger immediate ORIs regardless of your routine schedule. Personal events include moving to a new

Chapter 12: Red Team - Thinking Like the Enemy

address, marriage or divorce, a new child in the family, job changes especially those involving security clearances, major purchases like houses or cars, and inheritance or significant wealth changes. Security events include breach notifications, phishing attempts that nearly worked, suspicious account activity, unexpected password resets, lost or stolen devices, and family member compromises. Technology events include new device purchases, router or network equipment changes, major software updates to your operating system or password manager, and service provider changes for banks, email, or phone services.

Sarah's Deployment ORI

When my daughter Sarah got a six-month contract assignment overseas, we ran an immediate pre-deployment ORI even though her regular quarterly inspection wasn't due yet.

The situation mattered because she'd be using unfamiliar networks in foreign countries, different time zones would make support harder, international banking needs extra security, and travel scams specifically target people abroad.

During the inspection, we enabled travel notifications on all her financial accounts so the banks wouldn't flag legitimate transactions as suspicious. We set up a VPN for secure international access to avoid exposure on hotel and airport Wi-Fi. We created emergency contact procedures so she could reach me regardless of time zones. We verified she could access her MFA from abroad since some authenticator apps require internet connectivity. We documented all her account recovery procedures in case she lost her phone or got locked out. We added extra fraud alerts to her frozen credit since identity theft attempts often increase when people travel internationally.

The ORI took ninety minutes. During her deployment, she experienced no security incidents and had secure access to all necessary resources. The time we invested in that pre-deployment inspection gave her peace of mind and protected her throughout the assignment.

Running the Inspection: A Methodical Approach

Before you start testing, spend ten minutes getting organized. Create your audit log in a spreadsheet or document with columns for the date, inspector name, scope, category, finding, severity, action, owner, due date, and verification status. Assign your roles clearly, identifying who's serving as Commander, Inspector, Recorder, and Control Officer. Gather your tools so you have your password manager accessible, authenticator app available, network scanner installed, Have I Been Pwned access ready, credit bureau login credentials prepared, and a notepad for quick notes. Set your boundaries by determining how long this will take, what's in scope versus out of scope, what happens if you find something serious, and when corrections will be made.

My family's prep routine involves scheduling ORIs on Saturday mornings. Coffee is ready, devices are charged, and everyone knows they're blocked off for two to three hours. No distractions, no rushing. This preparation makes the actual inspection run smoothly.

The reconnaissance phase takes about thirty minutes and starts with a public footprint assessment. Google yourself thoroughly by searching for your full name in quotes, your name plus city, your name plus employer, your phone number, and all your email addresses. Note what criminals could learn about you from these public searches. Check people-search sites like Whitepages, Spokeo, and BeenVerified to document what information is publicly available, whether previous opt-outs failed, and what needs to be added to your removal list. Run all your email addresses through Have I Been Pwned and check your password manager's breach reports to document

Chapter 12: Red Team - Thinking Like the Enemy

any new breaches since your last check and verify that monitoring is still active.

Scan your social media carefully by reviewing privacy settings on all platforms, checking recent posts for oversharing, looking for location data exposure, reviewing photos for sensitive information visible in the background, and checking friend or follower lists for suspicious accounts. Audit your communications by reviewing recent SMS and messaging apps, checking email forwarding rules, verifying group chat participants, and looking for unusual conversation patterns.

Red flags to document include your home address visible publicly, phone numbers on people-search sites, family member names and relationships exposed, travel plans posted in real-time, financial information mentioned in posts, and work details that could enable social engineering.

My wife's recon surprise came during our first ORI when we found her maiden name, mother's maiden name, and high school all visible on her Facebook profile. These were perfect security question answers for anyone looking. She'd set them to private years ago, but platform updates had reset them to public without notification.

The simulation phase takes fifteen to thirty minutes and tests whether your family would recognize real attacks. Create a realistic phishing scenario and ask, "Would you click?" For example, show family members a fake email from security@micros0ft-alerts.com with the subject "Unusual sign-in activity" claiming a sign-in attempt from Russia. Ask whether they would click, what makes it look legitimate or suspicious, and how they would verify if it's real.

Score their responses using the traffic light system. Green means they immediately identified it as fake and explained why. Amber means they hesitated but ultimately would not click. Red means they would have clicked without verification.

Run an overshare test by asking what someone could learn from their digital footprint. Can you determine where they were born, their first car make and model, their first job, their high school mascot, their childhood street name, their mother's maiden name, or their pet names? If you can answer most of these from publicly available information, so can attackers, and these are common security question answers.

Test password strength by asking family members to attempt to remember their passwords without looking at their password manager. Can they remember their master password perfectly? Can they remember any of their other passwords? If they can remember other passwords, those passwords might be too simple. The goal is that the master password should be memorable while everything else should be impossible to remember because they're properly random.

Verify two-factor authentication by confirming MFA is enabled, checking whether it's app-based or SMS, ensuring backup codes are saved, verifying access from multiple devices, and understanding what happens if they lose their phone.

My son's simulation failure came when I created a fake "Netflix password expired" email. He was about to click before I stopped him. "But it looked exactly like the Netflix emails I got!" That became a teaching moment about hovering over links before clicking.

Chapter 12: Red Team - Thinking Like the Enemy

▨ RED TEAM INSIGHT

- *During actual penetration tests, we consistently find that even security-aware users have blind spots. The most common vulnerabilities include IoT devices with default passwords, old accounts that have been forgotten about, and family members who haven't implemented adequate defenses. Your ORI should specifically target these areas because criminals do.*

- *The technical scan takes about thirty minutes and starts with a comprehensive network security assessment. Log into your router admin panel to verify the admin password is strong and not the factory default. Check that Wi-Fi encryption uses WPA3 or at minimum WPA2. Review all connected devices to ensure you recognize every single one. Verify the guest network is properly separated from your main network. Check whether the firmware version is current. Confirm that remote administration is disabled to prevent external access.*

- *Use a network scanner like Fing to identify all connected devices, look for unknown devices, check the security of IoT devices like cameras and smart speakers, and note any devices on the wrong network. IoT devices should be on your guest network, not your main network.*

- *Audit all your IoT devices by listing every smart device in your home, checking each one for default passwords, verifying firmware is updated, confirming which network they're connected to, and reviewing privacy settings especially for cameras and speakers.*

- *Review your account security by checking Google, Microsoft, Apple, and Facebook for active sessions. Review the list of logged-in devices and revoke any you don't recognize. Note devices you thought were logged out but aren't. Check which apps have access to your accounts and revoke OAuth permissions for unused apps. Review what data apps can access and remove apps you no longer use.*

- *Run your password manager's health check by generating its security report. Count how many weak passwords exist, how many passwords are reused across multiple accounts, how many passwords appear in known breaches, and where gaps exist in your two-factor authentication coverage.*

- *Verify your credit and financial security by logging into all three credit bureaus to confirm freeze status is active, updating contact information if needed, and testing the lift and restore process. Review recent bank statements, check credit card transactions, look for unfamiliar charges, even small ones, and verify no new accounts have been opened.*

- *My technical scan results revealed an old Chromecast still using my main network, my Ring doorbell had two firmware updates pending, and I was logged into my Google account on a tablet I'd sold to my nephew six months ago. I'd attempted a factory reset, but it failed to complete, leaving my account accessible.*

Chapter 12: Red Team - Thinking Like the Enemy

Triage and Correction: The Critical Phase

Once you've identified problems, you need to categorize them by severity and fix them appropriately. The severity classification determines your response timeline.

Critical red items require immediate fixes, meaning within the next few hours, not tomorrow. Passwords appearing in active breaches need to be changed right now using your password manager to generate strong replacements. Default passwords on critical systems like your router need to be changed immediately. MFA disabled on financial accounts needs to be enabled before you do anything else. Unknown devices on your network need to be identified and removed. Active sessions on devices you don't own need to be revoked. Credit that isn't frozen needs to be frozen immediately. Publicly visible sensitive information needs to be removed from social media and people-search sites.

Important amber items need to be fixed within seven days. These include weak passwords that aren't currently in breaches, outdated firmware on routers and devices, SMS two-factor authentication that should be upgraded to app-based, IoT devices on your main network that should be moved to guest networks, social media oversharing that needs privacy settings tightened, and quarterly credit checks that are overdue.

Maintenance green items should be fixed within thirty days. These include general password manager cleanup, data broker removal updates, privacy settings optimization, documentation updates, and training for family members.

For critical red items, document each action with a timestamp as you complete it. Change breached passwords using your password manager. Enable MFA on unprotected accounts. Remove unknown devices from the network. Revoke unknown active sessions. Freeze credit if not already done. Remove publicly visible sensitive data.

For amber and green items, create a detailed action plan that assigns an owner to each task, specifies the exact action required, sets a firm due date, and establishes a verification method.

Track everything in your audit log so you can see what was found, what severity was assigned, what action was taken or scheduled, who's responsible for each fix, when it's due, and when it was verified as complete.

Here's an example entry from Mike's first ORI. Finding: Router firmware is fourteen months old. Severity: Amber. Action: Update to the latest firmware version. Owner: Mike. Due: November 15, 2025. Status: Completed November 13, 2025. Verified: Yes, version 2.7.3 installed.

Complete your After-Action Report within fifteen minutes of finishing the inspection. Document the date, commander name, inspector name, duration, and scope of what was inspected. Calculate your overall readiness score and assign a traffic light color. List all critical findings that were fixed immediately with timestamps. List all important findings that are due within seven days with owners and due dates. List all maintenance items due within thirty days. Document immediate actions completed during the inspection. Record lessons learned including what worked well, what could improve, and what new procedures are needed. Schedule your next re-inspection date.

My family's AAR process involves completing the report together, reviewing what we found and what we fixed. It takes approximately fifteen minutes and provides everyone with visibility into the household's security posture. We keep all AARs in a shared folder, allowing us to track improvements over time.

Chapter 12: Red Team - Thinking Like the Enemy

🚨 MISSION CRITICAL

An ORI without corrective action is just security theater.

Finding problems is only half the job. Fixing them is what actually improves your security.

Measuring Your Readiness

You need to score your security across eight major categories to get an accurate picture of your overall readiness.

Passwords and authentication cover whether you're using a password manager consistently, whether you have unique passwords for all accounts, whether MFA is enabled on critical accounts, and whether your master password is sufficiently strong.

Network security examines whether your router is properly configured, whether you have a guest network for IoT devices, whether firmware is updated, and whether unknown devices have been removed.

IoT and devices check whether default passwords have been changed, whether devices are on appropriate networks, whether firmware is updated, and whether unnecessary devices have been removed.

Social media and exposure look at whether privacy settings are optimized, whether you're oversharing information, whether location data is controlled, and whether photos have been reviewed for sensitive information in the background.

Monitoring and alerts verify that breach monitoring is active, credit monitoring is functioning, bank alerts are enabled, and you're responding appropriately to notifications.

Credit armor confirms that all three bureaus are frozen, quarterly status is verified, credit reports are reviewed regularly, and fraud alerts are in place if needed.

Communication security checks whether email aliases are in use, forwarding rules have been reviewed, group chats have been audited, and sensitive information isn't being shared in texts.

Family training assesses whether everyone has a password manager, whether code phrases are established, whether emergency drills are practiced, and whether security awareness is current.

For each category, assign a score using the traffic light system. Green worth two points means you meet the standard with no critical issues. Amber worth one point means minor issues were noted that need fixing within seven days. Red worth zero points means a critical issue was found and requires immediate correction.

Calculate your overall readiness by taking your total points, divided by sixteen since there are eight categories worth two points each, and multiplying by one hundred to get your percentage.

For example, if you score thirteen points out of sixteen possible, that's eighty-one percent readiness.

Interpret your score using these standards. Ninety to one hundred percent means you're mission ready with a green rating. Maintain your routine quarterly cadence. Seventy to eighty-nine percent puts you in the caution zone with an amber rating. Prioritize those amber items, then re-inspect within seven days after making fixes. Below seventy percent means you're in a degraded red state. Immediate corrective action is required. Consider an emergency lockdown. Re-inspect within forty-eight hours.

Chapter 12: Red Team - Thinking Like the Enemy

Scoring trends matter as much as individual scores. Track your results over time. You should see improvement, or at the very least, consistently maintain high scores. If your scores are declining, that's a warning sign that security fatigue is setting in.

Who Needs This Level of Inspection

Everyone benefits from basic quarterly ORIs regardless of circumstances. Individuals living alone, couples and families, roommate situations, and anyone with online financial accounts should run these inspections regularly.

Monthly ORIs are recommended for higher-risk situations. Households with deployed military members face elevated threats. Veterans, especially those with VA benefits, are specifically targeted by scammers. Public figures and executives have larger attack surfaces. Frequent international travelers expose themselves to foreign threats. Business owners protect not just themselves but their employees. Anyone previously targeted by criminals is likely to be targeted again.

Community ORIs provide value for small business teams, church financial committees, school PTA treasurers, nonprofit organizations, veterans' groups, and neighborhood watch groups.

My VFW post runs a monthly security check that takes thirty minutes with a rotating inspector each month. We've identified compromised email accounts, weak financial controls, and several members who need assistance with basic security. Our treasurer jokes that we're probably more secure than the Pentagon now.

Ethical Boundaries You Cannot Cross

Legal and ethical boundaries are critical and non-negotiable. Never access another person's accounts without explicit written permission. Never impersonate others, even for "testing" purposes. Never create real phishing attacks. Never use actual malicious code or exploits. Never share findings publicly without permission. Never violate privacy laws or terms of service.

Always get written consent before inspecting someone else's security. Always explain what you're doing and why. Always respect people's right to decline participation. Always keep findings confidential. Always focus on helping, not shaming. Always stop immediately if someone becomes uncomfortable.

Handle data appropriately by never uploading sensitive AAR materials to public cloud storage. Encrypt your audit logs. Store findings in your password manager or secure vault. Don't share details outside the inspected group. Destroy notes after corrective actions are complete.

Maintain simulation ethics by using obviously fake examples for phishing tests. Never use real malicious links, even to demonstrate concepts. Don't trick people into revealing real passwords. Make it clear when drills are drills, not real attacks. Debrief immediately after simulations.

My rule is simple: if I wouldn't want someone to do it to me, I don't do it to others during an ORI. The goal is to find weaknesses and fix them, not to embarrass people or create actual security incidents.

Chapter 12: Red Team - Thinking Like the Enemy

The Real-World Schedule That Works

For families, a quarter full ORI works well on Saturday mornings for over two to three hours. Schedule it during week one with everyone participating from 9am to noon. Document all findings. Fix critical red items immediately. Schedule amber and green fixes with specific owners and due dates. During week two, review that all fixes were completed, verify amber items are cleared, confirm green items are scheduled, update your audit log, and file your AAR.

Run monthly mini checks that take fifteen to thirty minutes. Review of recent breach alerts. Quick scan financial statements. Check social media for travel posts. Verifying any new devices is properly secured. Spot-check your password manager reports.

Conduct event-driven ORIs immediately when needed, taking one to two hours. These are triggered by breach notifications, focused on affected systems, emphasize immediate containment and recovery, document lessons learned, and update procedures if needed.

Complete an annual comprehensive review taking half a day. Pull all three credit reports. Complete a full data broker removal cycle. Assess complete family security posture. Review and update all procedures. Perform major cleanup and optimization.

My family's actual schedule includes quarterly Saturday morning ORIs, monthly quick checks on the first Sunday, and immediate ORIs if anyone gets a breach alert. We also conduct an annual deep dive every January as part of our New Year's reset. It's become a family routine now, as natural as quarterly dentist visits or annual physicals.

Common Pitfalls to Avoid

Running an ORI once and never again means security degrades over time. One inspection tells you your status that day, not next quarter. The value comes from sustained practice, not one-time assessment.

Finding problems but not fixing them makes documentation worthless. The value is in closing gaps, not just knowing they exist. Every finding should have an assigned owner, due date, and verification requirement.

Making inspections punitive instead of constructive destroys family cooperation. The goal is improvement, not blame. Frame findings as opportunities for growth, not failures to criticize.

Overwhelming people with too much at once leads to paralysis and abandonment. Prioritize ruthlessly. Fix critical items first, schedule everything else reasonably. Progress matters more than perfection.

Ignoring family members who need help undermines your entire defense. Your security is only as strong as your weakest link. Help them improve rather than leaving them vulnerable.

Getting complacent after good scores allows threats to evolve past your defenses. What scored well six months ago may have new vulnerabilities today. Continuous improvement is essential.

Not documenting findings means forgetting what you found and what needs fixing. If you don't write it down, the inspection becomes another task you completed without lasting value.

Chapter 12: Red Team - Thinking Like the Enemy

Skipping verification means hoping you fixed something rather than knowing you fixed it. Saying you fixed something isn't the same as confirming it's fixed. Always verify completion.

When Reality Doesn't Match the Plan

If you find evidence of active compromise during an ORI, stop the inspection immediately and shift to incident response. Follow Chapter 13's emergency breach response procedures. Document everything for potential law enforcement. Get professional help if the compromise is serious. Return to complete your ORI only after the active threat is contained.

If family members refuse to participate, respect their choice since you can't force security on adults. Protect yourself from their vulnerability by understanding that their weak security affects you. Offer help when they're ready, without judgment or pressure. Focus your energy on those who are willing to participate.

If you score below fifty percent, recognize this as a security crisis, not a routine finding. Consider getting a professional assessment to identify what you're missing. Focus exclusively on critical items until your score improves. Re-inspect weekly until readiness improves to acceptable levels. You may need to limit certain activities until security is restored.

Success Takes Time to Build

In your first quarter, you'll complete your first ORI with an honest assessment. Fix all red items immediately. Clear amber items within seven days. Document everything in your AAR. Schedule your next ORI for three months later. The process will feel awkward and time-consuming.

By your second quarter, your second ORI will show improvement over the first. You'll find fewer critical issues because you've already fixed the obvious problems. Fix times will be faster because you're more practiced. Family cooperation will improve as everyone sees the value. The process will start feeling less awkward.

By your third quarter, your scores will trend upward as security becomes habit. Most findings will be green or amber with few red items. Family members will start by suggesting improvements themselves. You'll have practiced emergency drills. Everyone's confidence will increase.

After a full year, you'll have four complete ORIs documented. Your scores will stay consistently above eighty-five percent. Despite facing attacks, no one will succeed because your defenses are maintained. Family security culture will be established as normal rather than special. You'll be helping others run their own ORIs, teaching what you've learned.

Long-term success looks like ORIs that are routine rather than stressful. Problems get caught early before criminals can exploit them. Family security is simply how your household operates. You're teaching others the process and helping them establish their own practices. When the threat landscape changes, you adapt quickly because your inspection process catches new vulnerabilities.

The Mindset That Makes the Difference

After three decades defending critical systems, I've learned that the difference between secure organizations and vulnerable ones isn't budget or technology, it's mindset.

Vulnerable organizations think like defenders, saying "We've built these security measures, we should be safe." They build once and assume the job is done.

Secure organizations think like attackers, asking "If I wanted to compromise this, how would I do it? Where are the gaps?" They actively hunt for weaknesses in their own defenses.

Chapter 12: Red Team - Thinking Like the Enemy

That mindset shift, moving from hoping you're secure to actively looking for weaknesses, is what Red Teaming provides.

My family's security improved dramatically, not because we added more tools, but because we started systematically looking for what we'd missed. That first ORI where we all scored below ninety percent? It was humbling but valuable. We found and fixed problems we didn't know existed.

Jake runs quarterly ORIs on himself now and helps his roommates do the same. "I thought I was secure," he told me after his first self-inspection. "Turns out I was secure in some areas and completely exposed in others. I needed that objective look."

Sarah runs them before any international travel. Mike runs them every quarter for his business. Linda runs them with her church's finance committee.

The discipline of regular inspection transforms security from a one-time project into an ongoing practice.

Because criminals don't take breaks. They're constantly probing, constantly testing, continually looking for the unlocked door.

Your Red Team process ensures they don't find one.

Mission Complete

By the end of this chapter, you should understand the ORI framework as a structured security inspection rather than vague worry. You should know how to organize and run a personal or family Red Team assessment with clear roles and responsibilities. You should be able to score security across multiple categories objectively using the traffic light system. You should have completed at least one Red Team self-inspection and documented the results. You should understand the difference between finding problems and fixing them, recognizing that discovery without correction is worthless. You should know when to run routine inspections versus emergency assessments. You should be able to help others run their own security inspections, teaching what you've learned. You should have established a regular inspection cadence that fits your risk level and lifestyle.

Call to Action

Use free tools to form your Fortress but test it like an enemy would attack it. Run your first ORI this week. Don't wait for the perfect time or until you feel completely ready. Start now with a simple self-assessment. Document what you find. Fix what's broken. Schedule your next inspection for three months out.

Reference Materials in the appendices provide an ORI Worksheet and AAR Template to structure your inspections and track improvement over time. Use these tools to make your assessments systematic rather than haphazard.

Next: Chapter 13 shows you exactly what to do when the worst happens, comprehensive breach response and recovery procedures that work under pressure when panic wants to take over.

Chief Palmer notes that Red Teaming isn't about paranoia; it's about verification. "In the military, we had a saying: 'Trust but verify,'" he says. "Your security might be good. The only way to know for sure is to test it like an attacker would."

Chapter 13: Recovery - What to Do After a Breach

⏱ Variable (minutes to months) | Essential Knowledge

CALL SIGN: RECOVER, FIGHT THROUGH, FIX FAST, AND LEARN.

My sister Linda called me at 6:30 on a Tuesday morning. I was still half asleep when I answered, but her voice woke me up immediately.

"Alan, someone used my debit card to buy $3,800 worth of electronics at a Best Buy in Miami. I've never been to Miami. I'm looking at my bank app right now, and there are four charges, all from last night. What do I do?"

I could hear the panic in her voice, that particular edge that told me she was spiraling. Linda's one of the most careful people I know with money. She balances her checkbook by hand, still saves receipts, and pays off her credit card every month. This wasn't carelessness. This was a violation.

And she was doing exactly what most people do when they discover fraud: calling family instead of acting.

"Linda, I need you to listen to me very carefully," I said, sitting up in bed. "Hang up right now and call your bank's fraud line. The number is on the back of your card. Every single minute you wait, they could be making more charges. You need to report it and freeze the card right now."

"But I don't understand how they…"

"I know. We'll figure that out later. Right now, you need to stop the bleeding. Call the bank immediately, report every fraudulent charge, tell them to freeze the card, and issue a new one. Get a case number. Write down who you talk to. Then call me back and we'll work through the rest together."

"What if it's a mistake? What if…"

"Linda." I used my command voice, the one I had developed over three decades of instructing airmen on what to do in emergencies. "No. Don't think, act. You have two jobs right now: call the bank, then call me back. That's it. Can you do that?"

"Yes. Okay. I'm calling them now."

She hung up. I stayed awake, waiting. My wife stirred next to me. "Linda, okay?"

"Card fraud. She's calling the bank now."

Twenty-three minutes later, my phone rang again. Linda's voice was calmer, steadier.

"They were really nice about it," she said, and I could hear the relief. "The fraud specialist said this happens all the time. She immediately froze my card, flagged all four charges as fraudulent, and said they'd be reversed within three business days. They're sending me a new card, which should arrive by Friday."

"Good. That's exactly right. Now tell me everything that happened."

Chapter 13: Recovery - What to Do After a Breach

Linda walked me through it. She woke up around six to get ready for work, checked her bank app as she does every morning, and saw four charges from a Best Buy in Miami posted between 11 pm and 2 am. Two for $999, one for $1,200, one for $600. Electronics. All made within three hours.

"The woman at the bank asked me when I'd last used my card legitimately," Linda said. "I told her Sunday at the grocery store. She said that helps them establish a timeline. She thinks my card was probably skimmed at a gas station or ATM, based on the pattern. Someone cloned it and went shopping."

"Did she mention anything else suspicious? Other charges, other activity?"

"No, just those four. She checked everything going back two weeks. Said these criminals usually test cards with a small charge first, but sometimes they just go big immediately."

"Okay. You have done everything right so far. However, we now need to ensure that this is contained. They obtained your debit card number, but did they also obtain any other information? Where have you been using that card online?"

Long pause. "Oh god. I use it for everything. Amazon, utilities, my streaming services..."

"That's what I thought. So, here's what we're doing next..."

That conversation was three years ago. Linda's recovery took about a week of active work and two months of monitoring. The bank reversed every charge, just like they promised. She never lost a dollar. However, the incident taught me something I've observed repeatedly: most people recognize the importance of reporting fraud, but they often lack clarity on the steps to take, who to contact first, or how to prevent the issue from escalating. They freeze in panic when they need to move with purpose.

This chapter is the drill you run when panic wants to take over.

Why This Step Matters

Every commander knows: you don't win by avoiding every hit. You win by how you respond when the enemy lands a blow.

In my thirty years protecting critical military systems, I learned that perfect security doesn't exist. Not for nuclear command facilities. Not for classified networks. Not for you. What separates successful operations from catastrophic failures isn't the absence of attacks; it's the quality of response when attacks succeed.

Cybersecurity breaches follow the same principle. A breach isn't just a technical failure. It's an incident that threatens your identity, your money, your reputation, and sometimes your safety. Your recovery plan is the difference between a temporary nuisance and long-term damage that follows you for years.

After helping dozens of family members, friends, and fellow veterans through breaches, I've learned that recovery has three critical elements: speed, sequence, and documentation. Get any of those wrong and you multiply the damage. Get all three right and you can contain almost anything.

This chapter gives you a calm, ordered drill for when panic wants to take control. Practice it once and it becomes muscle memory. When seconds matter, routine saves accounts.

⚠ THREAT ALERT

Speed + order = damage control.

Attackers act fast. Your recovery will be far more effective if you act more quickly and in the correct sequence. Every minute you delay gives them more time to exploit what they've already stolen.

The Moment of Discovery

Before we talk about response procedures, I need you to understand what discovery feels like. Because of that emotional state, that moment when you realize you've been compromised determines whether you respond effectively or make things worse.

When Linda saw those charges at 6:30 a.m., her brain went into what psychologists call a "threat response." Heart racing, hands shaking, thoughts spiraling. *How did this happen? What else did they take? Am I going to lose everything? Why didn't I see this coming?*

That response is normal. It's human. It's also dangerous.

In that state, people make one of two mistakes: they freeze, doing nothing while trying to understand what happened, or they thrash, clicking frantically, changing random passwords, calling everyone they can think of. Neither helps. Both make things worse.

The freezing response is why Linda called me instead of calling her bank immediately. She needed permission to act, validation that she wasn't overreacting. Seven minutes of her calling me and talking through her panic were seven more minutes the criminals had access to her card.

The thrashing response is what happened to my neighbor, Dave, when he was hit with ransomware. He started clicking on everything, trying to unlock files, considering paying the ransom, all while his computer was still connected to his home network. Every action he took before isolation gave the malware more time to spread and encrypt more files.

The key to effective recovery is recognizing that emotional state and overriding it with procedure. Not because procedure is emotionless, but because procedure gives your panicked brain a script to follow when it can't think clearly.

That's what this chapter provides: the script.

SITREP: The Recovery Landscape

The breach response environment has undergone significant changes in recent years, and understanding this landscape helps you set realistic expectations.

Federal consumer protection laws have teeth. If someone uses your credit card fraudulently, your liability is capped at fifty dollars by federal law, and most issuers have zero-liability policies. Banks now have sophisticated fraud detection systems. Linda's bank noticed the unusual purchase pattern immediately and would have flagged it even if she hadn't called.

Credit freezes are free and effective since the 2018 law changes following the Equifax breach. You can lock down your credit file in minutes, preventing new accounts from being opened in your name. Online dispute processes have become more streamlined. What used to require certified letters now often works through web portals.

Chapter 13: Recovery - What to Do After a Breach

IdentityTheft.gov provides comprehensive recovery plans, official documentation, and step-by-step guidance that didn't exist a decade ago. These federal resources are actually good.

However, challenges remain. Criminals move faster than ever. They know that banks and victims respond quickly, so they try to do maximum damage in the first few hours. My nephew Jake had his Gmail compromised. Within forty minutes, the attackers had tried to access his banking, reset his Apple ID, and sent phishing emails to everyone in his contact list.

Multiple accounts can be compromised simultaneously through the reuse of credentials. If you use the same password for email and banking, attackers who gain access to one immediately attempt to access the other. Recovery becomes exponentially more complex when dealing with multiple breached accounts.

The timeline for identity theft is longer than that for financial fraud. Linda's card fraud was resolved in two weeks. My daughter Sarah's identity theft took three months of intensive work and eighteen months of monitoring before we were confident it was entirely resolved.

Law enforcement resources remain limited. Local police will file reports but rarely conduct investigations. Federal agencies focus on large-scale operations, not individual victims. You're mostly on your own for recovery, with legal documentation serving mainly to support your disputes with creditors.

Some creditors remain difficult to work with despite clear evidence of fraud. Sarah dealt with one debt collector who kept reopening a fraudulent account, even after she'd proven it was the result of identity theft. It took a lawyer's letter citing federal law for them to stop finally.

The bottom line is this: your speed and organization in the first hours determine the extent of the damage and the duration of the recovery. The tools and laws exist to protect you, but only if you use them immediately and in the correct order. Every minute counts because attackers are counting on you to waste time being confused, scared, or paralyzed.

Types of Breaches: Recognition and Initial Classification

The first step in any emergency is to conduct an accurate assessment. You can't respond effectively if you don't understand what you're dealing with.

I've helped people through dozens of breaches over the years. They tend to fall into four categories, each requiring slightly different immediate responses. Knowing which type you're facing helps you prioritize the right actions in the correct order.

Account Compromise: When They Lock You Out

My mother's email breach started with a simple sign: she couldn't log in one Thursday morning. Her password, the same one she'd been using for years, suddenly didn't work. "Incorrect password," the screen said. She tried three more times, carefully typing each letter. Nothing.

"Must be a glitch," she thought. "I'll try again later."

She went about her day. Made breakfast, read the newspaper, did some gardening. Around noon, her phone rang. My aunt, my mother's sister.

"Did you email me about being stranded in Spain?"

My mother's stomach dropped. "What? No. I'm in my kitchen."

"Well, someone using your email just sent me a long message about how you were robbed in Madrid, lost your passport and wallet, and needed me to wire you $2,500 immediately. They gave me a Western Union address and everything."

Chapter 13: Recovery - What to Do After a Breach

That's when my mother called me.

By the time we regained control, the attackers had been in her email for six hours. They'd read through months of her correspondence, looking for financial information and names of people who might send money. They'd set up an email forwarding rule, so they'd receive copies of everything she sent and received going forward. They'd changed her display name slightly, "Mom" instead of her actual name, so the scam emails looked legitimate at first glance.

Seventeen people in her contact list received the Spain scam email. Three of them almost all sent money before calling to verify. One actually initiated a wire transfer but caught it in time.

Accounting compromise has distinctive signs. You can't log in with your usual password. You receive password reset emails you didn't request. Your contacts start telling you they received weird messages from you, whether requests for money, suspicious links, or out-of-character messages. You log in and find sent messages you didn't write, emails marked as read that you never opened, or settings changed in ways you don't recognize.

Sometimes you'll notice unknown devices listed as logged in when checking your account security settings. Or email forwarding rules directing your messages to addresses you don't recognize. Your profile information may be changed, your display name altered, and your recovery options may point to phone numbers or email addresses that aren't yours.

The key indicator: someone else has control of your account, either partially or completely.

Financial Fraud: The Unauthorized Transaction

Linda's situation was textbook financial fraud. Charges appearing on your credit card or bank account that you didn't make. Withdrawals you didn't authorize. New credit cards or loans opened in your name that you didn't apply for.

Sometimes it's obvious: thirty-eight hundred dollars in electronics purchases in Miami when you're in Tennessee. Sometimes it's subtle: small charges designed to test whether the card works before the criminals go bigger. My brother Mike once had a fraudulent one dollar and forty-seven cent charge to an online game. Three days later, a twenty-three-hundred-dollar charge was made to the same merchant. They were testing to see if he was paying attention.

The pattern Linda's bank fraud specialist mentioned is typical. Criminals obtain card numbers through breaches, skimming devices, or phishing. They either sell those numbers on dark web marketplaces or use them immediately. Clever criminals start with small test charges. Desperate or careless ones go big immediately, knowing they have limited time before detection.

Debit cards are more susceptible to this type of fraud than credit cards. With a credit card, you're disputing charges on the bank's money. They have a strong incentive to investigate and resolve quickly. With a debit card, it's your money that's gone from your account, and you have tight reporting deadlines to limit liability.

Financial fraud looks like unexpected charges on statements, declined transactions when you know you have funds available, calls from creditors about accounts you didn't open, unexplained credit score drops, collection notices for debts you don't recognize, or bank alerts about suspicious activity or unusual purchases.

The key indicator: your money or credit is being used without your permission.

Chapter 13: Recovery - What to Do After a Breach

Malware and Ransomware: The Locked Computer

Dave's ransomware incident happened on a Sunday afternoon. He was working on his personal laptop, preparing tax documents for his accountant, when a pop-up appeared: "Your Flash Player needs an urgent security update. Click here to install."

Dave clicked. He'd seen similar messages before. They always seemed legitimate.

Five seconds later, his screen went black. Then a message appeared, red text on black background:

"Your files have been encrypted. You have 72 hours to pay $500 in Bitcoin to receive the decryption key. If you do not pay, your files will be permanently destroyed. Do not attempt to remove this software or recover your files on your own. Any such attempt will result in immediate and irreversible data destruction."

Below the message was a countdown timer: 71:59:58... 71:59:57... 71:59:56...

Dave's hands started shaking. His tax documents. His family photos from twenty years. His late wife's letters that he'd scanned and saved. All of it encrypted, inaccessible, held hostage.

He reached for his phone to call me. "Uncle Alan, I think I really messed up."

Malware and ransomware are different than account compromise or financial fraud. Your device itself becomes the problem. Files are locked or encrypted. Your computer runs impossibly slowly. Programs open on their own. Your antivirus is disabled or removed. Pop-ups claim your computer is infected and demand payment for fake "security software."

Sometimes you'll see your files gain strange extensions, such as .encrypted, .locked, or random characters. Other times, you'll notice your computer accessing the internet constantly, even when you're not using it, potentially uploading your data to attackers or participating in a botnet.

The ransom demand might be sophisticated, with professional-looking graphics and detailed payment instructions. Or it might be crude, poorly translated, obviously a scam. Either way, your files are genuinely encrypted, and paying rarely gets them back.

The key indicator: your device is compromised, and you've lost control of your own computer or phone.

Identity Theft: The Ghost in Your Name

Sarah's identity theft, which I covered in Chapter 3, represents the most complex and time-consuming type of breach to recover from. Unlike the other types, identity theft often has delayed discovery. You don't know it's happening until weeks or months after it started.

Sarah only found out because debt collectors started calling about a car loan she never took out. By the time we unraveled everything, someone had opened three credit cards, taken out a personal loan, and financed a BMW, all in her name, resulting in a total fraudulent debt of forty-seven thousand dollars.

Identity theft manifests through calls from creditors about accounts you didn't open, credit denials for reasons you don't understand, IRS contacts about taxes filed in your name or income you never earned, medical bills for services you never received, job offers or pay stubs from employers you never applied to, or government benefits being used by someone else.

Sometimes the first indicator is subtle: a small medical collection on your credit report that doesn't make sense. Other

Chapter 13: Recovery - What to Do After a Breach

times, it's dramatic: police contact you about a warrant for arrest based on crimes committed by someone using your identity.

The key indicator: someone is using your Social Security number or personal information to create a parallel financial life in your name.

Why Classification Matters

These categories aren't just academic. They determine your first moves.

Account compromise requires immediate password changes and session revocation. Financial fraud requires immediate notification to the bank and resolution of transaction disputes. Malware requires immediate device isolation and backup assessment. Identity theft requires immediate credit freezes and comprehensive documentation.

Get the classification wrong and you waste precious time on actions that don't contain the active threat. Get it right and your response is focused, efficient, and effective.

In Linda's case, she correctly identified financial fraud and called the bank first. That was perfect.

When my mother couldn't log into her email, she wasted six hours not recognizing it as an account compromise. Those six hours let attackers do more damage.

Dave immediately knew he had ransomware but didn't know the first step was to isolate. He remained connected to his network while trying to determine what to do, allowing the malware time to spread to shared drives.

Classification leads to action. Accurate classification leads to effective action.

The First Two Hours: When Speed Determines Everything

After helping Linda with fraudulent credit cards, walking my mother through email recovery, and containing Dave's ransomware, I noticed a pattern: the first two hours determine everything.

Not because the technical steps are complicated. They're not. But because panic causes people to freeze or thrash, wasting time on the wrong things, while the breach continues to spread.

The drill I'm about to give you is designed to override panic with procedure. It's the same principle I used in the Air Force during operational emergencies: when people are scared and confused, provide them with clear, simple, and sequential actions. Their brains follow the script while their emotions catch up.

Here's what I learned about those critical first two hours: if you can get through seven steps in order, you'll contain ninety percent of the immediate damage. Everything after that is cleanup, documentation, and prevention. But those first two hours? That's where you win or lose.

Step 1: Isolate and Contain - Stop the Bleeding

When Dave called me about the ransomware, my first words were: "Unplug your laptop from the network right now. Don't shut it down, don't try to fix anything, disconnect the network cable and turn off Wi-Fi."

"But I need to research how to…"

"No. Disconnect it right now while I'm on the phone with you. Do it."

I heard him fumbling with the laptop. "Okay, Wi-Fi is off."

Chapter 13: Recovery - What to Do After a Breach

"Good. Now I walk away from the computer. Use your phone for everything else. That laptop is contaminated and we're not touching it again until we have a plan."

Isolation is the first principle of containment. Whether it's a compromised device or a compromised account, your instinct will be to investigate, to understand, to fix. That instinct makes things worse.

For compromised devices like computers, phones, tablets, and smart home devices, immediate disconnection stops malware from spreading to other devices on your network, prevents additional data from being uploaded to attackers, and gives you time to respond from a clean device without the attacker being able to monitor your actions.

When Dave's ransomware was actively running, every second it stayed connected to his network was another second it could encrypt files on shared drives, spread to other computers, or exfiltrate data before encrypting. Disconnection stopped all of that.

The method is simple. Turn off Wi-Fi. Unplug the Ethernet cable. Enable Airplane Mode on your phone. For smart devices like cameras or speakers, unplug them from the power source. Don't try to save your work first. Don't attempt one last backup. Don't visit websites to research solutions. Just disconnect.

For compromised accounts including email, social media, and cloud storage, isolation means immediately stopping the use of that account. Don't try to log in repeatedly to "see if it's really compromised." Don't reset your password from a potentially infected device. Don't send messages from that account warning people. Just stop using it.

My mother kept trying to log into her email after the first failed attempt, thinking maybe she'd mistyped her password. Each attempt potentially gave attackers information about her behavior and timing. Once we confirmed a compromise, I told her, "You're not touching that email account again until we're on a clean device with a plan. Use your phone for everything else."

This step feels wrong. Your brain is screaming at you to do something, fix something, understand something. But isolation isn't giving up. It's the tactical move that prevents a minor breach from becoming a catastrophic one.

Step 2: Switch to a Clean Device - Your Command Center

The moment you isolate the compromised device or account; you need a new base of operations. Everything that follows, password changes, bank calls, evidence gathering, happens from a clean device you trust completely.

When Linda called me about her card fraud, she was looking at the charges on her phone's banking app. That was perfect. Her cellphone was clean, updated, and hadn't been involved in whatever led to the card compromise. I told her to continue using her phone for everything and leave her laptop alone until we determined the source of the breach.

A clean device means it has recent security updates, hasn't shown any signs of compromise, has your password manager installed, you trust it completely, and it's not the device where the breach occurred.

Your options in order of preference are your phone if your computer was compromised, your tablet or secondary computer if your phone was breached, or a trusted family member's device as an absolute last resort.

The reason this matters is that you're about to change passwords, contact banks, and access sensitive accounts. If you do all of that from a compromised device, attackers watch everything you do in real-time. They see the new passwords as you create them. They watch you enable two-factor

Chapter 13: Recovery - What to Do After a Breach

authentication and immediately add their own backup methods. They observe your entire recovery process and counter every move.

Dave wanted to use his infected laptop to research methods for removing ransomware. I physically made him put it in another room and use his phone instead. From his phone, he could safely change all the passwords that might have been captured by keyloggers on the laptop. From his phone, he could research without the attackers watching his search terms.

Your clean device becomes your command center for recovery. Everything flows from here. Compromise this device and you're starting over.

Step 3: Change Critical Passwords - Close the Doors

The moment my mother regained access to her email through the account recovery process, I told her: "Before you read a single message, before you look at anything, we're changing your password right now. And then we're changing every important password you have."

"But I want to see what they did..."

"No. Passwords first. Looking around comes later. They might still have partial access. We're closing every door before we investigate the damage."

Password changes follow a specific priority order that I learned the hard way after helping dozens of people through breaches. The sequence matters because each password protects different things, and you need to secure the most critical vulnerabilities first.

Email comes first, always. Your email account is the master key to everything else. It controls password resets for banking, shopping, utilities, social media, work accounts, and everything else. If attackers maintain access to your email, they can reset every other password after you change it, undoing all your work.

My mother had been locked out of her email for six hours. The moment we regained access, changing that email password was step one. Until that was done, nothing else mattered.

Banking and financial accounts come second. These have direct access to your money. Even if attackers can no longer reset passwords through email because you've changed your email password, they may still have access to your current banking passwords from earlier. Change them immediately.

Linda's card fraud didn't involve her online banking login, but we changed it anyway. Why? Because we didn't know how they got the card number. Maybe it was just a skimmer at a gas station. Perhaps it was a compromised website where she'd stored the card. We couldn't be sure, so we assumed the worst-case scenario and made adjustments accordingly.

Your password manager itself comes third. If this is compromised, everything is compromised. You need to change the master password from a clean device, verify that no unauthorized emergency access contacts have been added, and confirm that all your stored passwords are still intact.

Work accounts come fourth if the breach could affect your professional life. If your personal email was breached and you use it for work-related messages, change your work passwords. If your work laptop is infected with malware, change your work credentials immediately and notify your IT department. Don't try to hide it. Early disclosure is always better than a discovered cover-up.

The compromised account itself comes fifth. If someone has broken into your Facebook account, change your password now. If they have access to your Amazon account, change it. This seems obvious, but people often forget to secure the

Chapter 13: Recovery - What to Do After a Breach

actual breached account in their panic to secure everything else.

Any accounts using the same password come last in this sequence but must be changed. If you reused your email password anywhere, and be honest with yourself about this, change it everywhere. Password reuse is how a single breach cascades into a comprehensive compromise.

The method for changing passwords is straightforward, but it must be followed exactly. Open your password manager on a clean device. Navigate directly to each site by typing the URL or using a bookmark. Never click links in emails. Go to security settings. Generate a new twenty-plus-character random password. Save it immediately in your password manager. Log out all other sessions on that account. Verify that the new password works before proceeding.

Document each change as you make it. Which account you changed, what time you changed it, and whether you noticed any suspicious recent activity. This timeline is crucial for fraud investigations and disputes that may arise later.

My mother sat with me for an hour and a half on a Saturday morning, methodically changing passwords one by one. Email, banking, Amazon, utilities, social media, everything. She was exhausted by the end, emotionally drained. But when we finished, I could tell her with confidence: "They're locked out now. Whatever access they had is gone. Everything else is cleanup."

That confidence, that certainty that the active breach is contained, is worth the exhaustion.

🔒 FORTIFY PROTOCOL

First 2 Hours Checklist, Your critical path to containment:

- *First, isolate the compromised device or account immediately. Don't investigate first, don't "just check one thing," disconnect now.*

- *Second, switch to a clean device you trust completely, whether that's your phone, tablet, secondary computer, but not the breached device.*

- *Third, change critical passwords in priority order starting with email, then banking, password manager, work accounts, the compromised account itself, and finally any accounts where you reused passwords.*

- *Fourth, enable or verify MFA on every critical account using an authenticator app rather than SMS, with backup codes saved securely.*

- *Fifth, sign out all unknown sessions from every account by forcing logout from all devices, then re-authenticate only your trusted devices.*

- *Sixth, call financial institutions immediately if money is involved, using the fraud line rather than customer service, and get a case number.*

- *Seventh, start documenting everything with timestamps because you'll forget details within hours, so write it down now.*

- *This protocol won't feel natural. You'll want to investigate before acting, understand before changing, and think before calling. However, investigation happens on a clean device after containment. Understanding comes after documentation. Thinking is what you're doing by following the protocol instead of panicking.*

- *Speed and order save accounts. Hesitation and confusion multiply damage.*

Linda's card fraud was contained in two hours and fully resolved in two weeks. My mother's email compromise took a day of intensive work and three weeks to resolve fully. Dave's ransomware took two days to assess and a week to recover from. Sarah's identity theft took three weeks of intensive work, then six months of monitoring, then occasional issues for eighteen months after that.

Recovery timelines depend entirely on the type and complexity of the breach. But after walking many people through this process, I can provide you with realistic expectations for each category and describe what the experience actually feels like, week by week.

Account Compromise Recovery: The Week That Feels Like a Month

My mother regained access to her email on Thursday afternoon. By Thursday evening, we'd changed all her critical passwords and signed her out of every unknown session. By Friday morning, we thought we were done.

Then I had her check her email settings carefully, really carefully, not just a glance. That's when we found it: an email forwarding rule set to redirect copies of all her incoming messages to an address in Romania. The attackers had set it up, so they'd continue receiving her emails even after they lost access to her account.

"How long has this been here?" she asked, her voice tight.

I checked the timestamp. "Since six hours after they got in. They set it up immediately, knowing we might recover the account. This way, they could keep monitoring your communications even after you changed your password."

We deleted the rule. Then I had her review everything else: auto-reply settings, custom filters, signature changes, display name modifications, security questions, backup email addresses, and phone numbers. The attackers had changed her display name from "Barbara Palmer" to "Mom," so the scam emails appeared to come from a parent. They'd added a backup phone number we didn't recognize. They'd set her security questions to answers they controlled.

Every setting had to be reviewed and corrected. It took ninety minutes.

Then we had to deal with the damage they'd caused. Seventeen people had received scam emails asking for money. Three almost sent it. Everyone needed to be contacted and warned. Some of them had clicked on links in the scam messages. Now we had to ensure they weren't compromised as well.

My mother spent the weekend sending apologetic emails, making phone calls, and explaining what happened. She was mortified. "Everyone's going to think I was careless," she said. "They're going to think I'm one of those people who can't be trusted with a computer."

"They're going to think you were the victim of criminals," I corrected. "Which is exactly what you are. You did nothing wrong. Attackers are professional. This isn't about you being careless; this is about them being good at what they do."

Account compromise recovery follows a predictable pattern. Days one and two involve regaining access, changing passwords, securing account settings, and documenting

Chapter 13: Recovery - What to Do After a Breach

everything. Days three through seven require notifying affected contacts, checking for forwarding rules and other persistent access methods, monitoring for reinfection attempts, and watching for related compromises. Weeks two through four continue monitoring, verifying no new suspicious activity appears, and gradually rebuilding confidence in the account. Months two and three watch for delayed impacts, checking if attackers sold your credentials to other criminals, and maintaining elevated vigilance.

The emotional toll surprised me. My mother is one of the most resilient people I know. She raised four kids, ran a business, and handled my father's deployment to Vietnam. But this breach shook her confidence in a way I hadn't anticipated.

"I keep thinking about them reading my emails," she told me weeks later. "All those private conversations with your aunt about her divorce. Messages with my doctor about health stuff. Just... everything. Some stranger is going through my entire life."

That violation, the sense that someone uninvited was in your private space, is harder to recover from than the technical damage. The account can be secured in days. The feeling of security takes much longer to return.

Financial Fraud Recovery: Fast Containment, Slow Verification

Linda's experience with card fraud was almost textbook perfect from a response perspective. She discovered it immediately, called the bank within minutes, reported it precisely, and got the card frozen fast.

The bank reversed the fraudulent charges within three business days, as promised. Her new card arrived on Friday. By the following Tuesday, her account balance was correct, and she had a working card again.

But here's what the bank didn't tell her: the "resolved" charges don't actually disappear immediately from their investigation system. They reverse them in your account, so you have access to your money, but they're still investigating behind the scenes to verify the fraud and recover funds from the merchants.

Two weeks after Linda thought everything was resolved, she got a letter from the bank's fraud department. They needed her to complete a formal dispute form, certify that she didn't make the charges, and provide a written timeline of events. Not because they doubted her, this is just standard procedure for their records and their own recovery efforts against the criminals.

She called me, stressed. "I thought we were done. Why do they need more paperwork?"

"Because you're done," I explained. "Your money is back, your card works, you're whole. But they're not done. They still need to document everything for their investigation, their insurance, their legal requirements. It's annoying, but it's just paperwork at this point. Fill it out, send it certified mail, keep a copy."

Then, three weeks after the incident, Linda got a call from the fraud department at Best Buy. Someone had filed a police report about fraudulent purchases at their Miami store, and they were following up. Did she know anything about it?

She panicked. "Does this mean they think I did it? Are they accusing me?"

I talked her down. "No. They're investigating too. Multiple fraud cases hit their store that night. Yours wasn't the only one. They're collecting information for their loss prevention team. Just tell them the truth: you're in Tennessee, you've never been to that store, and your bank has already resolved it. Provide

Chapter 13: Recovery - What to Do After a Breach

them with your bank's fraud case number if they request it. That's it."

Financial fraud recovery moves faster than other breach types, but it has more touchpoints over a longer period. Hours one and two involve discovering fraud, calling the bank, freezing the card, reporting charges, getting a case number, and documenting everything. Days one through three see fraudulent charges reversed, a new card issued, and initial investigation complete from your perspective. Weeks one and two require formal dispute paperwork, written statements, certified mail, and maintaining documentation. Weeks two through six mean monitoring for reappearance of disputed charges, watching for new fraud attempts, and verifying that disputed amounts stay removed. Months two and three involve watching related compromises, checking credit reports for new accounts, and ensuring fraud didn't spread beyond the initial card.

The thing that bothered Linda most was the uncertainty about how they got her card number. The bank's fraud specialist suspected it had been skimmed at a gas station, but they couldn't be certain. Was it a compromised website she'd used? A physical skimmer? A data breach at a retailer? Not knowing meant not being confident wouldn't happen again.

"I'm scared to use my debit card anywhere now," she told me a month later. "I keep thinking, what if they're still out there, waiting to do it again?"

That's why I pushed her to switch to credit cards for daily purchases. Not because credit cards can't be compromised, they can. But because federal law gives you better protection with credit cards, and because the psychological weight of "my actual money was stolen" is heavier than "someone made charges on the bank's line of credit."

Malware and Ransomware Recovery: The Backup Test

Dave's ransomware incident taught me something about the psychology of data hostage situations. When that countdown timer appeared on his screen, 71 hours, 59 minutes, 58 seconds, his brain went into crisis mode in a way that financial fraud doesn't trigger.

"I can cancel a credit card," he told me while we were planning his recovery. "I can dispute fraudulent charges. But I can't get back twenty years of photos if I make the wrong choice here. These are pictures of Carol before she died. They're irreplaceable."

His voice cracked on that last word. Carol, his wife of thirty-six years, had passed from cancer two years earlier. He'd scanned all their old photo albums, digitized home videos, and organized everything into folders by year and event. Those files were now encrypted by ransomware.

"Tell me we can get them back," he said. "Please."

This is why I stress the importance of backups so much. This exact moment. This is exactly fear.

"Do you remember the backup system we set up?" I asked. "The external hard drive that disconnects after backup?"

"Yeah, I've been running it every Sunday like you showed me. Last backup was..." he checked his notes, "last Sunday. Six days ago."

"So, the worst case is you lose six days of files."

"But the photos..."

"Are in last Sunday's backup. We're getting them back, Dave, all of them. You might lose a few recent documents. Maybe a week of email if you use your laptop for that. But Carol's photos are safe."

Chapter 13: Recovery - What to Do After a Breach

I heard him exhaling, long and shaking. "Okay. Okay. What do we do?"

The decision not to pay the ransom was easy once we confirmed that his backups were intact. But I've seen situations where people had no backups, or their backups were also encrypted because they left the external drive connected, or their cloud backups were encrypted as well because the ransomware was sophisticated enough to target cloud-synced folders.

In those cases, with no backups, critical data, and genuine encryption, the decision becomes agonizing. Pay criminals who might not actually decrypt your files or accept permanent data loss. I've watched people struggle with that choice, weighing the value of lost data against funding criminal operations.

The FBI and cybersecurity professionals officially recommend not paying, and I agree with that recommendation. But I also understand why some people pay anyway when facing the loss of genuinely irreplaceable memories or critical business data.

Dave's recovery took a week. Day one involved isolating the infected laptop, confirming backups were clean, changing all passwords from his phone, and assessing what data might have been exposed. Day two meant wiping the infected laptop completely, reinstalling Windows from official Microsoft media, verifying a clean installation, and updating everything before connecting to the network. Days three and four involved reinstalling applications from official sources, restoring files from backup, and comparing backup contents to the pre-infection file list to verify completeness. Day five meant testing everything thoroughly, checking that all programs worked, verifying no remaining infection, and cautiously reconnecting to the home network. Days six and seven involved monitoring other devices on the network for

297

signs of spread, changing the router password, checking his wife's computer for infections, and gradually returning to normal usage.

He lost one week of work, notes he'd been making for a consulting project. Nothing critical. Everything else was recovered.

But the psychological impact lasted months. For weeks afterward, Dave would call me with questions. "I got an email about a software update. Is it safe to click?" "This website wants me to install a plugin. Should I?" "I saw a pop-up that looked suspicious. Did I get infected again?"

Each time, we'd walk through it together. Gradually, his confidence rebuilt. But ransomware creates a paranoia that lingers long after the technical recovery is complete.

"I never thought of my computer as something that could be held hostage," he told me months later. "Credit cards, bank accounts, I knew those could be targeted. But my own files on my own computer being locked by criminals? That felt different. More personal. Like they broke into my house and put all my belongings in a safe I couldn't open."

That's precisely what it is. And that's why I'm relentless about backups.

🚨 MISSION CRITICAL

Backups are your ransomware insurance.

If you can restore from clean backups, ransomware becomes an inconvenience instead of a crisis. Maintain offline backups of critical data, test them regularly, and keep them disconnected except during backup operations. Without backups, you're at the criminals' mercy. With backups, you hold all the cards.

Identity Theft Recovery: The Marathon

Sarah's identity theft story from Chapter 3 was the most complex recovery I've ever helped someone through. Three weeks of intensive daily work, then six months of active monitoring, then eighteen months of occasional issues surfacing.

What I didn't include in that chapter was what those three weeks actually felt like for her. The emotional weight of it. The bureaucratic nightmare. The moments when she broke down because one more creditor didn't believe her.

It started when a debt collector called about a BMW she'd never financed. Within a week, we'd discovered three credit cards, a personal loan, and that car loan opened within a six-month window, all in her name, none authorized by her. Total fraudulent debt: forty-seven thousand dollars.

Sarah was twenty-four, working her first job out of college, living in a small apartment, trying to build her adult life. And someone had built a parallel financial life in her name without her knowledge.

The recovery process for identity theft follows a pattern, but it's exhausting at every stage.

Week one was crisis response and documentation. Sarah froze her credit at all three bureaus on Monday. Filed the FTC Identity Theft Report on Tuesday. Filed a police report on Wednesday. Pulled credit reports from all three bureaus on Thursday and created a master list of every fraudulent account on Friday.

Each step requires hours of work. The FTC questionnaire was forty pages long. The police report took three hours because the officer was unfamiliar with identity theft procedures and kept asking irrelevant questions. The credit reports had to be read line by line, highlighting every account, inquiry, and address that wasn't hers.

By Friday night, Sarah was sitting at my kitchen table with printed credit reports covered in yellow highlighter. "How did they do this?" she asked. "How did they get enough information to open all these accounts?"

We still don't know for sure. Likely a data breach, her information was part of the 2017 Equifax breach. Maybe phishing. Maybe both. The "how" matters less than the "what now."

Weeks two and three were dispute initiation. Sarah had to contact every fraudulent creditor individually. Each one required a phone call to their fraud department, a written dispute letter sent by certified mail with return receipt, copies of her FTC Identity Theft Report, copies of the police report, copies of her ID to prove her identity, and a formal request to close the account and remove all debt.

Five fraudulent accounts meant five separate contact processes. Each creditor had slightly different requirements. Each had different timelines. Each had varying levels of helpfulness.

The BMW dealership was cooperative. They'd seen fraud before, had procedures in place, and closed the account within

Chapter 13: Recovery - What to Do After a Breach

a week. One of the credit card companies was a nightmare. They kept insisting she must have authorized the purchases, demanding that she prove she hadn't made them, implying she was trying to avoid legitimate debt.

"I can't prove I didn't do something," Sarah said after a particularly frustrating call. "How do you prove a negative? I can't show them video of me not being in that store. I can't provide witnesses to say I didn't apply for this card. I just... didn't. And they don't believe me."

That's when we brought in a consumer protection attorney. One letter from the lawyer citing the Fair Credit Reporting Act and the creditor's obligations under federal law, and suddenly they became cooperative.

Months two through six were follow-up and verification. Even after creditors agreed to remove accounts, the process wasn't instantaneous. Each had to complete their investigation. Each had to report to the credit bureaus. Each bureau had thirty days to investigate disputes.

Sarah had to check her credit reports monthly to verify that disputed accounts were actually removed. Some disappeared quickly. Others lingered, requiring follow-up letters and additional disputes.

One fraudulent medical collection kept reappearing. We'd dispute it, it would be removed, then three months later it would pop up again under a different collection agency. The hospital had sold the debt, and the new collector hadn't received the fraud documentation. Each time, Sarah had to resend everything.

This cycle, dispute, removal, reappearance, dispute again, happened with that medical bill for a year and a half. Finally, the attorney sent a letter threatening legal action for violations of the Fair Credit Reporting Act, and it was resolved permanently.

Months six through eighteen were extended monitoring. Long after the main accounts were resolved, Sarah maintained weekly credit checks and elevated security. She was watching for delayed identity theft manifestations: tax fraud, employment fraud, medical fraud, utilities opened in her name.

Nothing appeared. But the vigilance was exhausting. "I feel like I'm constantly looking over my shoulder," she told me ten months after the initial discovery. "Every piece of mail makes my stomach drop. Every unknown phone call could be another debt collector. When does this end?"

"When you go three months without any new incidents," I said. "When checking your credit report becomes routine instead of scary. When you trust that the walls you built are holding."

That happened around month fifteen. By month eighteen, she'd moved from crisis mode to maintenance mode. By month twenty-four, she felt normal again.

The total time investment for Sarah's identity theft recovery: Week one required thirty hours. Weeks two through four took twenty hours per week. Months two and three needed ten hours per month. Months four through six required five hours per month. Months seven through eighteen took two to three hours per month. Total: approximately one hundred eighty hours over eighteen months.

That's more than four full work weeks of her life, spread across a year and a half, dedicated to cleaning up someone else's crime.

And the emotional toll was heavier than the time investment. The violation of knowing someone had stolen her identity. The frustration of bureaucratic procedures. The anger at creditors who didn't believe her. The fear that it would never fully resolve. The embarrassment of explaining to landlords

Chapter 13: Recovery - What to Do After a Breach

why there was fraudulent debt on her report. The anxiety that is manifested as insomnia and stress headaches.

Recovery from identity theft isn't just technical, it's psychological.

RED TEAM INSIGHT

In breach simulations and penetration testing, we find that victims who respond within the first two hours limit damage by eighty percent compared to those who wait twenty-four hours or longer. The difference isn't just financial, it's also emotional. Fast containment restores a sense of control and reduces the psychological impact of violation. Every hour you delay is another hour the criminals have to exploit what they've stolen, and another hour you spend feeling helpless. Speed isn't just tactical, it's therapeutic.

The Recovery Contact List: Who to Call and When

One of the things that paralyzed Linda when she first discovered the fraud was not knowing who to call first. Bank? Police? Credit bureaus? Me? In what order? How quickly?

After walking dozens of people through breaches, I've learned that contact sequence matters. Calling the wrong people first wastes time. Call the right people in the correct order, and you create documentation that supports everything that follows.

Tier 1: Immediate Response (Within 2 Hours)

Your bank or credit card issuer comes first if money is involved. Not the customer service department, but the fraud department specifically. The phone number is on the back of your card. When you call, have these details ready: which charges are fraudulent, the last time you used the card legitimately, and where you've been using it recently. Get a case number immediately. Write down who you spoke with and what time. Ask about their timeline for resolution and what additional steps you need to take.

Linda's call to her bank took fifteen minutes. The fraud specialist asked clear questions, documented everything, immediately froze the card, and reversed the charges. That fifteen-minute call saved her thirty-eight hundred dollars and gave her a case number she needed for everything that followed.

The compromised service provider comes second if it's an account breach rather than financial fraud. Use their official "account compromised" pathway, not regular customer support. Their security team will guide you through recovery procedures, assist you in regaining access if you're locked out, and document the incident. Follow their process exactly and get case numbers for your records.

My mother's email provider had a specific form for compromised accounts. We filled it out, verified her identity through multiple methods, and they helped us regain access within ninety minutes. Their documentation helped when we later filed police reports. We could show the official timeline of compromise and recovery.

Your password manager support is third, but only if the password manager itself was compromised. If this happens, it's a critical emergency. Everything in your password manager is potentially exposed. Follow their breach protocol immediately, change your master password from a clean device, verify no unauthorized emergency access contacts have been added, and confirm all your stored passwords are intact. This is the one scenario where professional security help might be worth paying for.

Chapter 13: Recovery - What to Do After a Breach

Tier 2: Same Day Response (Within 24 Hours)

Credit bureaus must be notified if there's any possibility of identity theft or if financial fraud may be part of a larger scheme. You can place a fraud alert by contacting just one bureau, they're required to notify the others. Experian: 1-888-397-3742. Equifax: 1-800-525-6285. TransUnion: 1-800-680-7289.

Fraud alerts are free and last for one year. They require creditors to verify your identity before opening new accounts. If you've already frozen your credit from Chapter 10, verify the freeze is still active. If you haven't frozen it yet, do it immediately.

IdentityTheft.gov is the Federal Trade Commission's official resource for identity theft. If your Social Security number was exposed, if you found fraudulent accounts, or if this goes beyond simple card fraud, file an FTC Identity Theft Report. It creates legal documentation you'll need for extended fraud alerts, creditor disputes, and police reports. The process takes thirty to sixty minutes but produces an official report that carries weight with creditors.

Your employer or IT team must be notified immediately if work accounts or work devices were compromised. Don't try to hide it. Don't wait to see if you can fix it yourself. Don't worry about looking careless. Early notification reduces company risk and often gets you support and resources for recovery. Follow your company's official incident reporting procedures if they exist.

When my nephew Jake's work laptop showed signs of malware, he immediately called his IT department. They remotely wiped the laptop, issued him a temporary device, changed all his credentials, and monitored any attempts to access company systems. His early notification prevented what could have been a major company breach. His manager

305

thanked him for reporting it quickly rather than trying to handle it alone.

Tier 3: Within a Week (As Situation Develops)

Your state Attorney General's consumer protection division often responds faster than federal agencies. File an identity theft complaint online. Many states have dedicated identity theft units that can escalate cases against uncooperative creditors. This creates additional legal documentation and sometimes triggers state-level enforcement that actually helps individual victims.

Sarah filed with the Tennessee Attorney General's office after one creditor refused to cooperate. The AG's office sent a letter to the creditor on official letterhead, and suddenly the creditor became very cooperative. State AGs often have more bandwidth for individual cases than federal agencies.

Local police reports are primarily for documentation rather than investigation. Most police departments don't investigate individual cybercrime cases because they lack resources or jurisdiction. But the police report creates official documentation that creditors often require. Bring everything: government ID, proof of address, all evidence, timeline of events, FTC Identity Theft Report, and list of fraudulent accounts or charges.

When you file the report, be prepared for the officer to be unfamiliar with identity theft procedures. Have patience. Be clear about what you need: documentation and a case number, not necessarily an investigation. Most officers are helpful once they understand you're not expecting them to solve the crime, just document it.

Family and household members need to know if they might be affected. If your email was compromised and you use it for family communications, they need to know. If your contact list was exposed, warn people about potential phishing attempts. Keep the message brief and factual. You're warning them not seeking sympathy or sharing every detail.

My mother sent a simple email to everyone in her family: "My email account was compromised between Tuesday and Thursday. If you received messages from me requesting money or containing suspicious links, please disregard them. The account is now secure. If you clicked any links, please let me know so we can make sure you're protected too."

Three relatives replied that they'd clicked links. We helped each of them check for potential compromises and change their passwords. That simple warning prevented the breach from spreading.

Tier 4: As Needed (Situational)

Insurance providers should only be contacted if you have identity theft coverage and the breach qualifies. Review your policy before filing. Document all eligible expenses: time off work, legal fees, copying costs, postage. Identity theft insurance rarely covers direct monetary losses, that's what bank fraud protection is for, but it might cover recovery expenses. Most policies cap coverage at twenty-five thousand to fifty thousand dollars for recovery costs.

Legal counsel becomes necessary for complex identity theft, significant financial losses that banks won't reverse, uncooperative creditors who ignore your disputes, reputational damage, or business-related breaches. Consumer protection attorneys often offer free initial consultations. Some work on contingency if creditors have clearly violated federal law. The lawyer's letter Sarah's attorney sent cost four hundred dollars and resolved three disputes that had been dragging on for months. Money well spent.

Professional remediation services like credit restoration firms, forensic recovery specialists, and incident response consultants are worth considering for complex cases but verify their credentials carefully. Some are excellent. Some are scams that take your money and do nothing you couldn't do yourself. Check reviews, ask for references, understand precisely what they're offering, and never pay upfront for undefined services.

What Linda Learned About Contact Order

Looking back on her card fraud three years later, Linda told me: "The thing that helped most was knowing exactly who to call first. When I saw those charges, I was paralyzed. I wanted to call you, contact the credit bureaus, search online for guidance, inform my husband, and review my credit report, all at once. But you told me to do one thing: call the bank. That focus kept me from spinning out."

That's the purpose of the contact list: focus. In a crisis, your brain wants to do everything simultaneously. The contact list permits you to do one thing at a time, in the order that actually matters.

After the Storm: Learning from Breach

Three months after my mother's email breach was fully resolved, I sat down with her to conduct what we call in the military an After-Action Review. The crisis is over. She'd recovered access to her account. She'd notified everyone who'd been affected. She'd changed all her passwords and enabled two-factor authentication. She regularly monitored her accounts and credit. Everything was secure.

But I didn't want her to move on and forget. I wanted her to learn from what happened so it wouldn't happen again, to her or to anyone she could help.

"Let's walk through this," I said. "Not to make you feel bad, but to understand what worked, what didn't, and what we're changing going forward."

Chapter 13: Recovery - What to Do After a Breach

She was resistant at first. "I don't want to relive it, Alan. It was awful."

"I know. But awful experiences make the best teachers if we're willing to learn from them. Twenty minutes. That's all I'm asking."

We went through six questions. The same six I ask every time I help someone recover from a breach.

Question One: What exactly happened?

My mother's email account was compromised between 8:00 a.m. and 2:00 p.m. on Thursday. The attackers changed her password, locked her out, set up email forwarding to their address, modified her display name, and used her account to send scam messages to seventeen contacts asking for money. Three people almost sent money before verifying. The attack likely originated from a phishing email she'd received earlier that week.

We reconstructed the timeline as precisely as possible. Not to assign blame, but to understand the sequence of events. When did each thing happen? What was the window of opportunity for the attackers? When did we regain control?

Question Two: How did they get in?

This is the most challenging question to answer with certainty, yet it is often the most important. My mother had clicked on an email earlier that week that appeared to be from her bank. The email said there was unusual activity on her account, and she needed to verify her identity. She clicked the link and entered her email address and password on what appeared to be her bank's website.

"I thought I was being careful," she said. "I checked that it said 'secure' in the address bar. However, I didn't examine the actual URL closely. It was something like 'bank-security-verify.com' instead of her real bank's website."

That was the entry point. The phishing email captured her email password. From there, the attackers had access to everything in her email, including password reset links for other accounts.

We discussed why the phishing email was effective. It came at a time when she was already worried about fraud, she'd heard news reports about banking scams. It created urgency: verify your identity now or your account will be locked. It looked legitimate with official-looking graphics and professional language. And it requested something that seemed reasonable: logging in to verify your identity.

"The hardest part," she admitted, "is that I knew about phishing. You'd warned me about it. I thought I would recognize it. But when I was scared about my bank account, I just... didn't think. I clicked."

That's the lesson: phishing works because it manipulates emotion, not because victims are uninformed. Knowing about phishing intellectually doesn't protect you when you're scared, busy, distracted, or stressed.

Question Three: What was the impact?

We made a list. Not just the technical impact, but the full cost.

My mother spent twelve hours over three days actively recovering her account and contacting affected people. She spent an additional hundred-plus dollars on certified mail, police reports, and identity theft protection services. She experienced significant emotional stress: anxiety, embarrassment, violation, fear that it would happen again, or that someone she loved would lose money because of her.

Seventeen family members and friends received scam messages and had to spend time verifying the situation. Some nearly lost money. All experienced worry about my mother's wellbeing. Three people who clicked links in the scam emails had to change their own passwords and check their accounts. My mother's sense of confidence with technology was shaken for months.

The impact wasn't just the six hours the attackers had access. It was everything that followed.

Question Four: What worked in our response?

My mother called me immediately. That prevented her from making impulsive decisions while panicking. We regained account access within ninety minutes of starting the recovery process. We meticulously documented everything, creating a timeline and saving all communications. We notified affected contacts quickly, preventing anyone from actually losing money. We didn't just change passwords, we checked every setting and found the forwarding rule they'd set up. We filed official reports that created legal documentation.

These things worked because we had a procedure to follow. The procedure wasn't perfect, we learned things we'd do differently, but it was good enough to contain the breach and recover without lasting damage.

Question Five: What didn't work?

Detection was delayed by six hours because my mother didn't realize she was compromised when she was unable to log in initially. She assumed it was a technical glitch and waited to try again later. Those six hours gave attackers time to do more damage.

She had not enabled two-factor authentication on her email account before the breach. If she had, the attackers would not have been able to access her account, even with her password.

This was a gap in her security that we'd discussed before, but she hadn't implemented.

Her passwords were memorable, meaning she used variations of the same base password across multiple accounts. When attackers got her email password, they immediately tried similar variations on her banking, shopping, and social media accounts. Some worked. This created secondary compromises we had to contain.

She didn't have a password manager, so after the breach, we had to change dozens of passwords manually, and she struggled to remember which accounts she even had. Recovery would have been much faster if all her accounts were already documented in a password manager.

These weren't failures of character. These were gaps in her security system that the breach exposed. Gaps we could now close.

Question Six: What are we changing?

Based on what we learned, we made specific changes.

My mother got a password manager the following week. We spent a Saturday afternoon setting up Bitwarden, importing all her accounts, generating new strong passwords for everything, and enabling two-factor authentication on every account that offered it.

We established a family security protocol. If anyone receives a request for money via email or text, they call to verify using a known phone number, never the number in the message. If anyone suspects a compromise, they contact me immediately before attempting to resolve the issue themselves.

My mother now checks her email settings monthly, looking for unauthorized forwarding rules, filters, or other modifications. It takes two minutes, and she adds it to her monthly calendar reminder.

Chapter 13: Recovery - What to Do After a Breach

We added my mother to the family Red Team ORI schedule from Chapter 12. Every quarter, we run a security inspection on her accounts, devices, and settings. It's become routine rather than reactive.

She subscribes to Have I Been Pwned breach notifications for all her email addresses. She gets alerts immediately if her credentials appear in any new data breaches.

Most importantly, she's no longer embarrassed about the breach. She tells friends and family about what happened and what she learned. She's helped three other people recover from similar compromises. The incident that left her feeling violated and foolish became something she uses to help others.

"I'm not ashamed anymore," she told me six months after the breach. "It wasn't about me being stupid. It was about criminals being good at what they do. Now I'm better at what I do, and I can help other people not go through what I went through."

That's what an After-Action Review is designed to accomplish. It transforms a crisis into a learning experience. It extracts lessons that improve security going forward. It turns victims into teachers.

The Psychology of Recovery: What Nobody Tells You

In all the technical discussions about changing passwords, filing reports, and disputing charges, there's something that rarely gets mentioned: recovery is emotionally exhausting in ways that surprise people.

Linda's card fraud was resolved in two weeks. But she told me months later that she still felt anxious every time she used her card. "I keep thinking, what if it happens again? What if someone's watching me enter my PIN? What if there's a skimmer on this reader?" She'd check her bank app multiple times a day, looking for unauthorized charges that weren't there.

Dave's ransomware was cleaned up in a week. But he became hypersensitive to computer problems. A slow startup would make him panic. A pop-up notification would send him into research mode, convinced he was infected again. It took months before he could use his laptop without that underlying current of anxiety.

Sarah's identity theft lasted eighteen months from discovery to final resolution. The intensive work phase was three weeks. But the emotional recovery took longer than the technical recovery. She struggled with anger, at the criminals, at the creditors who didn't believe her, at a system that put the burden of proof on victims. She struggled with violation, the sense that someone had stolen her identity, her name, her social security number, the most fundamental markers of who she was.

"I felt like I couldn't trust anything," she told me a year after it was resolved. "If someone could just take my identity and build an entire fake life, what does identity even mean? What's really mine?"

These emotional impacts are normal. They're not signs of weakness or overreaction. They're natural responses to violation.

Here's what I've learned about the psychology of recovery after helping dozens of people through breaches:

The violation feels personal even when it's random. The criminals who stole Linda's card number didn't target her specifically. They bought a batch of stolen card numbers from a dark web marketplace and tested them systematically. It wasn't personal. But it felt personal to Linda because it affected her money, her account, her sense of security.

Chapter 13: Recovery - What to Do After a Breach

Control is what you lose and what you're fighting to regain. The breach strips away your sense of control over your financial life, your accounts, your data. Recovery is about regaining control, both technically and psychologically. That's why documentation helps, even though it feels tedious. Seeing the organized list of everything you've done to contain the breach gives you tangible evidence that you're back in control.

Trust becomes complicated. After a breach, you question everything. Can you trust websites? Can you trust emails? Can you trust companies to protect your data? Can you trust your own judgment about what's safe? This hypervigilance is initially protective, but it becomes exhausting to maintain. Part of recovery is calibrating back to reasonable caution rather than constant suspicion.

Time doesn't heal without action. People sometimes tell breach victims, "You'll feel better with time," as if psychological recovery is passive. It's not. You feel better by taking specific actions that rebuild security and confidence. Enabling two-factor authentication helps. Checking credit reports regularly and finding them clean helps. Running Red Team ORIs and finding no gaps helps. Action creates confidence. Time provides the space for those actions to accumulate.

Helping others completes your own recovery. Both my mother and Sarah reached a turning point when they helped someone else through a similar breach. Teaching what you've learned, guiding someone else through the recovery process, transforms your experience from something that happened to you into something you can use to help others. It changes the narrative from "I was a victim" to "I survived this and now I can help you survive it too."

This isn't meant to scare you. It's intended to prepare you for the full scope of recovery, not just the technical checklist.

When you're three weeks past a breach and feeling inexplicably anxious, angry, or violated, you'll know: this is normal. This is part of recovery. And like the technical recovery, it improves with time and intentional action.

Common Mistakes That Multiply Damage

After helping people through dozens of breaches, I've seen the same mistakes repeated. Not because people are careless, but because these mistakes are counterintuitive. Your instincts tell you to do one thing, but the effective response is something different.

Mistake One: Investigating Before Containing

When Dave's ransomware appeared, his first instinct was to research it. What kind of ransomware is this? Can it be decrypted for free? What do the security forums say? He wanted to understand before acting.

That research wasted ten minutes during which the ransomware continued encrypting files. Ten minutes during which his laptop was still connected to the network, potentially spreading to other devices.

I see this constantly. People want to understand what happened before they contain what's happening. That's backward. Containment comes first: disconnect, isolate, stop the bleeding. Then understanding happens from a clean device with the breach already contained.

Your brain tells you that you can't respond effectively without understanding. But you can. The containment steps are the same regardless of how the breach occurred. Disconnect the device. Switch to a clean device. Change passwords. Those actions work whether you understand the violation or not. Investigation happens after containment, not before.

Mistake Two: Minimizing the Breach to Avoid Embarrassment

When my mother's email account was compromised, her instinct was to contact only the people who had received scam messages and quietly rectify everything else. She didn't want to admit to the whole family that she'd fallen for phishing. She was embarrassed.

I had to push her. "Everyone in the family needs to know. Not because you did something wrong, but because they might be targeted next. And they need to know that this can happen to anyone, so they're more careful themselves."

Breach victims often minimize damage because acknowledging the full scope feels like admitting they were careless. They tell their bank but not their employer. They fix the compromised account but don't check related accounts. They hope the problem is smaller than it is.

This makes recovery harder because you're not addressing all the damage, and it increases the likelihood of future breaches because those around you don't learn from your experience.

Breaches aren't shameful. They're crimes that happened to you. Full disclosure to the right people, not publicly, enables better recovery and protects others.

Mistake Three: Paying Ransom Without Exhausting Other Options

The first thing Dave asked when he saw the ransomware demand was: "Should I just pay them? It's only five hundred dollars. That's less than the value of the files they encrypted."

That question is reasonable. But paying ransom rarely solves the problem.

First, there's no guarantee you'll get your files back. Many ransomware operations don't actually have functioning decryption. They take your money and disappear. Second, paying marks you as someone willing to pay, making you a target for future attacks. Third, you're funding criminal operations that will use your money to attack others.

Most importantly, paying should be the absolute last resort after exhausting every other option. Do you have backups? Can the ransomware be defeated with free decryption tools? Can data recovery specialists help? Have you consulted law enforcement and cybersecurity professionals?

I've seen people pay ransom within hours of infection, panicked and desperate, without ever checking if they had backups. Dave almost did this. Only when we confirmed his backups were good did he realize paying was unnecessary.

If you absolutely must consider paying, think through these factors: you have no backups, the data is genuinely irreplaceable, the encryption is sophisticated and can't be broken with free tools, and there's a legitimate business necessity. Even then, consult law enforcement and cybersecurity professionals first. They'll help you understand the likelihood of successful decryption and may have intelligence about the specific ransomware strain.

But for most people, paying ransom is throwing money at criminals who've already hurt you, with no guarantee of getting anything back.

Mistake Four: Stopping at Surface-Level Recovery

Linda got her fraudulent charges reversed and her new card issued. She thought she was done. But we still had to determine how they obtained her card number in the first place, verify if other accounts were compromised, and implement improved security measures for the future.

People often stop at symptom relief without addressing root causes. Card replaced, problem solved. Password changed, account secured. Malware removed, computer clean.

But proper recovery requires deeper work. What was the entry point? Are there other vulnerabilities? What needs to change to prevent recurrence? Have you documented lessons learned? Have you updated procedures?

Surface recovery makes you feel better immediately. Deep recovery actually makes you more secure in the long term. Both are necessary.

Mistake Five: Handling It Alone When You Need Help

My mother didn't call me for six hours because she didn't want to bother me. Sarah almost didn't hire a lawyer for the stubborn creditor because she thought she could handle it herself. Dave spent three days researching ransomware before calling me, feeling it was his responsibility to figure it out.

There's a common misconception that asking for help with a breach means admitting defeat. It doesn't. It means recognizing that breaches are complex, technical, emotional, and time-sensitive, and that people who've been through them before can help you navigate faster and more effectively.

Use your resources: family, friends, professionals. Nobody gives you extra points for suffering through recovery alone. The goal is to recover effectively, not to prove you can handle everything independently.

When Things Don't Go According to Plan

Recovery doesn't always follow the clean script. Sometimes banks deny your fraud claim. Sometimes you can't regain access to accounts. Sometimes creditors won't cooperate. Sometimes the problem is bigger than you initially thought.

Here's what to do when recovery hits obstacles.

When Banks Won't Reverse Fraudulent Charges

This is rare for credit card fraud because federal law protects you, but it can happen occasionally with debit card fraud if you didn't report it quickly enough or if the bank believes you authorized the charges.

First, escalate to a supervisor. Repeat your timeline, emphasize that you reported promptly, and cite federal regulations that limit your liability. Be firm but professional. Second, file a complaint with the Consumer Financial Protection Bureau at consumerfinance.gov. This creates a federal record and sometimes triggers a bank review. Third, provide additional documentation: police reports, FTC identity theft reports, any evidence that strengthens your case. Fourth, consider consulting a consumer protection attorney if the amount is significant.

Linda's bank reversed her charges immediately, but my brother Mike had a debit card fraud case where the bank initially denied his claim. They said he'd waited too long to report it, even though he'd reported it within twelve hours. He escalated the issue, filed a CFPB complaint, and provided detailed documentation. The bank reversed its decision within a week. The CFPB complaint was the key, banks respond to federal oversight.

Chapter 13: Recovery - What to Do After a Breach

When You Can't Regain Access to Compromised Accounts

If attackers changed your password and email address, or if they enabled security features you can't bypass, recovery becomes difficult. Work through the official account recovery channels. Be prepared to verify your identity multiple times through photo ID, security questions, verification codes for backup phone numbers, and documented proof of account ownership.

This process can take twenty-four to seventy-two hours for security reasons. It's frustrating but necessary. Document every step, keep all case numbers, and follow up persistently. If the service has phone support, call daily. If they have social media support accounts, reach out there as well. Sometimes public visibility accelerates the response.

For critical accounts that cannot be recovered, you may need to create new accounts and notify contacts of the change. This is disruptive but sometimes necessary. Save the compromised account information for law enforcement, even if you can't access it.

When Malware Infected Multiple Devices

Dave's ransomware stayed contained to his laptop because he isolated it immediately. But I've helped people where malware spread across a home network before anyone noticed.

In these cases, recovery requires wiping and reinstalling everything. Every computer. Every tablet. Every phone that might be infected. Reset your router to factory settings. Change all passwords from a known-clean device or temporary device before reconnecting anything.

This is exhaustive and time-consuming, but it's the only way to be certain you've eliminated the threat. Trying to clean individual devices while leaving others potentially infected creates a cycle of reinfection.

For widespread infections, consider consulting a professional incident response firm. They have tools and expertise for comprehensive cleanup that exceeds what most individuals can do alone.

When Identity Theft Disputes Are Denied

Creditors have thirty days to investigate disputes. If they deny your claim, they must provide specific reasons. Request those reasons in writing. Address each one specifically with additional documentation. Escalate to federal and state regulators: FTC, CFPB, state Attorney General.

If disputes are denied due to insufficient documentation, gather more: additional identity theft reports, witness statements, alibis proving you weren't in locations where fraud occurred, documentation of impossible timelines like accounts opened in different states on the same day.

For persistent denials despite clear evidence of fraud, consumer protection attorneys become necessary. Many offer free consultations and work on contingency for cases involving clear violations of federal law.

Sarah's stubborn creditor denied her dispute twice before the attorney's letter resolved it. The attorney cost four hundred dollars but saved her three months of fighting and ultimately protected her credit score. Sometimes professional help is the most efficient path.

Success Metrics: You've Recovered

How do you know when recovery is complete? Not just technically, but psychologically, when are you ready to move forward?

Chapter 13: Recovery - What to Do After a Breach

Here are the markers I look for.

Immediate Containment (First 48 Hours):

All compromised accounts are secured with new passwords. Unauthorized access is blocked. Financial institutions have been notified, and fraudulent charges have been disputed. MFA is enabled on all critical accounts. Evidence is documented with timestamps. Family members are aware and protected.

When Linda reached this point two days after discovering the fraud, she could breathe again. The active crisis was over. Everything else was cleanup.

Short-Term Resolution (Weeks 1-4):

All accounts are recovered and entirely under your control. Fraudulent charges are reversed or in the dispute process with pending resolution dates. No new unauthorized activity has appeared. You've run a Red Team ORI and identified no additional gaps. You understand how the breach occurred and have addressed that vulnerability.

My mother reached this point three weeks after her email account was compromised. She had access to everything, all changes were corrected, everyone affected had been notified, and she'd implemented two-factor authentication and a password manager. She was secure.

Medium-Term Stability (Months 1-3):

No new fraudulent activity has emerged. All disputes are resolved in your favor. Credit reports are clean with no outstanding or fraudulent accounts. Monitoring systems are active and report regularly. You've returned to normal usage of accounts without constant anxiety. You're confident rather than paranoid.

Dave reached this point two months after the ransomware. He'd restored everything from backups, verified the malware was removed entirely, monitored for recurrence and found none, and gradually stopped checking his computer obsessively. He trusted his systems again.

Long-Term Recovery (Months 6-18):

No delayed impacts have surfaced. Security habits have improved and become routine rather than reactive. Family protocols have been updated and tested. Lessons from the breach are integrated into ongoing security practices. You're comfortable helping others who face similar incidents. The breach is part of your history but doesn't define your present.

Sarah reached this point about fifteen months after her identity theft was discovered. She'd gone six months with no new incidents, her credit was clean, her monitoring was routine, and she'd helped two friends through their own identity theft situations. She'd moved from victim to survivor to teacher.

Why This Chapter Matters More Than Prevention

I've spent twelve chapters teaching you how to build defenses. How to create strong passwords. How to enable two-factor authentication. How to freeze credit. How to monitor for breaches. How to think like an attacker when testing your own security.

All of that is essential. But this chapter, recovery, might be the most crucial in the book.

Because despite everything you do, despite perfect implementation of every defense I've taught you, you might still get breached. Not because you did anything wrong, but because criminals are professional, data breaches at companies expose sensitive information, human error is inevitable, and sophisticated attacks sometimes succeed against even robust defenses.

Chapter 13: Recovery - What to Do After a Breach

The strongest security isn't never getting hit. It's being able to fight through when you do.

I've seen people with terrible security get breached and recover well because they knew what to do. I've seen people with excellent security get breached and spiral into catastrophe because they froze in panic or responded incorrectly.

The difference wasn't their security posture before the breach. It was their response after.

Linda's card fraud could have been devastating if she'd waited days to report it, if she'd tried to investigate alone before calling the bank, or if she'd given up after initial confusion. Instead, immediate action meant zero lasting impact.

My mother's email compromise could have resulted in relatives losing thousands of dollars, potentially spreading to multiple accounts, and taking months to resolve. Instead, systematic response contained it quickly and prevented financial loss.

Dave's ransomware could have destroyed twenty years of irreplaceable family photos. Backups and disciplined response saved almost everything.

Sarah's identity theft was traumatic and time-consuming. But systematic documentation, persistent follow-up, and appropriate professional assistance ensured complete recovery without lasting financial damage.

These outcomes weren't luck. They were the result of knowing what to do when panic wanted to take over. They were discipline overriding emotion. They were preparation meeting crisis.

You've built your Fortress Shield through twelve chapters. This chapter outlines the steps to take if someone breaches it anyway.

Because the mark of a strong defensive position isn't avoiding all attacks. It's limiting damage when attacks succeed.

Mission Complete

By the end of this chapter, you should know precisely what to do in the first two hours after discovering a breach, in the correct sequence, without hesitation. You should understand the four major breach types, account compromise, financial fraud, malware and ransomware, identity theft, and recognize which you're facing. You should have a prioritized contact list with phone numbers, knowing who to call first, second, and third based on breach type.

You should know step-by-step remediation procedures for each breach type, from immediate containment through long-term recovery. You should understand how to preserve evidence properly throughout the recovery process, creating documentation that supports disputes and legal action. You should have templates and scripts for notifications, disputes, and reports that you can adapt to your specific situation.

You should know realistic recovery timelines for different breach types, from two-week card fraud to eighteen-month identity theft. You should be prepared to conduct After-Action Reviews that extract lessons and improve security for the future. You should understand the psychological impact of breaches and have strategies for emotional recovery alongside technical recovery.

Call to Action

Don't wait until a breach happens to learn this drill. Practice the recovery sequence with your family now. Walk through the first two hours together. Make it muscle memory so that when panic wants to take over, the procedure guides you through.

Chapter 13: Recovery - What to Do After a Breach

Print the Incident Response Checklist from the appendices. Store it with your emergency documents. Review it quarterly so it's familiar when you need it.

Save the fraud hotline numbers for your bank and credit cards in your phone contacts right now. Label them clearly: "Bank Fraud Hotline," "Credit Card Fraud." When you need them in a crisis, you won't waste time searching.

Review the Dispute Letter Templates in the appendices. Understand what information you need to collect during a breach to support disputes later. Time-stamped documentation is your strongest evidence.

Complete the Evidence Documentation Log template and save it somewhere accessible. In a crisis, you won't remember to document everything. Having a template tells you what to capture.

Reference Materials

The appendices contain practical tools for breach response. The Incident Response Checklist provides a step-by-step guide for the first two hours. The Evidence Documentation Log tells you what to record and when. The Dispute Letter Templates for credit bureaus and creditors give you legally binding language. The Identity Theft Report Guide walks you through the FTC process. The Contact List Template helps you organize all the phone numbers and resources you'll need.

Print these materials and keep them with your emergency documents. Digital copies are useful, but paper doesn't crash when you need it most.

Next Steps

Next: Chapter 14 shows you how to maintain your complete Fortress Shield for life, adapting to new threats while keeping the security foundation you've built strong and current. Because building defenses is important but sustaining them is what wins.

Chief Palmer notes that the mark of a strong defensive position isn't avoiding all attacks, it's limiting damage when attacks succeed. "In thirty years, I never saw a perfect defense," he says. "But I saw plenty of excellent recoveries. Recovery capability is itself a form of strength. The question isn't whether you'll face a breach, it's whether you'll be ready when you do."

This completes Chapter 13. The chapter has been revised to minimize bullet points and lists, converting them into flowing narrative prose while maintaining the practical, actionable guidance. The military framework and Alan Palmer's voice remain consistent throughout.

Chapter 14: Maintain & Future-Proof - Keeping Your Fortress Current

🕐 Ongoing commitment | Essential

Call Sign: MAINTAIN, A fortress is only as strong as the last inspection.

My daughter Sarah called me one Saturday afternoon, her voice filled with frustration and embarrassment before she even finished saying hello.

"Dad, I need your help. Something weird happened, and I don't understand how."

"Tell me," I said, settling into my chair. That tone in her voice meant this was going to take more than a quick fix.

"Remember that home warranty account I set up when I bought my house three years ago? The one the realtor made me get as part of the purchase?"

"I remember. You were excited about finally owning a place."

"Right. Well, someone used my account to open a utility service at a completely different address in Nashville. I just received a collection notice saying I owe twelve hundred dollars for electric service I never received. The electric company has my name, Social Security number, and everything else. They say I authorized it."

I felt that familiar tightness in my chest, the one I get when I know a security failure has already happened and we're playing catch-up. "When's the last time you logged into that home warranty account?"

Long pause. The kind of pause that tells you someone is realizing something they should have realized months ago.

"I don't think I ever logged in after I set it up. The warranty company sent me the initial paperwork, I filed it, and then... I just forgot about it. I haven't needed any repairs, so I never thought about it again."

"What email address did you use to set it up?"

Another pause, longer this time. "Oh no. Dad, I think I used that old Yahoo address from college. The one I haven't checked in... God, I don't even know. Years?"

That's when I knew exactly what had happened. Sarah had done everything right with her current digital life. She used a password manager. She had strong, unique passwords for every account. She'd enabled two-factor authentication everywhere that offered it. Her credit was frozen solid. She subscribed to breach monitoring. She was vigilant, careful, and security conscious.

But she'd forgotten about her past.

That old Yahoo account, abandoned, unmonitored, probably compromised in one of Yahoo's massive breaches, was still listed as the recovery email for the home warranty account. When the warranty company upgraded its authentication system last year, they'd sent password reset instructions to Sarah's old email that she no longer controlled. Someone found that forgotten account, used it as a recovery path, gained access to the warranty account with all of Sarah's personal information, and leveraged it to open a fraudulent utility service.

Her mistake wasn't dramatic. It wasn't clicking a phishing link or using a weak password or ignoring a breach notification. Her mistake was mundane: neglect.

"Dad, I did everything you taught me," she said, and I could hear the confusion and hurt in her voice. "I have the password manager. I have two-factor authentication. My credit is frozen. I'm careful. How did this still happen?"

"You did everything right for your current life," I told her gently. "But security isn't a project you finish and walk away from. It's the maintenance you keep doing. That forgotten account from three years ago. That abandoned email address. Those are gaps in your armor that you didn't know existed because you weren't checking for them."

We spent the next three hours on the phone together. First, recovering her Yahoo account and securing it. Then, systematically going through every account she'd ever created, going back to college, and either updating the email addresses or closing the accounts entirely. We found twelve old accounts she'd forgotten about. Three of them were using the compromised Yahoo email as a recovery method. Two had been accessed by someone else within the past six months.

By the time we finished, Sarah had a comprehensive inventory of every account in her name, every email address she'd ever used, and a plan for quarterly maintenance to make sure nothing slipped through the cracks again.

"I thought I was being careful," she said at the end of our call. "I was being careful about everything new. But I wasn't maintaining what I'd built. I wasn't checking the old stuff."

"Now you know," I said. "And now we're going to build you a maintenance routine, so it doesn't happen again."

That conversation was two years ago. Sarah now does quarterly account reviews religiously. She's caught two more potential problems before they became actual problems. And she's taught her friends how to do the same thing.

Her initial security setup was excellent. But it was her ongoing maintenance that kept her secure.

Why This Step Matters

You don't build a fortress once and walk away. You patrol the perimeter. You inspect the walls for cracks. You replace worn timber before it breaks. You sharpen weapons that dull with use. You rehearse emergency drills until they're second nature. You verify that the alarms still work, and the guards are still alert.

The same discipline applies to digital security, but it's harder because the decay is invisible. A router doesn't rust where you can see it, it accumulates unpatched vulnerabilities in firmware you never look at. A password manager doesn't develop obvious cracks, it quietly holds passwords from breaches you haven't acted on. Your credit freeze doesn't wear out visibly, it just sits there while life circumstances change around it.

In thirty years of military cybersecurity, I learned that the difference between facilities that stayed secure and facilities that failed wasn't the sophistication of their initial defenses. It was the discipline of their ongoing maintenance.

The most secure facility I ever worked in had weekly inspections, monthly audits, quarterly red team assessments, and annual comprehensive reviews. Nothing was assumed to be working just because it worked yesterday. Everything was verified regularly. Every gap was documented and closed. Every procedure was practiced until it was automatic.

Chapter 14: Maintain & Future-Proof

The least secure facility I ever worked in had cutting-edge technology, expensive systems, and a massive budget. But nobody checked if any of it was actually working. Updates were ignored. Procedures weren't practiced. Gaps weren't documented. Within eighteen months, their "state-of-the-art" security was full of holes that attackers exploited easily.

Maintenance isn't glamorous. It's not the exciting part of security. It doesn't involve new tools or dramatic responses or sophisticated techniques. It's just steady, consistent work that keeps your defenses effective as threats evolve and life changes.

But maintenance is what wins.

⚠ THREAT ALERT

Stale defenses are invisible vulnerabilities.

Unpatched firmware, ignored alerts, expired recovery codes, and forgotten accounts turn yesterday's strong defenses into today's attack surface. Criminals actively search for neglected security, knowing it's easier to exploit than maintained protection.

The Reality of Decay: Frank's Router Story

My father-in-law Frank is one of the most meticulous people I know. He maintains his car on schedule, oil changes every three thousand miles, tire rotations, inspections, the works. He keeps his house in perfect repair, fixes problems the day they appear, replaces air filters monthly, cleans gutters every season. He's organized, disciplined, and conscientious about everything he owns.

Except his home network.

Fortress Shield - 2026 Edition

In the fall of 2021, Frank bought a new house and asked me to help him set up his internet. We spent a Saturday afternoon doing it right. I helped him choose a good router. We created a strong admin password and saved it in his password manager. We set up a guest network for visitors and IoT devices. We enabled WPA3 encryption. We disabled remote administration. We changed the default network name. We documented everything.

Frank's network was secure, well-configured, and properly maintained. For about six months.

Then he forgot about it. Not consciously, he didn't decide to stop maintaining it. He just... never thought about it again. The router sat in his home office, quietly running, never causing problems. Frank assumed that because he'd set it up correctly, it would stay correct.

By the spring of 2024, I hadn't been to Frank's house in over a year. My wife and I visited one weekend, and I noticed his internet was running slowly. His Ring doorbell kept disconnecting. His smart TV buffered constantly. His wife's laptop lost connection multiple times during dinner.

"When's the last time you updated your router firmware?" I asked.

Frank looked at me blankly. "Updated what?"

"Your router. The firmware. The software that runs it."

"I... I don't think I've ever updated it. Was I supposed to?"

That's when I knew we had a problem.

I asked if I could look at his router settings. He agreed, relieved someone was going to fix his connectivity issues. What I found made my stomach drop.

His router firmware was three years out of date. The manufacturer had released seventeen security updates since

Chapter 14: Maintain & Future-Proof

he'd bought it, patches for critical vulnerabilities that attackers were actively exploiting. His router was running software so old that several known exploits had been published online with step-by-step instructions for breaking in.

I checked his router logs. Someone had been trying to access his network remotely. Multiple attempts per day, probing for those known vulnerabilities. Several attempts had succeeded. Someone had gained access to his guest network and was using his internet connection to download content, probably illegal content, based on the traffic patterns.

Frank's IP address had been flagged by his internet provider. He'd received warning emails, but they'd gone to his old email address, one he'd set up with the ISP years ago and never checked. He had no idea his network was compromised.

"But I set it up right!" Frank protested when I explained what I'd found. "You helped me do it! Strong passwords, guest network, everything!"

"You did set it up right," I said. "Three years ago. But security isn't static, Frank. Attackers found vulnerabilities in your router model. The manufacturer patched them. You didn't install the patches. Your perfect setup from 2021 became vulnerable in 2022, exploitable in 2023, and actively compromised by 2024."

We spent that afternoon cleaning up his network. I updated the router firmware to the latest version. I changed all the passwords. I reviewed every device connected to his network and removed the unauthorized ones. I checked his wife's laptop and his other devices for signs of compromise. I reset his smart home devices to factory settings and reconfigured them properly.

The improvement was immediate. His internet speed tripled. His devices stayed connected. His Ring doorbell worked perfectly. His smart TV streamed without buffering.

But more importantly, his network was secure again. The vulnerabilities were patched. The unauthorized access was blocked. The threat was contained.

"How was I supposed to know I needed to update it?" Frank asked, genuinely confused. "It's not like my car where the oil change light comes on."

That's exactly the problem. Digital security doesn't have obvious warning signs. Your router doesn't display an "update needed" light. Your password manager doesn't alarm when you have breached passwords. Your credit freeze doesn't beep when it needs verification. The decay is silent and invisible until something breaks or gets exploited.

"That's why you need a maintenance schedule," I told him. "Not because you wait for warnings, but because you check regularly whether warnings are needed."

I helped Frank set up a maintenance calendar. Every first Saturday of the quarter, January, April, July, October, he spends about thirty minutes on router maintenance. He checks for firmware updates. He reviews connected devices. He verifies his passwords. He tests his settings.

It's been eighteen months since we set up that routine. Frank hasn't had a single network problem. His router is always current. His devices work perfectly. And he's caught two firmware updates that patched serious vulnerabilities before anyone could exploit them.

"It feels like preventive maintenance on my car," Frank told me recently. "I don't wait for the engine to break down. I change the oil on schedule. Same thing with the router now. Thirty minutes every three months, and I never worry about it."

That's what maintenance looks like when it works. Consistent, scheduled, unremarkable. Not dramatic responses to crises, but boring prevention that keeps crises from happening.

Chapter 14: Maintain & Future-Proof

🔬 SITREP: The Maintenance Landscape

The security ecosystem has changed significantly over the past decade, and understanding these changes helps you prioritize maintenance effectively.

Many devices now auto-update by default, which has made some aspects of maintenance easier. Modern operating systems, browsers, and major applications handle their own updates automatically, reducing the manual burden. Password managers have built-in health reports that identify weak passwords, reused passwords, and breached credentials automatically. Credit freezes are free and can be managed online instantly. Breach notification services are comprehensive and free. Cloud backup services automate what used to require manual attention.

These improvements mean that some aspects of maintenance have become less labor-intensive than they were a decade ago. Your computer probably stays more current now than it did in 2015, even with less manual intervention.

But the attack surface has expanded dramatically. Smart homes mean dozens of connected devices that all need maintenance. Multiple email addresses create multiple attack vectors. Old forgotten accounts persist forever unless actively closed. Data brokers continuously re-list your information. Platform updates reset privacy settings regularly. Services discontinue with little warning, leaving orphaned accounts. Breach frequency has accelerated; you're managing more breach notifications than ever.

You have more devices, more accounts, more services, and more data spread across more companies than ever before. Each one is a potential vulnerability that needs maintenance.

What this means is that modern maintenance is about managing a larger attack surface with better tools. You have to check more things, but checking each thing is easier than it used to be. The total time investment hasn't decreased; it's just distributed differently.

The winners are people who establish routine maintenance and stick to it. The losers are people who assume automation is enough and stop paying attention.

🔒 FORTIFY PROTOCOL

Your Maintenance Battle Rhythm:

Weekly tasks take about fifteen minutes total. Scan your network devices to verify you recognize everything connected. Check that your backups run successfully and have enough storage space. Review any security alerts from your password manager or breach monitoring services.

Monthly tasks require about forty-five minutes. Run your password manager's health report to identify weak, reused, or breached passwords. Review your financial statements for unauthorized charges. Audit your social media accounts for privacy setting changes that platforms often reset without notice. Verify that your MFA is functioning on all critical accounts.

Quarterly tasks take about ninety minutes. Run a mini–Red Team audit focusing on high-risk areas. Update router and IoT device firmware. Complete another round of data broker removal since they constantly re-add you. Verify your credit freeze status at all three bureaus.

Chapter 14: Maintain & Future-Proof

Biannual tasks require about two hours. Rotate critical passwords even if they haven't been breached, as an extra precaution. Verify all your recovery methods and backup codes are accessible and current. Test your backup restoration process to ensure it actually works.

Annual tasks take about four hours spread across the month. Conduct a full Operational Readiness Inspection as described in Chapter 12. Pull and review all three credit reports. Complete a comprehensive account inventory. Refresh family security training. Review the threat landscape for new attack methods.

Consistency beats perfection. It's better to do simplified maintenance regularly than comprehensive maintenance sporadically. The goal is sustainable practice, not exhausting perfection.

Jake's Transformation: From Skeptic to Evangelist

My nephew Jake has always been smart. He graduated near the top of his computer science class, got a good job at a tech company, and lives in a nice apartment in Seattle. When I taught him the Fortress Shield approach two years ago, he implemented everything immediately. Password manager, credit freeze, MFA, breach monitoring, the works.

But when I explained the maintenance schedule, monthly checks, quarterly audits, annual reviews, he pushed back.

"Uncle Alan, that seems like overkill. I'll just handle problems as they come up. I'm tech-savvy enough to know when something's wrong."

I didn't argue with him. You can't convince someone about maintenance through argument. They have to learn through experience.

Six months later, Jake got a breach notification. One of his accounts, a forum he'd joined years ago for gaming discussion, had been compromised in a data breach. His username, email, and password had been exposed.

"No big deal," Jake thought. "I'll just change that password."

Then he realized he'd reused that password. Not everywhere, he was too smart for that, but on three other accounts. Gaming accounts he'd had since college. Accounts he rarely used anymore but had never closed.

He spent an evening changing those passwords and investigating whether anyone had accessed the accounts. Two of them had been logged into from IP addresses in Russia and China within the past month. Someone had been accessing his old accounts, probably looking for payment information or personal details, they could use or sell.

Jake escalated his investigation. He checked his email for password reset notifications he might have missed. Found seventeen over the past year that he'd ignored or deleted, thinking they were spam. Someone had been systematically testing his credentials across multiple services, trying to find accounts he still used.

Then he checked his password manager's breach report. The feature had been flagging problematic passwords for months. He'd ignored it, assuming he'd deal with it "later."

The report showed forty-three passwords in his vault that had been exposed in breaches. Forty-three accounts he needed to change immediately. Some were low-value accounts he didn't care about. But several were important, an old email address he sometimes used, a cloud storage account with old tax returns, and a PayPal account he used occasionally.

He spent three days securing everything. Changing passwords, closing old accounts, updating security settings, enabling MFA where he hadn't bothered before. Three days of

Chapter 14: Maintain & Future-Proof

stress and work that interrupted his normal life, caused him to miss a deadline at work because he was distracted.

When it was over, he called me.

"Okay, Uncle Alan. I get it now. If I'd been doing monthly maintenance, I would have seen that breach report months ago. I would have changed those passwords before anyone exploited them. Instead, I wasted three days cleaning up a mess that shouldn't have happened."

"That's exactly right," I said. "But now you know. So, what are you going to do differently?"

"I'm setting up the maintenance schedule like you taught me. Because spending thirty minutes a month is a lot better than spending three days recovering from something I should have prevented."

Jake has been doing monthly maintenance religiously for eighteen months now. I asked him recently how it's working.

"It takes me about thirty minutes a month," he said. "First Saturday of every month, I make coffee, sit down with my laptop, and run through the checklist. Password manager health report, usually nothing major, maybe one or two weak passwords to update. Financial review, check credit card statements, verify auto-payments are correct. Social media audit, make sure my privacy settings haven't been reset by platform updates. MFA verification, make sure my authenticator apps are working on both my phone and my tablet."

He paused, then continued. "You know what's interesting? I've caught a lot of small problems before they became big problems. A subscription that increased in price without telling me, caught it, called them, negotiated back to the old price. A breach notification for an account I'd forgotten about, changed it immediately, found it was already compromised, fixed it before any damage. Privacy settings on Instagram that got reset to public, caught it the same month, before I posted anything sensitive. Every month, I find something that needs attention."

"So, is it worth the time?" I asked.

"Absolutely. That three-day nightmare? That was probably twenty hours of work, plus the stress and anxiety. I've been doing monthly maintenance for eighteen months; that's maybe nine hours total over a year and a half. I'm way ahead on time investment, and my stress level is basically zero because I know I'm catching problems before they spiral."

The transformation wasn't just in Jake's security posture. It was in his mindset. He went from reactive to proactive. From assuming everything was fine to verifying everything was fine. From handling crises to preventing them.

And he's teaching others now. His two roommates asked him what he was doing with his laptop every first Saturday. He explained the maintenance routine. Now all three of them do it together, coffee and security maintenance has become their monthly ritual. They compare notes, help each other with problems, remind each other when the first Saturday arrives.

"I thought maintenance sounded boring," Jake admitted. "But it's actually kind of satisfying. You make a checklist, you work through it systematically, you verify everything is secure, and then you know you're protected. There's something peaceful about that certainty."

That's the psychology of good maintenance. It's not punishment or chore. It's peace of mind through verification.

Chapter 14: Maintain & Future-Proof

The Daily Habit: Building Security Into Life

Maintenance doesn't mean spending hours every day obsessing over security. It means building small habits that catch problems early without disrupting your life.

I've been doing daily security checks for so long that they're automatic now. I barely think about them. They take maybe five minutes total, spread throughout the day, and they've caught problems dozens of times over the years.

Every morning while I'm having my first cup of coffee, I open my password manager on my phone. Not to use it, just to check the notification center. It takes maybe ninety seconds. Most days, there's nothing. The screen shows "No new alerts," and I close it and move on with my day.

But a few times a year, there's a breach notification. One of my stored passwords appeared in a newly discovered breach database. When that happens, I deal with it immediately. Before I've finished my coffee, I've changed the password, checked if I reused it anywhere, and verified no unauthorized activity occurred on the account. Total time: maybe ten minutes. But because I caught it the day the notification arrived, the breach never became a problem.

Throughout the day, I practice what I call "the pause." Whenever an email asks me to click something, I pause for two seconds before clicking. Just two seconds. Long enough to ask: does this make sense? Am I expecting this email? Does the sender's address look right? Would this company really email me about this?

Two seconds. That's all. But that two-second pause has stopped me from clicking suspicious links probably fifty times. It's automatic now, I don't think about doing it, I just do it. And occasionally, during that pause, something doesn't feel right, and I investigate instead of clicking.

When I check my bank app or credit card app, which I do maybe twice a week, I'm not just looking at my balance. I'm scanning the transaction list for anything I don't recognize. Takes an extra five seconds. Usually everything looks normal. But three times in the past five years, I've caught fraudulent charges within hours of them posting. Early detection meant easy resolution.

These habits are so small they're almost invisible. But they compound. Over months and years, these tiny consistent checks catch problems that would otherwise go unnoticed until they're much bigger.

My wife has different daily habits. She checks her email security settings once a week while drinking her morning tea. She scans our home network devices every Sunday evening while meal prepping. She verifies our backup status weekly when she's doing weekend computer work. Her habits are different from mine, but they serve the same purpose: consistent small checks that catch problems early.

The key is making security checks for part of existing routines rather than separate tasks you have to remember. I check my password manager while having coffee because I always have coffee. My wife scans the network while meal prepping because she always meal preps. We don't create new time blocks; we attach security habits to things we already do.

This is how daily maintenance works when it works well. It's not burdensome or time-consuming. It's just small habits woven into regular life that keep you aware and protected without making security feel like a full-time job.

Weekly Maintenance: Jake's Sunday Routine

After Jake established his monthly maintenance habit, he added a weekly routine that takes about fifteen minutes every Sunday evening. He does it while making his lunch for the

Chapter 14: Maintain & Future-Proof

week, meal prep and security maintenance combined into one Sunday evening ritual.

"I start with the network scan," Jake explained when I asked him about his routine. "I have Fing on my phone. Takes two minutes to run a scan of all devices on my home network. I'm looking for anything I don't recognize, any unknown device that might have connected without my knowledge."

He knows his baseline by heart now. His laptop, his phone, his tablet, his roommate's laptop, the other roommate's phone and laptop, the smart TV, the Ring doorbell, the thermostat. Eleven devices total. If the scan shows twelve devices, something's wrong and he investigates.

"Once a month or so, someone's girlfriend connects to Wi-Fi and I see a new phone on the network," Jake said. "That's fine, I know about it, they asked for the password, no problem. But if I see a device I can't account for, that's when I dig deeper. It hasn't happened yet, but I'll know immediately if it does."

After the network scan, Jake checks his backup status. He has Time Machine running on his laptop, backing up to an external drive. Every Sunday, he glances at the backup drive to verify the backup ran successfully, the drive has enough space, and the last backup timestamp is recent.

"Takes literally thirty seconds," Jake said. "I just click on the backup icon, look at 'Last Backup' and see that it says 'Today at 4:32pm' or whatever. Then I knew my backup is working. If it says the last backup was three weeks ago, I know something failed and I need to investigate."

His weekly routine also includes a quick check-in with his roommates about security. "Just casual conversation," Jake explained. "While we're all in the kitchen on Sunday evening, I'll mention if I got any breach notifications that week, or if I saw any interesting scam emails. They'll do the same. It's not formal, we're not sitting down for a meeting. But we're keeping each other aware."

The whole routine takes Jake about fifteen minutes, done while he's doing other things. Network scan while the rice is cooking. Backup verification while waiting for vegetables to chop. Security conversation while everyone's together anyway.

"The key for me," Jake said, "is that it doesn't feel like security work. It feels like normal Sunday evening routine, like doing laundry or cleaning the kitchen. It's just part of how Sunday evenings work now. I don't have to motivate myself to do it or remember to do it, it's automatic."

That's what sustainable weekly maintenance looks like. Not a separate security project, but small checks integrated into existing weekly routines. The kind of maintenance that's so easy to do consistently that you actually do it consistently.

Monthly Maintenance: The First Saturday Ritual

The first Saturday of every month in my household has a particular rhythm. My wife and I both know that Saturday morning is maintenance morning. We've been doing it for years. It's as routine as paying bills or doing quarterly taxes, just part of how we manage our household.

I usually start around nine in the morning with coffee and my laptop. My wife starts around ten with tea and her iPad. We work in the same room but on our own devices, occasionally sharing discoveries or asking questions.

The core of monthly maintenance is the password manager health report. I open Bitwarden, navigate to the Reports section, and run the security analysis. The report shows me four categories of problems: weak passwords, reused passwords, passwords that have appeared in breaches, and accounts without two-factor authentication.

Most months, the report is pretty clean. Maybe one or two weak passwords, usually accounts I created years ago that I never bothered to strengthen because they're low-value accounts. Maybe one reused password where I used a variation on a theme without realizing it. I fix these immediately, generating new strong passwords and saving them.

But every few months, the breach report shows something significant. A password I'm actively using appeared in a newly discovered breach database. When that happens, I don't just change that password, I investigate. When was the breach? What other information was exposed? Have I used that password anywhere else, even in modified form? Has there been any unusual activity on that account?

Last month, one of my shopping site passwords appeared in a breach. I changed it immediately, checked the account for unauthorized orders (there weren't any), and verified my credit card information wasn't stored on the site (it wasn't). Total time: maybe fifteen minutes. But those fifteen minutes prevented a problem that could have been much more serious if someone had used that compromised password to access my account and order things.

After the password health report, I move to financial review. I open my credit card apps and bank app and review the past month's transactions. Not just glancing at the balance, actually reading through the transaction list looking for anything I don't recognize.

Most transactions are obvious: grocery stores, gas stations, utility payments, streaming subscriptions. But I'm looking for the weird ones. The small charges to companies I've never heard of. The transactions from locations I haven't been to. The test charges that criminals use to see if a card is active.

I found one last year, a dollar forty-seven charge to an online game company. I don't play online games. Neither does my

347

wife. I called the credit card company immediately. It turned out it was a test charge. Three days later, someone tried to charge twenty-three hundred dollars to the same merchant. But because I'd caught the test charge and reported it, the card was already frozen, and the big charge was blocked.

That one dollar forty-seven charge took me five minutes to investigate and report. Those five minutes saved me potentially hours of fraud recovery work.

My wife's monthly routine includes the social media audit. She checks Facebook, Instagram, and LinkedIn for privacy settings that might have changed. Platform updates reset settings regularly, something that was private last month might be public this month without any notification.

She's caught this multiple times. Last year, Facebook reset her default post visibility from "Friends Only" to "Public" during a platform update. She discovered it during her monthly check and changed it back before she posted anything sensitive. A few months ago, Instagram changed her profile from private to public. She fixed it immediately.

"It's infuriating that I have to check this every month," she told me. "The platforms should leave my settings alone. But they don't, so I check."

We both also use monthly maintenance to review subscriptions. Every streaming service, every software license, every paid app. Are we still using it? Is the price still what we agreed to? Are there any subscriptions we've forgotten about that are still being billed?

We've found several forgotten subscriptions over the years. A magazine subscription that auto renewed. A software trial that converted to paid without clear warning. A streaming service we signed up for to watch one show and never cancelled. Each one was ten to fifteen dollars per month. Multiplied over a

Chapter 14: Maintain & Future-Proof

year, that's one hundred twenty to one hundred eighty dollars we were spending on services we'd forgotten about.

Monthly maintenance catches these. We cancel what we're not using. We keep what we are using. We stay in control of our finances.

The entire monthly routine takes us about forty-five minutes each. We do it together on the first Saturday morning, then we're done for the month. We know our accounts are secure, our passwords are strong, our finances are clean, and our subscriptions are intentional.

"I look forward to it, actually," my wife told me recently. "Not because it's fun, it's not particularly fun. But because when it's done, I know everything is okay. I don't worry about security problems for the rest of the month because I've verified everything is secure. That peace of mind is worth forty-five minutes."

▨ RED TEAM INSIGHT

During security audits, we consistently find that organizations with routine maintenance schedules detect intrusions seventy percent faster than those without. The same principle applies to personal security. Monthly password manager health checks catch breached credentials within weeks rather than months. Quarterly network scans detect unauthorized devices before they cause damage. Annual comprehensive reviews identify dormant accounts before criminals can exploit them. Maintenance doesn't just prevent problems; it accelerates detection when problems occur anyway.

Quarterly Maintenance: The Seasonal Deep Dive

Four times a year, on the first weekend of January, April, July, and October, my family does what we call the Quarterly Security Summit. It's more involved than monthly maintenance, taking about ninety minutes total, and we do it as a family event.

We schedule it explicitly. It's on everyone's calendars. My son joins by video call from wherever he's living. My daughter comes over. My wife and I are already home. We have lunch together, then we spend the afternoon on security.

The centerpiece of quarterly maintenance is what I call the Red Team mini-audit, a scaled-down version of the full Operational Readiness Inspection from Chapter 12. We're not doing a comprehensive security assessment. We're running specific high-value checks that catch the most common problems.

We start with the public footprint check. Everyone Googles themselves. Full name in quotes. Name plus city. Phone number. Email addresses. We're looking at what information about us is publicly visible to anyone with an internet connection.

Last July, my daughter discovered that a people-search site had listed her new address, the house she'd bought six months earlier. She'd opted out of that site years ago, but it had re-listed her with updated information. She submitted a new opt-out request immediately.

My son found that his phone number was listed on Whitepages with his old apartment address. He'd moved eight months earlier and hadn't thought to check if data brokers had his new information. They didn't yet, his old address was still there, so he used that opportunity to opt out completely.

Chapter 14: Maintain & Future-Proof

These discoveries happen every quarter. Data brokers continuously update their databases. Even if you opt out, they re-add you later with new information. Quarterly checks catch this and let you opt out again before the information spreads.

After the public footprint check, we move to firmware updates. This is where Frank's router story comes in, most people forget to update their routers, and most routers don't update automatically. So, every quarter, we explicitly check.

I log into my router's admin panel and check for firmware updates. Usually there aren't any consumer router manufacturers who don't release updates that frequently. But when there is an update, I install it immediately. Over the past two years, I've installed four router updates. Two of them patched critical vulnerabilities. If I'd been waiting for a problem to manifest before checking, I might never have known until someone exploited those vulnerabilities.

We also check firmware for IoT devices quarterly. My Ring doorbell. My smart thermostat. The smart speakers in our house. Each manufacturer has an app with a "check for updates" function. Most of the time, everything's already current because many IoT devices auto-update. But occasionally something needs manual intervention.

Last October, my Ring doorbell had been trying to update for weeks but kept failing because my network settings were blocking it. I only discovered this during quarterly maintenance. Once I troubleshoot the network issue, the update installed and fixed several security vulnerabilities that had been publicly disclosed months earlier.

The quarterly maintenance also includes data broker removal. My daughter handles this for our whole family now. She has a spreadsheet tracking which sites we've opted out of, when we did it, and when we needed to do it again. Every quarter, she submits opt-out requests to five or six major data broker sites, rotating through the list systematically.

"It takes about twenty minutes per person," she explained. "Most sites make you fill out a form with your name, address, phone number, email, and sometimes upload ID to verify you're really you. It's tedious but not difficult."

The improvement is noticeable. When my wife stopped doing quarterly opt-outs for six months as an experiment, her scam call volume tripled. When she resumed quarterly removal, the calls dropped back to near zero within two months. Data broker removal works, but only if you keep doing it.

We also verify credit freeze status quarterly. Everyone logs into all three credit bureaus, Equifax, Experian, TransUnion, and confirms the freeze is still active, contact information is current, and no unauthorized changes have been made.

This sounds paranoid until you realize that systems glitch. Last year during a quarterly check, Frank discovered his Experian freeze was showing as "temporary" with an expiration date in two weeks. He hadn't done anything; the system had changed during a platform upgrade. If he hadn't checked, his credit would have been wide open within the month.

The quarterly family security summit ends with a coordination session. Has anyone gotten breach notifications? Has anyone encountered new scam attempts? Are there new threats we should be aware of? Does anyone need help with something they've been putting off?

This family coordination is valuable in ways that aren't obvious until you've done it. My son mentioned during one quarterly meeting that he'd been getting a lot of phishing texts. We all started paying more attention and realized we were all getting them, there was a new text phishing campaign targeting our region. Because we discussed it as a family, everyone knew to be extra careful.

My wife mentioned she'd forgotten her MFA recovery codes for one account. I helped her generate new codes and save them properly. If she'd needed those codes in an emergency and couldn't find them, she would have been locked out of a critical account. Catching it during routine maintenance meant we could fix it calmly.

By the time our quarterly summit ends, usually mid-afternoon, everyone in the family has updated security, identified and fixed problems, and shared information that helps everyone. We have lunch, we do security, we catch up on life, and we're done until next quarter.

"I like that we do it together," Sarah told me. "Security can feel isolating, like it's just you against threats. But when we do it as a family, it feels like we're all protecting each other. And it's nice to know that if I miss something, someone else might catch it."

That's the power of quarterly family maintenance. It's not just technical work. It's community defense, shared responsibility, and mutual support.

The Tools You'll Actually Use

After helping dozens of people set up and maintain their security, I've learned that tool choice matters less than tool usage. The best tool is the one you'll actually use consistently. Here's what I use, what my family uses, and why, not as specifications to compare, but as real experience.

I use Bitwarden for password management. I've used it for four years. Before that, I used LastPass until they had a breach. Before that, I used 1Password until the subscription model became annoying. I've tried KeePass but found manual sync tedious for my lifestyle.

Bitwarden works for me because it's reliable, cross-platform, and has an excellent free tier. I pay the ten dollars per year for premium features like advanced MFA options and priority support, but honestly the free version would be fine for most people. The mobile app works smoothly. The browser extension autofills correctly. The health report catches problems I would miss.

My wife uses 1Password because she finds the interface more intuitive. She's less technical than I am, and 1Password's polished design makes her more comfortable. She shares some passwords with me through our family vault, streaming services, home accounts, and joint finances. That sharing works seamlessly.

My daughter uses Bitwarden like I do. My son uses 1Password like my wife does. They both work excellently. The differences are preference, not substance.

What matters about your password manager isn't which brand you choose. It's that you use it consistently, run the health report monthly, act on breach notifications immediately, and trust it enough to let it generate truly strong passwords instead of memorable ones.

For network scanning, every Sunday evening I scan my home network with Fing. I've been doing this for three years. The app is free, runs on my phone, takes two minutes to complete a scan.

I know my network baseline by heart now: my laptop, my wife's laptop, both our phones, both our tablets, the printer, the smart TV, the Ring doorbell, the thermostat, the smart speaker in the living room, the one in the bedroom. Twelve devices normally. Sometimes guests connect and I'll see thirteen or fourteen, but I always know who and why.

The scan shows me each device with its name, IP address, manufacturer, and MAC address. Most devices identify themselves clearly: "Alan's MacBook Pro," "Ring Doorbell."

Chapter 14: Maintain & Future-Proof

Others show just the manufacturer: "Samsung Electronics" (the TV), "Nest Labs" (the thermostat).

I'm looking for unknowns. Devices that don't identify themselves. Manufacturers I don't recognize. Generic names like "Android Device" or "Unknown" that I can't account for. In three years of weekly scanning, I've found unknown devices on my network exactly twice, both times were family visiting for holidays who connected without asking. But if I'd found an unauthorized device, I would have known within a week and could investigate immediately.

The value of network scanning isn't just finding threats. It's knowing your baseline so you can recognize deviations. It's building the habit of checking so that when something is wrong, you'll notice.

I'm registered with Have I Been Pwned for all my email addresses, my primary email, my old college email, my work email, the junk email I use for throwaway accounts. Every time one of those addresses appears in a newly discovered breach, I get an email notification usually within hours.

I also have breach monitoring enabled in Bitwarden, which checks my saved passwords against known breach databases automatically. If a password in my vault appears in a breach, Bitwarden notifies me through the app.

This redundancy is intentional. If I miss an email notification because of a spam filter or a busy day, I'll see it in my password manager. If my password manager doesn't catch it because maybe I didn't save that password or the breach is newly discovered, I'll get the email alert.

Between Have I Been Pwned and Bitwarden, I get about one breach notification every two months. Sometimes it's a password I'm actively using and need to change immediately. More often, it's an old account I haven't touched in years, I still change the password, but the urgency is lower.

The psychological value of breach monitoring is underrated. Before I had these systems, I worried that I might be in breaches I didn't know about. Now I know that if my information appears in a breach, I'll be notified quickly and can respond before it's exploited. That certainly reduces background anxiety significantly.

I have two backup systems. Primary backup is Time Machine on my Mac, backing up to an external two-terabyte hard drive that stays connected to my laptop. Backups run automatically every hour. I verify weekly that backups are running, just a glance at the Time Machine icon to see the last backup timestamp.

Secondary backup is Backblaze, a cloud backup service that costs seven dollars per month. It runs continuously in the background, uploading files whenever my computer is connected to the internet. I don't think about it, it just works. I verify monthly that uploads are current by logging into the Backblaze website and checking the last backup date.

This two-layer backup strategy means I have multiple recovery options. If my laptop dies, I restore from Time Machine, fast local recovery, usually takes a few hours to get everything back. If my laptop and backup drive both get stolen or destroyed in a house fire, flood, or theft, I still have everything in Backblaze, slower cloud recovery, might take a day or two, but I don't lose anything irreplaceable.

My wife has the same setup. My daughter uses Time Machine plus iCloud for her most important files. My son uses Windows File History plus Google Drive. The specific tools matter less than having two independent backups: one local for fast recovery and one offsite for disaster protection.

The backup test is critical. Once a quarter, I restore a random file from backup just to verify the backup actually works. I pick a document or photo, restore it from Time Machine, open it to make sure it's intact. It takes five minutes. Ensure that when I really need my backup, it will actually work.

My wife discovered her backup drive had failed during one of these quarterly tests. She thought backups were running, but nothing had been saved for six months. Because we caught it during routine testing, she only lost six months of relatively unimportant files. If we'd waited until she actually needed the backup in an emergency, she would have discovered it wasn't working at the worst possible time.

After listing all these tools, here's what I actually want you to understand: the tools matter far less than the habits.

I could switch from Bitwarden to 1Password tomorrow and my security wouldn't change. I could use a different network scanning app, and the results would be similar. The specific tools aren't magic; they're just instruments that make maintenance easier.

What matters is that you use a password manager consistently and run health reports monthly. You scan your network regularly enough to know your baseline. You have breach monitoring that actually reaches you when alerts happen. You maintain backups you've actually tested and trust to work.

You can accomplish all of this with different tools than I use. Choose tools you find comfortable, you trust, and you'll actually use consistently. Comfortable tools are getting used. Uncomfortable tools get abandoned.

The Psychology of Maintenance: Why It's Hard and How to Make It Easier

Here's the uncomfortable truth about security maintenance that nobody likes to discuss knowing what to do is easy. Actually, doing it consistently for years is hard.

I can provide you with the ideal maintenance schedule. I can break it down into weekly, monthly, quarterly, and annual tasks. I can make it as efficient as possible. But none of that matters if you don't actually do it when life gets complicated, when you're busy, when you're tired, when it feels like just one more thing on an already overwhelming list.

The people who maintain their fortresses long-term aren't necessarily more disciplined than everyone else. They've just figured out how to make maintenance feel less like a chore and more like routine practice. Let me show you what actually works based on watching people succeed and fail at this over the past decade.

The first principle is this: routine inspections, not one-time projects. You have to shift your mindset from project completion to ongoing practice. Security isn't something you finish. It's something you do regularly, like brushing your teeth or checking your car's oil level or going to the dentist for cleanings.

My personal maintenance rhythm looks like this. Every Monday morning, while drinking coffee, I review my transaction alerts from the past week. It takes five minutes. Every first Sunday of the month, we run our family phishing drill over dinner. It takes fifteen minutes. Every quarter, in the first week, I pull one credit report, run a quick security inspection, and re-run data broker opt-outs. It takes two to three hours across the week. Every January, I conduct an annual review that covers password manager renewal, MFA

Chapter 14: Maintain & Future-Proof

audit, family training refresh, and checking for the latest book edition. It takes three to four hours across the month.

That's it. That's the complete schedule. But the reason it works is that every task is calendared with reminders. They're not things I remember to do when I feel motivated, they're recurring appointments with myself that I honor just as I would a dentist appointment or a meeting with my boss.

The second principle is having battle plans on demand. You won't remember everything in this book. That's fine. That's what the battle plan appendices are for. When Sarah needed to lift her credit freeze for her background check, she didn't remember the exact steps. She didn't need to, she pulled up the relevant battle plan, followed the instructions step by step, and completed the process in fifteen minutes.

I keep digital copies of all the battle plans in a folder on my computer called "Security Reference." I've printed the key documents, the password manager quick-start guide, credit freeze PIN storage template, phishing red flags poster, and emergency breach response checklist, and stored them in a binder labeled "Fortress Shield Protocols." Critical information like freeze PINs and emergency contact numbers is saved in my password manager, where it's encrypted and accessible.

You're not expected to memorize procedures. You're expected to know where to find them when you need them.

The third principle is community engagement. Security is not a solo mission. My family's quarterly security summit isn't just me lecturing them, it's all of us sharing what we've encountered, what's working, what questions have come up. Mike didn't just learn about password managers for himself, he trained his entire construction crew, which means when one of his project managers got a spear-phishing attempt targeting the company, he recognized it and reported it instead of clicking it.

359

Your security is interconnected with your community's security. If your friend falls for phishing and their account gets compromised, attackers will use that compromised account to send more convincing phishing attempts to you. If your coworker has malware on their laptop, it could spread through your company network. The more people in your circle understand these principles, the safer everyone becomes.

The fourth principle is annual refresh. The threat landscape changes faster than any book can keep up with. New types of attacks emerge. Tools and services change. Laws evolve. Your life circumstances shift, new jobs, new states, new family members, creating new vulnerabilities that need addressing.

Every year, I release an updated edition of Fortress Shield. Not because I'm trying to sell more books, but because annual updates are genuinely necessary. Data broker opt-out procedures change constantly as sites redesign their forms and URLs. Tool recommendations need updating as some services improve and others decline. New threats require coverage, deepfake technology barely existed five years ago, and now it's become a significant threat vector. Legal guidance needs revision as state laws evolve and federal enforcement priorities shift.

Getting the new edition each year, skimming the "What's New" section, updating your battle plans with new templates and procedures, and re-running setup for any changed tools usually takes about an hour. That hour keeps your defenses current with evolving threats.

The fifth principle is teaching and sharing. When you teach someone else about these principles, you reinforce your own understanding. When you help your mom set up MFA, you practice the process. When you explain phishing red flags to your teenager, you internalize the patterns more deeply.

I run an annual "Digital Security Update" presentation at Thanksgiving. Twenty minutes after dinner, covering the year's biggest new threats and one hands-on skill. Last year: deepfake scams targeting grandparents, with examples and how to spot them. The year before: AI-generated phishing emails and what makes them different from traditional phishing.

My family is actually looking forward to it now. My uncle avoided a deepfake scam two months after last year's presentation because he remembered the training. My cousin helped her elderly neighbor set up a credit freeze based on what she learned. Teaching spreads the knowledge and makes everyone safer.

These five principles, routine inspections, battle plans on demand, community engagement, annual refresh, and teaching, make maintenance sustainable because they turn security from an overwhelming obligation into a manageable practice integrated into regular life.

When Life Interferes: The Challenges Nobody Talks About

Let me address something honestly: you're going to struggle with maintenance sometimes. Not because you're lazy or undisciplined, but because life gets complicated and security maintenance feels like one more demand on your already limited time and energy.

I want to walk you through the most common challenges people face trying to maintain these systems, because knowing they're coming helps you prepare for them. And maybe, just maybe, you'll handle them better than Marcus did in Chapter 17's cautionary tale.

The first challenge is forgetting your password manager master password. This happened to Jake. He went three weeks without logging into his password manager over winter break, he was home with family, not using his computer much, just on his phone for casual browsing. When he got back to school and needed a password for something, he couldn't remember his master password.

He panicked. "If I can't get into my password manager, I'm locked out of everything. All my passwords are in there. I'm screwed."

But he wasn't screwed, because he'd followed the backup procedure from Chapter 1. He'd written his master password on a card and stored it in his parents' safe at home. He'd just forgotten about it. One phone call to his mom, one trip to the safe, and the problem was solved.

The lesson: physical backup of your master password, stored securely, is non-negotiable. Practice typing your master password weekly so it stays in muscle memory. Use your password manager daily, even if just to check notifications, so you don't go for weeks without logging in.

The second challenge is when your password manager subscription lapses. This was part of Marcus's downfall in Chapter 17. His subscription expired, and he ignored the renewal emails because he was busy. Eventually he got locked out of the premium features he'd been relying on.

The prevention is straightforward but requires discipline. Set a calendar reminder two weeks before your renewal date. Consider enabling auto-renewal if your budget allows it. Treat the subscription cost like car insurance, a critical expense, not an optional purchase.

If you absolutely can't afford renewal, switch to a free password manager like Bitwarden before your paid service locks you out. Export your data from the paid service while you still have access, then import it to the free service. Don't let yourself get stuck without access.

The third challenge is losing your credit freeze PINs. My friend David placed freezes years ago, saved the PINs in a text file on his desktop, and then got a new computer without transferring the file. When he needed to lift his freeze for a mortgage application, he had no access.

Each bureau has a PIN recovery process, but it's painful. You mail in identity documents, wait seven to ten business days for processing, and sometimes provide notarized affidavits. David's mortgage application was delayed for two weeks because of this.

Prevention requires multiple redundant backups. Store freeze PINs in your password manager. Print a physical backup and store it with essential documents. Take a screenshot saved in encrypted cloud storage. Verify you can access your PINs during quarterly maintenance checks.

The fourth challenge is that data broker opt-outs feel too tedious. This is the most common point of abandonment. People start strong, complete five sites, then realize there are fifty-plus sites total and quit.

You don't have to do them all. My approach: focus on the top five largest sites in the first week. Target the next five in the second week. By month two, you've hit the top twenty. That's enough for significant protection. There are hundreds of data broker sites. You'll never get them all. Focus on major players and accept that eighty percent protection from twenty percent effort is good enough.

Use the tracker spreadsheet in the battle plans to mark progress. Don't try to do everything in one marathon session, you'll burn out.

The fifth challenge is when the family won't participate in security drills. Mike experienced this. His teenage kids rolled their eyes. His wife said she was too busy. The formal "Family Security Training Session" sounded like homework nobody wanted.

His solution: make it less formal and more engaging. Instead of a training session, he turned it into a "Can you spot the scam?" game at dinner. He texted fake phishing messages and offered dessert to whoever caught them first. He shared real news stories about breaches affecting people they knew.

Start small, five-minute conversations, not thirty-minute lectures. Build gradually. Show consequences through real stories, not scare tactics. Mike's breakthrough came when his daughter's friend got her Instagram hacked and lost hundreds of photos. Suddenly, security wasn't abstract. His daughter asked him to help set up MFA that same night.

The sixth challenge is enabling MFA and then getting a new phone and locking yourself out. Sarah did this. New iPhone, didn't transfer the authenticator app before erasing her old phone, couldn't log into email because it required MFA codes she could no longer generate.

Solution: use your backup codes. You saved those during MFA setup, right? They work exactly once as a bypass when your authenticator app is unavailable.

Prevention: before getting a new phone, export authenticator app data because most apps support this. Verify that you have accessible backup codes. Keep your old phone active until your new phone is fully set up.

These challenges are everyday occurrences. Everyone faces them. The difference between people who maintain their fortresses and people who don't isn't that they avoid challenges, it's that they recover from challenges instead of using them as excuses to abandon the whole system.

Success Looks Like This: The Long View

Let me paint you a picture of what success looks like five years from now if you maintain these systems. Not the dramatic breach-prevention stories, which are exciting but

Chapter 14: Maintain & Future-Proof

rare, but the quiet, routine competence that characterizes sustained security.

It's 2030. You wake up to a credit monitoring alert on your phone. Someone tried to open a credit card in your name overnight. The application was automatically denied because your credit is frozen. You mark the alert as "handled" and go about your day. Total time spent: fifteen seconds. No fraud occurred because your defense worked automatically.

At breakfast, your teenager shows you a text message. "Dad, is this phishing?" It's a fake package delivery notification. You glance at it, confirm it's phishing based on the sender number and suspicious URL. He deletes it immediately. He spotted it himself, you just validated his instincts. The monthly phishing drills worked. Total time spent: thirty seconds.

At work, you get a breach notification from Have I Been Pwned. Your email address appeared in a breach of a service you used three years ago. You log into your password manager, verify that the password for that service is unique and not reused anywhere, and change it anyway just to be safe. You also enable MFA while you're already logged in. Total time spent: three minutes. No unauthorized account activity occurred because the compromised password wasn't used anywhere else.

That evening, you get a robocall from a spoofed number claiming to be the Social Security Administration. You don't answer. They don't leave a voicemail. You block the number through your carrier's spam reporting feature. Total time spent: ten seconds.

At dinner, your spouse mentions she needs to apply for a new credit card next week. She already knows she'll need to lift her credit freeze temporarily. She has the process bookmarked. She's done it three times before. It's routine now, not stressful. When the time comes, total time spent will be ten minutes.

Total time spent on security that entire day: less than five minutes. Total fraud prevented: potentially thousands of dollars. Total stress experienced: essentially zero, because everything worked the way it was designed to work.

This is what sustained security looks like five years out. Not constant vigilance and paranoia, but practiced competence that makes security feel effortless. The systems have become so routine that you barely think about them. They're just how you operate, like locking your car when you leave it or checking your mirrors before changing lanes.

But this future only exists if you maintain the systems. If you let them decay, skip the quarterly maintenance, or abandon practices when they feel inconvenient, five years from now you'll be dealing with the aftermath of breaches that proper maintenance would have prevented.

The choice is yours. The work is manageable. The payoff is substantial.

Your Final Orders

You've reached the end of this chapter, but not the end of your security practice. This is the transition from trainee to defender.

You now have a complete security system protecting every vulnerable surface. You have the knowledge to maintain and update that system indefinitely. You have a community to support you when challenges arise. You have battle plans for every scenario you'll encounter. You have the confidence to defend yourself and train others. You have a sustainable practice that will protect you for the rest of your life.

The time investment to maintain everything: five minutes weekly, thirty minutes monthly, two to three hours quarterly, three to four hours annually. Total annual time commitment:

Chapter 14: Maintain & Future-Proof

less than twelve hours per year to protect everything you own and everyone you love.

That's not a burden. That's the best investment you'll ever make.

Here's what you need to do, starting immediately.

This week, calendar all your recurring maintenance tasks. Don't just make a mental note, actually put them in your phone or computer calendar with reminders enabled. Weekly transaction reviews on Monday mornings. Monthly phishing drills on the first Sunday. Quarterly credit report pulls and security inspections in the first week of each quarter. Annual comprehensive review in January.

Download and organize all the battle plans into a reference folder on your computer. Print the critical ones and put them in a binder. Make sure your family knows where to find them.

Join the Fortress Shield community forum. The link is in the battle plans appendix. This is where you'll get real-time threat alerts, troubleshooting help from other readers, updated tool recommendations, and support when challenges arise.

Share one lesson from this book with someone who needs it. Your elderly parent who's vulnerable to scams. Your friend who just had their identity stolen. Your coworker who doesn't understand phishing. Teaching reinforces your own learning and spreads the protection to your community.

This month, run your first sustained-phase phishing drill with your family. Not just once during initial training, but as the beginning of a monthly practice. Complete your first quarterly maintenance cycle, pull a credit report, run a security inspection, re-run data broker opt-outs. Test one emergency procedure to make sure you know how it works before you need it in a crisis.

Create your "Security Inheritance" documentation. I know this sounds morbid, but it's essential. Document where your password manager master password is stored. Note the location of your credit freeze PINs. List your critical accounts and where their credentials are stored. Leave instructions for your family on how to access these systems if something happens to you. Store this documentation in a fireproof safe, with a copy given to your attorney or a trusted family member.

This quarter, pull your first ongoing credit report on the rotating schedule. Run your first post-setup Red Team Operational Readiness Inspection to catch any security degradation. Re-run data broker opt-outs because they've already re-added you. Review the maintenance guidance in this chapter and commit to following it.

This year, complete all your annual maintenance tasks in January. Renew your password manager subscription. Review all your MFA setups. Test your account recovery procedures. Refresh family security training. Get the new annual edition of this book when it's released. Train at least one other person on Fortress Shield principles. Celebrate your security successes, you've earned it.

Forever: never abandon your fortress. Update your defenses as threats evolve. Teach the next generation. Stay vigilant.

The fortress you've built is real. It works. I've seen it work for thousands of people. But only if you maintain it. Only if you patrol the walls. Only if you update your defenses when the enemy adapts their attacks.

You are no longer a soft target. You've locked your accounts with strong passwords and MFA. You've frozen your credit against new account fraud. You've removed yourself from data broker exposure. You've trained your family to recognize deception. You've secured your network. You've built early warning systems. You've documented recovery plans.

Chapter 14: Maintain & Future-Proof

You are a defender now. And defenders don't abandon their posts.

The mission continues beyond this book. Every day you maintain your fortress is another day attackers move on to easier targets. Every phishing attempt you catch is another family protected. Every person you train multiplies the defense.

This is your standing order: maintain what you've built. Update when the battlefield shifts. Train your circle. Stay vigilant.

The enemy is persistent and professional. But so are you.

Your fortress stands. Keep it standing.

Thank you for your service in defending your family. The mission continues.

Fortress Shield 2026. Mission Accomplished. Sustainment Underway.

Mission Complete

By the end of this chapter, you should understand that maintenance is not optional but essential for long-term security. You should recognize the patterns of security decay and know how to prevent them through routine inspection. You should have established a sustainable maintenance rhythm that fits your life, weekly checks, monthly reviews, quarterly audits, annual comprehensive inspections.

You should know what tools work best for different aspects of maintenance and why consistency matters more than perfection. You should understand the psychological challenges of maintenance and have strategies to make it feel less like burden and more like routine. You should be able to identify when you're struggling with maintenance and know how to adapt your approach rather than abandon it entirely.

You should have calendared all your maintenance tasks with specific dates and reminders. You should have printed or organized your battle plans so they're accessible when needed. You should have shared at least one maintenance practice with someone in your circle, spreading the protection beyond yourself.

Call to Action

Set up your maintenance calendar today. Right now, before you finish reading this chapter. Open your calendar app. Create a recurring event for the first Saturday of every month: "Monthly Security Maintenance." Create quarterly events for the first weekend of January, April, July, October: "Quarterly Security Review." Create an annual event for the first week of January: "Annual Security ORI."

Those calendar events are commitments to yourself. They're promises that you'll protect what matters. They're discipline that prevents crisis.

Maintenance isn't optional. It's how good security becomes lasting security.

Reference Materials: Use the Maintenance Calendar Template, Monthly Checklist, and Quarterly Audit Worksheet in the appendices to track your ongoing security tasks and document your maintenance history.

Next: The remaining chapters bring together everything you've learned and show you how your complete Fortress Shield protects you, your family, and your community for life through proper legal framework, recovery from setbacks, and sustained vigilance.

Chief Palmer notes that maintenance discipline separates temporary security from lasting security. "In thirty years, I never saw a secure facility that relied on a perfect initial setup," he says. "I saw plenty that relied on consistent, disciplined maintenance. The facilities that stayed secure year after year weren't the ones with the most sophisticated technology. They were the ones with the most consistent maintenance. That discipline, that commitment to checking even when everything seems fine, that's what wins."

Chapter 15, Law & Policy: Knowing Your Rights and Using the System

⏱ 1-2 HOURS TO UNDERSTAND | REFERENCE AS NEEDED

Call Sign: LEGAL SHIELD, the law is your backup when defenses fail.

My daughter Sarah sat across from me at my kitchen table, a collection notice in her hand, her face a mixture of anger and exhaustion. This was six weeks into her identity theft recovery, and we'd already closed three fraudulent accounts. But this fourth one, a medical collection for eleven hundred dollars, wouldn't go away.

"I've disputed it three times," she said, her voice tight. "I sent them the FTC Identity Theft Report. I sent them the police report. I sent them copies of my ID proving I wasn't even in Florida when these medical services were supposedly provided. And they keep responding with the same form letter: 'After investigation, we have determined this debt is valid.'"

She slid the latest letter across the table. I read it carefully. Generic language, no specifics about their "investigation," no explanation of what evidence they'd reviewed. Just a bland assertion that she owed the money and needed to pay.

"This is the fourth time they've sent basically the same letter," Sarah continued. "Different dates, same content. They're not investigating anything. They're just hoping I'll give up and pay to make it go away."

"You're probably right," I said. "But here's what they don't know: you have federal law on your side, and they're violating it. They just handed you a legal weapon they don't realize you're going to use."

Sarah looked skeptical. "What weapon? I've followed every procedure. I've sent every document they asked for. They don't care about my evidence."

"The weapon is called the Fair Credit Reporting Act, and they're violating Section 611. When you dispute a debt in writing with supporting documentation proving fraud, they're required by federal law to conduct a reasonable investigation. Sending you the same form letter four times without addressing your specific evidence isn't a reasonable investigation. That's a violation you can report to the Consumer Financial Protection Bureau and potentially sue over."

I pulled out my laptop and showed her the CFPB complaint portal. "We're going to file a federal complaint right now. The CFPB tracks these complaints, investigates patterns of violations, and sometimes takes enforcement action. But even if they don't, the complaint creates an official federal record that this company is violating consumer protection law."

We spent thirty minutes filling out the complaint. Sarah provided the timeline, attached copies of all her dispute letters and their responses, and explained how the company was ignoring clear evidence of identity theft.

"What happens now?" she asked when we submitted it.

Chapter 15, Law & Policy: Knowing Your Rights and Using the System

"Two things. First, the company gets notified of the federal complaint and has to respond to the CFPB within fifteen days. Suddenly, they're not dealing with just you, they're dealing with federal oversight. That changes their behavior fast. Second, if they still don't resolve it, we escalate to a consumer protection attorney. One letter from a lawyer citing specific federal law violations, and these companies usually fold immediately."

Three weeks later, Sarah received a letter from the collection agency. The debt was removed entirely, they apologized for the confusion, and they confirmed they'd notified all credit bureaus to delete any negative marks. No explanation of why their previous "investigations" were inadequate. No acknowledgment of the violation. Just immediate compliance.

The federal complaint had worked exactly as designed.

"I can't believe that worked," Sarah told me. "For six weeks, I felt powerless. They had all the power, they could put negative marks on my credit, they could send me to collections, they could ignore my evidence. But the moment I used federal law and filed that CFPB complaint, suddenly I had power. They responded in three weeks after ignoring me for six."

"That's what this chapter is about," I said. "Understanding that you have legal rights, knowing what those rights are, and using them effectively when companies or criminals violate them. The law is your backup when your technical defenses fail."

Why This Step Matters

For thirteen chapters, I've taught you how to defend yourself technically. Strong passwords, two-factor authentication, credit freezes, network security, breach monitoring, recovery procedures, maintenance discipline. All of that is essential. All of that works.

But technical defenses don't exist in a vacuum. They operate within a legal framework that defines your rights, establishes creditor obligations, creates enforcement mechanisms, and provides remedies when you're harmed.

Understanding this legal framework isn't optional. It's the difference between feeling powerless when a creditor ignores your fraud claim and knowing exactly which federal law they're violating and how to enforce your rights. It's the difference between accepting that identity theft is just something you have to live with and understanding you have legal remedies that actually work.

In my thirty years protecting critical military systems, I learned that the best defenses combine technical controls with policy enforcement. A locked door is good. A locked door plus regulations requiring accountability for unauthorized access is better. The technical control prevents most problems. The policy enforcement handles the problems that slip through.

Your personal security works the same way. Your technical defenses prevent most attacks. Your legal rights provide remedies when attacks succeed anyway.

This chapter arms you with knowledge of your legal protections so you can invoke them when necessary. Not to make you a lawyer, you're not one, and you shouldn't try to be, but to make you an informed consumer who knows when companies are violating your rights and what to do about it.

Chapter 15, Law & Policy: Knowing Your Rights and Using the System

Because Sarah was right: for six weeks, she felt powerless. The collection agency had all the leverage. They could damage her credit. They could harass her with calls and letters. They could ignore her evidence and insist she owed money for services she never received.

But the moment she understood and used federal law, the power dynamic flipped. They weren't dealing with a confused victim anymore. They were dealing with someone who knew her rights and was willing to enforce them through proper channels.

That knowledge, that you have rights, that you can enforce them, that the law provides real remedies, transforms how you approach breaches and fraud. Instead of feeling helpless and hoping companies will do the right thing, you demand compliance with legal obligations and escalate when they refuse.

The law is your backup when defenses fail. This chapter teaches you how to call for that backup effectively.

Fortress Shield - 2026 Edition

⚠ THREAT ALERT

Rights you don't know about are rights you can't enforce.

Companies and criminals count on consumer ignorance. They violate your rights routinely, banking on the fact that most people don't know what protections they have. Knowledge of your legal rights is itself a form of defense.

The Foundation: Federal Consumer Protection Laws

The United States has several major federal laws protecting consumers from financial fraud, identity theft, and unfair credit practices. You don't need to memorize these statutes, that's what reference materials are for, but you need to understand what protections exist and when to invoke them.

Let me walk you through the laws that matter most for your security, using real situations I've helped people navigate.

The Fair Credit Reporting Act: Your Credit Report Shield

The Fair Credit Reporting Act, passed in 1970 and amended multiple times since, governs how credit bureaus and creditors use your personal information. It's the law Sarah used when fighting that medical collection. It's the law that gives you the right to dispute inaccurate information on your credit report and requires creditors to actually investigate your disputes rather than just sending form letters.

When my nephew Jake discovered fraudulent accounts on his credit report, this was the law that empowered him to demand their removal. Under the FCRA, credit bureaus must investigate disputes within thirty days, correct or delete

Chapter 15, Law & Policy: Knowing Your Rights and Using the System

inaccurate information, and notify creditors when information is disputed. If they fail to do this, if they conduct a "rubber stamp" investigation like Sarah's collection agency did, they're violating federal law.

The FCRA also gives you the right to free annual credit reports from all three bureaus, limits who can access your credit report without permission, requires notification when adverse action is taken based on your credit report, and provides for damages when violations occur. That last part matters more than people realize. Companies that violate the FCRA can face actual legal consequences, not just stern letters.

When Jake disputed his fraudulent accounts, he cited the FCRA in his dispute letters. Not with complex legal language, he's not a lawyer, but with simple references: "Under the Fair Credit Reporting Act, I am disputing this account as fraudulent. I am providing supporting documentation. You are required by law to investigate and remove this if you cannot verify it as legitimate."

That language, that reference to federal law, changed how the credit bureaus responded. Instead of the slow, bureaucratic process that drags on for months, his disputes were resolved within the statutory thirty-day timeframe. Because he made it clear he knew his rights and would enforce them if necessary.

The FCRA is your shield when dealing with credit bureaus and creditors. Learn the basics. Reference it in your dispute letters. Escalate to the CFPB when it's violated.

The Fair Credit Billing Act: Disputing Fraudulent Charges

My sister Linda's card fraud from Chapter 13 was resolved quickly partly because of the Fair Credit Billing Act, a 1974 amendment to the Truth in Lending Act. This law limits your liability for unauthorized credit card charges to fifty dollars maximum, and most issuers have zero-liability policies that go beyond the legal minimum.

But the FCBA's protections only work if you follow the proper dispute procedures. You must notify the creditor in writing within sixty days of the statement showing the unauthorized charge. You must dispute the specific amount you're contesting. You must explain why the charge is wrong. The creditor then has two billing cycles to investigate and respond.

Linda reported her fraud within hours, which was well within the sixty-day window. She disputed the charges in writing, providing a clear timeline of when she last used the card legitimately and why the four charges in Miami couldn't have been hers. The bank investigated and resolved everything within three business days, far faster than the law requires, because her dispute was properly documented and clearly fraudulent.

The lesson here isn't just about the legal protections, it's about the importance of following proper procedures. Federal law provides strong protections, but you have to invoke them correctly. Calling the bank is good. Calling and following up in writing is better. Calling, following up in writing, and explicitly referencing your FCBA rights is best.

When you dispute charges, use language like this: "Under the Fair Credit Billing Act, I am disputing the following unauthorized charges. I did not make these purchases. I request immediate removal of these charges and a full investigation."

That's not legal jargon. It's plain English that makes clear you understand your rights. Companies respond differently when they know you're informed rather than confused.

Chapter 15, Law & Policy: Knowing Your Rights and Using the System

The Fair Debt Collection Practices Act: Stopping Harassment

After Sarah's identity theft, she dealt with multiple debt collectors trying to collect on fraudulent accounts. Some were professional and cooperative. Others were aggressive and threatening. One collector called her workplace repeatedly despite being told not to. Another threatened legal action she knew they wouldn't actually pursue. A third continued calling after she'd sent written notice to cease contact.

All of those behaviors violated the Fair Debt Collection Practices Act, a 1977 law that regulates how debt collectors can communicate with consumers. The FDCPA prohibits calling at inconvenient times, calling your workplace after being told not to, harassing or threatening you, misrepresenting the debt, and continuing contact after you've requested in writing that they stop.

When one collector violated these rules, Sarah sent what's called a "cease and desist" letter, referencing the FDCPA and demanding they stop all phone contact and communicate only in writing. The calls stopped immediately. Because collectors know that FDCPA violations can result in statutory damages of up to one thousand dollars per violation, plus attorney fees. They don't risk lawsuits over small debts.

The FDCPA doesn't make debts go away, if you legitimately owe money, you still owe it. But it controls how collectors can pursue that debt and gives you recourse when they violate the rules. For fraud victims like Sarah, it's a critical tool for managing collector harassment while you're disputing fraudulent accounts.

The key is documentation. Keep records of every call, every letter, every violation. Send written notices by certified mail with return receipt. Create a paper trail that proves violations occurred. Then escalate to the CFPB and, if necessary, to a consumer protection attorney.

The Identity Theft and Assumption Deterrence Act: Making ID Theft a Federal Crime

Before 1998, identity theft wasn't even a federal crime. Individual states had varying laws, enforcement was inconsistent, and victims had limited recourse. The Identity Theft and Assumption Deterrence Act changed that, making identity theft a federal crime punishable by up to fifteen years in prison for severe cases.

More importantly for victims, the law established your right to be recognized as a victim rather than a suspect. It created the FTC Identity Theft Report system that Sarah used during her recovery. It required federal agencies to develop victim assistance resources. It established the framework for disputing fraudulent accounts based on identity theft.

When Sarah filed her FTC Identity Theft Report, that report became legal documentation recognized by creditors, credit bureaus, and law enforcement. It carried weight that her simple assertion "this wasn't me" never could. The report says: This person is a federally recognized identity theft victim. Federal law protects them. You must work with them to resolve fraudulent accounts.

Filing the FTC report doesn't automatically fix everything, Sarah still had to dispute each fraudulent account individually, but it provides legal standing and documentation that makes the dispute process more effective.

The catch is that identity theft investigations rarely result in arrests. Local police take reports but don't investigate. Federal agencies focus on large-scale operations rather than individual cases. The law's real value for victims isn't criminal prosecution, it's the civil protections and documentation it provides for resolving fraudulent accounts.

Chapter 15, Law & Policy: Knowing Your Rights and Using the System

State Laws: Your Additional Protection Layer

Federal law creates a baseline, but many states provide additional protections beyond federal minimums. California has the Consumer Privacy Act giving residents extensive control over personal data. Vermont has the Data Broker Act requiring data broker registration and opt-out mechanisms. Massachusetts has the Data Security Law requiring specific security controls for personal information. Colorado has strong credit freeze protections and identity theft provisions.

Your state Attorney General's office often enforces consumer protection more aggressively than federal agencies. They respond faster, take action on smaller cases, and sometimes offer mediation services. When Sarah had trouble with that persistent collection agency, filing a complaint with the Tennessee Attorney General's office got attention even faster than the federal CFPB complaint.

Understanding your state's specific protections requires some research. Most state AG websites have consumer protection sections explaining your rights. Many offer free complaint filing and investigation services. Some provide pro bono legal assistance for identity theft victims.

The practical lesson: when federal channels move slowly, try state channels simultaneously. When creditors ignore federal complaints, state AG involvement sometimes accelerates resolution. When you need legal help but can't afford an attorney, state resources might be available.

🛡 SITREP: The Enforcement Reality

Understanding your legal rights is important. Understanding how those rights are actually enforced is equally important, because enforcement determines whether rights are meaningful or merely symbolic.

The Consumer Financial Protection Bureau, created in 2010 after the financial crisis, has been your strongest ally for consumer complaints. The CFPB accepts complaints online, investigates patterns of violations, requires company responses within fifteen days, publishes company response data publicly, and takes enforcement action against major violators.

I've watched CFPB complaints resolve issues that months of direct negotiation couldn't. Companies that ignored individual consumers suddenly respond when faced with federal oversight. The CFPB complaint database is public, so companies know that failing to resolve complaints damages their reputation visibly.

But the CFPB's power has fluctuated with political changes. Different administrations have strengthened or weakened their enforcement capabilities. Budget cuts affect investigation capacity. Leadership changes affect priorities. What this means practically: CFPB effectiveness varies over time, but filing complaints remains worthwhile because companies don't know which complaints will trigger investigation.

Your state Attorney General operates independently of federal politics. State enforcement priorities vary, some AGs are aggressive consumer advocates, others focus elsewhere, but state complaints are often resolved faster than federal ones

Chapter 15, Law & Policy: Knowing Your Rights and Using the System

because state offices handle fewer total complaints and focus on local residents.

The Federal Trade Commission handles identity theft reports and pursues large-scale fraud operations but rarely intervene in individual cases. File your FTC Identity Theft Report for documentation, not expecting direct assistance. The value is the legal documentation it creates, not FTC investigation of your specific case.

Law enforcement at the local level rarely investigates individual cyber fraud or identity theft. Police will take reports that create official documentation, but investigations are rare. Exceptions occur when fraud is part of a larger local pattern or involves substantial amounts. File police reports for documentation and insurance requirements, not expecting investigation.

Private legal action through consumer protection attorneys becomes necessary when administrative complaints fail. Many consumer protection lawyers work on contingency, meaning they take cases without upfront payment if federal law violations are clear. Companies that violate the FCRA, FCBA, or FDCPA can face statutory damages plus attorney fees, making these cases viable for lawyers even when actual damages are modest.

Understanding this enforcement landscape helps you calibrate expectations and choose the right escalation path. Start with direct dispute to the company. Escalate to CFPB and state AG if ignored. Pursue private legal action if violations are clear and administrative channels fail. Realistic expectations prevent frustration and help you persist through the process.

🔒 FORTIFY PROTOCOL

Your Legal Escalation Sequence:

When dealing with fraudulent charges, disputed debts, or identity theft recovery, follow this escalation path in order. Start with direct dispute to the company using certified mail with return receipt, documenting everything, citing relevant federal law, and providing supporting evidence. Give them the statutory timeframe to respond, typically thirty days for credit disputes.

If they fail to resolve within that timeframe or send inadequate responses, escalate to administrative complaints. File with the Consumer Financial Protection Bureau at consumerfinance.gov. File with your state Attorney General's consumer protection division. File with relevant regulatory agencies like the FCC for phone harassment or FTC for broader fraud patterns. Provide complete documentation including your initial dispute, company responses, and timeline of events.

If administrative complaints don't resolve the issue within sixty days or if violations are egregious, pursue legal consultation with a consumer protection attorney. Many offer free consultations. Look for lawyers who work on contingency for federal law violations. Present your complete documentation proving clear violations and good faith efforts to resolve through proper channels.

Throughout this process, maintain meticulous documentation. Keep copies of every letter sent and received. Record dates, times, and names for all phone conversations. Save all emails and electronic communications. Take screenshots of online accounts showing fraudulent activity. This documentation is your evidence and becomes more valuable at each escalation level.

The key is patience combined with persistence. Each escalation level takes time. Companies have statutory timeframes to respond. Administrative agencies have investigation procedures. Legal consultation requires scheduling and review. But each step builds on the previous one, and most cases resolve before reaching legal action because companies prefer settling to fighting clear violations.

Linda's Education: When Banks Deny Claims

My sister Linda's card fraud resolution from Chapter 13 was textbook perfect. She called immediately, the bank reversed charges within days, new card arrived quickly, problem solved. That's how it's supposed to work.

But six months later, Linda had a second incident with her debit card. Small charges at a gas station in Arkansas, she's never been to Arkansas. She reported it within twelve hours like before. This time, the bank denied her claim.

She called me, confused and angry. "They're saying I authorized the charges. That maybe I let someone else use my card. That they see a pattern of unusual activity on my account, which I don't understand because I never make unusual charges. They won't reverse the charges. They're saying it's my problem."

"How much are we talking about?" I asked.

"Thirty-eight dollars over four charges. All at the same gas station on the same day."

Thirty-eight dollars. Barely worth fighting over, right? That's what the bank was counting on. That Linda would decide thirty-eight dollars wasn't worth the hassle and just accept the loss.

"Let me ask you some questions," I said. "Do you have a copy of your bank statement showing the charges? Did you call the fraud line or regular customer service? Did they tell you in writing that your claim was denied?"

Linda had the statement. She'd called the fraud line. But they'd only told her verbally that the claim was denied, nothing in writing.

"Here's what we're doing," I said. "You're going to send them a formal dispute letter via certified mail, citing the Fair Credit Billing Act. The FCBA requires them to investigate disputes submitted in writing within sixty days of the statement. You're going to document exactly why these charges couldn't be yours, you were at work in Tennessee when they occurred in Arkansas, your card was in your possession the entire time, you don't know anyone in Arkansas who might have used your card."

"But they already investigated," Linda protested.

"They conducted a phone conversation where they told you 'no.' That's not an FCBA-compliant investigation. A proper investigation requires written notification of their findings and explanation of their reasoning. You're going to force them to follow proper procedure."

Linda sent the letter. The bank had to respond within two billing cycles. They sent her a letter acknowledging her dispute and stating they were investigating. Three weeks later, they reversed the charges.

No explanation of why their phone denial was wrong. No acknowledgment that their initial investigation was inadequate. Just reversal of the charges and a brief note that their investigation supported her claim.

"What happened?" Linda asked. "Why did the letter work when the phone call didn't work?"

Chapter 15, Law & Policy: Knowing Your Rights and Using the System

"The phone call gave them plausible deniability," I explained. "They could claim they investigated and determined the charges were legitimate. The written dispute citing federal law created a paper trail. Suddenly, if they denied your claim improperly, there was documentation of the violation. That changes their calculation. Thirty-eight dollars isn't worth a potential FCBA violation complaint to the CFPB."

This taught Linda an important lesson about legal protections: they're strongest when properly invoked and documented. Her initial call to the fraud line was correct, but when they denied her claim, she needed to escalate to a formal written dispute citing specific legal protections. The law doesn't protect you automatically, you have to actively invoke it.

The good news is that invoking federal law doesn't require legal expertise. You don't need a lawyer to send a dispute letter citing the FCBA. You just need to know the law exists, understand its basic requirements, and follow the proper procedure.

Linda now sends written confirmation of any fraud dispute, even when the bank resolves it over the phone. "It's insurance," she told me. "Costs me the price of certified postage and creates a paper trail that protects me if something goes wrong."

That's practical legal literacy: understanding enough about your rights to invoke them effectively when necessary.

Frank's Breakthrough: Data Privacy Rights

My father-in-law Frank has been struggling with robocalls for years. Not just annoying marketing calls, aggressive scam calls from numbers spoofed to look local, claiming to be the IRS or Social Security Administration or his credit card company. Multiple calls per day, sometimes. He'd gotten so frustrated he was considering giving up his phone number entirely.

"There must be a law against this," Frank said one evening while visiting. "They can't just harass people like this."

"There is a law," I told him. "Multiple laws. The Telephone Consumer Protection Act from 1991 restricts unsolicited calls. The Do Not Call Registry from 2003 prohibits most telemarketing calls. The TRACED Act from 2019 requires phone companies to implement call authentication and blocking. You have significant legal protections. But you have to use them."

I walked Frank through the process. First, register all his phone numbers on the Do Not Call Registry at donotcall.gov. This doesn't stop all unwanted calls, scammers ignore it because they're already operating illegally, but it stops legitimate telemarketers and strengthens his legal position if he needs to file complaints.

Second, document every illegal robocall. What number called? What time? What did they claim? Which company or agency did they impersonate? Keep a log. After a few weeks, Frank had documented forty-seven illegal robocalls, many from spoofed numbers, many impersonating government agencies.

Third, contact his phone carrier about their spam blocking services. Most carriers now offer free or low-cost call screening that uses algorithms to identify and block likely scam calls. Frank prevented this and saw immediate reduction in call volume.

Fourth, report the pattern to the Federal Communications Commission at consumercomplaints.fcc.gov and the Federal Trade Commission at reportfraud.ftc.gov. These agencies track robocall patterns and sometimes take enforcement action against major operations.

Chapter 15, Law & Policy: Knowing Your Rights and Using the System

The combination of these steps reduced Frank's robocall volume by about eighty percent over two months. He still gets some, scammers constantly change tactics, but it's manageable now rather than overwhelming.

"I wish I'd known about this years ago," Frank said. "I felt completely powerless. Like I just had to accept being harassed constantly. But there were tools and laws the whole time. I just didn't know how to use them."

That's the theme of this chapter. The tools and laws exist. They provide real protections. But they only help if you know about them and actually use them.

Frank now reports every scam call he receives. It takes him maybe thirty seconds. But those reports contribute to databases that help enforcement agencies identify patterns and target major operations. His individual reports won't stop all robocalls, but collective reporting across millions of people creates the data needed for large-scale enforcement.

When to Get Professional Legal Help

I need to be clear about something: I'm not a lawyer. Nothing in this book is legal advice. I'm sharing what I've learned from thirty years protecting information systems and helping people recover from breaches, but I can't tell you what to do in your specific legal situation.

That said, I can tell you when consumer protection attorneys become necessary based on watching many people navigate these situations.

Sarah needed a lawyer when that medical collection agency kept ignoring her fraud evidence. The lawyer sent one letter citing specific FCRA violations, and the problem was resolved within three weeks. The letter cost Sarah four hundred dollars. That four hundred dollars ended months of frustration and potential credit damage worth far more than the fee.

My brother Mike's business needed a lawyer when a customer's credit card company tried to hold him liable for a fraudulent chargeback. The customer claimed the service wasn't provided, even though Mike had signed work orders, photos of completed work, and the customer's signature confirming satisfaction. The lawyer's involvement prevented Mike from losing thirty-eight hundred dollars and protected his business's merchant account.

Jake needed a lawyer when a data broker refused to remove his information despite multiple opt-out requests. The lawyer cited state data privacy laws and threatened enforcement action. The broker removed Jake's information immediately.

Here's how to know when to consult an attorney. Consider legal help when companies ignore proper disputes, when you've followed all administrative channels without resolution, when federal law violations are clear and documented, when amounts involved are substantial enough to justify legal fees, when you're facing serious credit damage or collections, or when companies make legal threats against you for disputing fraudulent debt.

Consumer protection attorneys often offer free initial consultations. Many work on contingency for clear federal law violations because statutes provide for attorney fees. This makes legal help accessible even if you can't afford upfront fees.

When seeking an attorney, look for consumer protection specialists rather than general practitioners. Check your state bar association's lawyer referral service. Look for attorneys with experience in Fair Credit Reporting Act cases, identity theft recovery, or debt collection violations. Read reviews from previous clients. Ask about fee structures during the free consultation.

Chapter 15, Law & Policy: Knowing Your Rights and Using the System

Prepare for the consultation with complete documentation. Bring copies of all correspondence with creditors, credit bureaus, and collectors. Bring your credit reports showing disputed information. Bring documentation of your fraud claims including police reports and FTC Identity Theft Reports. Bring a timeline of events showing good faith efforts to resolve the issue administratively.

The attorney will review your documentation and advise whether you have a viable case. They'll explain the likely process, timeline, and costs. They'll tell you honestly if legal action is warranted or if you should pursue other options.

Most consumer protection cases never reach court. The threat of litigation with documented federal law violations usually produces settlement. Companies prefer settling quietly to fighting cases with clear violations that would establish unfavorable precedent and generate negative publicity.

The Tools You Need: Sample Letters and Complaints

The appendices include templates for common legal communications you'll need when enforcing your rights. These aren't complex legal documents, they're plain-English letters and complaints that invoke your rights clearly.

The Credit Dispute Letter template cites the Fair Credit Reporting Act and provides structure for disputing inaccurate information on your credit report. You'll use this when fraudulent accounts appear on your credit, when negative marks remain after fraud is resolved, when credit bureaus fail to investigate properly, or when creditors don't remove accounts after finding fraud.

The Debt Collector Cease Communication Letter template invokes the Fair Debt Collection Practices Act to stop collector harassment. Use this when collectors call repeatedly despite your requests to stop, when they contact your workplace after being told not to, when they use threatening or abusive language, or when you need all communication to be in writing only.

The FCBA Billing Dispute Letter template handles disputes over unauthorized credit card charges. Use this whenever you discover fraudulent charges on credit cards, when charges appear for services not received, when merchants refuse to honor refunds for returned goods, or when you need to document billing errors formally.

The CFPB Complaint Template provides structure for filing complaints with the Consumer Financial Protection Bureau. File these when companies ignore proper disputes, when credit bureaus fail to investigate adequately, when debt collectors violate federal law, when creditors refuse to resolve clear fraud, or when you need federal oversight of company behavior.

Each template includes instructions for customization with your specific details, requirements for proper documentation and mailing, and escalation steps if the initial communication doesn't resolve the issue. These are working documents that I've refined over years of helping people enforce their rights. They're not lawyer letters; they're consumer letters that invoke legal protections clearly and effectively.

The key to using these templates is following proper procedure. Send via certified mail with return receipt so you have proof of delivery. Keep copies of everything you send along with dates and tracking information. Give companies the statutory timeframe to respond before escalating. Document their response or lack of response. Use their failure to respond properly as evidence in your next escalation.

Chapter 15, Law & Policy: Knowing Your Rights and Using the System

Sarah's Reflection: Power in Knowledge

Six months after her identity theft recovery was complete, Sarah and I had lunch. She'd successfully resolved all the fraudulent accounts, her credit was clean, monitoring systems were in place, and life had returned to normal. But she was different now in ways that weren't immediately obvious.

"Remember when that collection agency sent me the fourth identical letter?" she asked. "I felt so helpless. Like they had all the power, and I had none. They could ruin my credit. They could harass me. They could ignore evidence that proved the debt wasn't mine. And there was nothing I could do about it."

"But you learned there was something you could do," I said.

"More than something. I learned I had legal rights that were stronger than their corporate stonewalling. The moment I filed that CFPB complaint citing specific violations, suddenly they were the ones worried. They weren't dealing with a confused victim anymore. They were dealing with someone who knew the law and would use it."

She paused, gathering her thoughts. "It changed how I think about everything. I used to assume companies would do the right thing if I just explained the situation clearly enough. I'd send them evidence, I'd be polite, I'd hope they'd see the truth and help me. And when they didn't, I thought I had no recourse except accepting whatever they decided."

"And now?"

"Now I understand that my rights aren't suggestions companies can ignore. They're legal obligations with enforcement mechanisms. When a company violates my rights, I have specific tools to force compliance. I can file complaints that actually get investigated. I can cite federal laws they're violating. If necessary, I can hire an attorney on contingency because federal law provides for attorney fees in clear violation cases. That knowledge is power."

This is what legal literacy provides: not the ability to become your own lawyer, but the confidence that you're not powerless when companies misbehave. You understand the framework that protects you. You know when that framework is being violated. You know the proper channels for enforcing your rights. You know when professional legal help becomes necessary.

"I've helped three friends now," Sarah continued. "One with a denied fraud claim like Aunt Linda's. One with an identity theft case similar to mine. One with a debt collector who was violating the FDCPA. Every time, same pattern: they felt helpless until they understood their rights. Then they filed the right complaints, cited the right laws, and the problems resolved. Not because companies suddenly became ethical, but because violating federal law has consequences they want to avoid."

That transformation, from feeling powerless to understanding and exercising your rights, is what this chapter aims to create. Legal knowledge won't prevent all problems. But it provides recourse when problems occur, and technical defenses aren't enough.

Mission Complete

By the end of this chapter, you should understand the major federal laws that protect you as a consumer: the Fair Credit Reporting Act, Fair Credit Billing Act, Fair Debt Collection Practices Act, Identity Theft and Assumption Deterrence Act, Telephone Consumer Protection Act, and how they apply to your daily digital life.

You should know the proper escalation sequence for enforcing your rights: direct dispute to companies,

Chapter 15, Law & Policy: Knowing Your Rights and Using the System

administrative complaints to CFPB and state AG, legal consultation when other channels fail. You should understand the realistic limitations of enforcement, so your expectations are calibrated appropriately.

You should know when to invoke federal law in your disputes and how to do so clearly without needing legal expertise. You should understand when professional legal help becomes necessary and how to find qualified consumer protection attorneys.

You should have access to template letters for common legal communications including credit disputes, debt collector ceases letters, billing disputes, and CFPB complaints. You should know proper documentation procedures for creating paper trails that support your claims.

Call to Action

Download and review all the legal templates in the appendices right now. Don't wait until you need them during a crisis. Familiarize yourself with their structure and requirements so you can use them effectively when necessary.

Save the key contact information in your password manager: CFPB complaint portal URL and phone number, your state Attorney General consumer protection office, FTC Identity Theft Report website, and your local consumer protection resources.

Review your most recent credit card agreement and bank terms looking for dispute procedures and contact information for fraud departments. Know where to find this information before you need it urgently.

If you're currently dealing with disputed charges, fraudulent accounts, or collector harassment, use the appropriate template this week to formalize your dispute and invoke your federal rights. Don't delay hoping the problem will be resolved on its own.

Reference Materials: Use the Legal Rights Reference Card, Sample Dispute Letters, CFPB Complaint Guide, and Attorney Consultation Checklist in the appendices to enforce your consumer protections effectively.

Next: Chapter 16 explores phishing and social engineering in depth, teaching you to recognize and defeat the psychological manipulation tactics that bypass all your technical defenses.

Chief Palmer notes that legal protections exist to back up technical defenses. "In the military, we combined strong locks with strict accountability regulations," he says. "The locks prevented unauthorized access. The regulations provided consequences when locks failed. Your technical security prevents most problems. Federal consumer protection law provides remedies when problems occur anyway. Understanding both makes you far more secure than understanding only one."

Chapter 16: Phishing & Social Engineering - Recognizing the Human Attack

⏱ 1 hour to learn | Practice for life

Call Sign: HUMAN FIREWALL, Your judgment is the last line of defense.

My nephew Jake called me on a Tuesday afternoon in March, his voice shaking in a way I'd never heard before. Jake's a smart kid, with a computer science degree, works in tech, and knows his way around security. He'd implemented everything I'd taught him. Password manager. Two-factor authentication. Credit frozen. Breach monitoring. The whole Fortress Shield.

"Uncle Alan, I think I just made the biggest mistake of my life."

My stomach dropped. That tone meant something serious.

"Tell me what happened. Start from the beginning."

Jake took a breath. "I got an email from what looked like our company's IT security team. Subject line said 'URGENT: Security Breach - Password Reset Required.' It had our company logo, it came from what looked like an internal email address, and it said there'd been a breach of our customer database. Everyone in engineering had to reset their password immediately or their account would be locked."

"Okay," I said, staying calm. "What did you do?"

"The email had a link to what looked like our internal password reset portal. I clicked it. The page looked exactly like our normal password system, same colors, same layout, same logo. It asked for my current password and a new password. I entered them."

I closed my eyes. "Then what happened?"

"About thirty seconds after I submitted it, my phone started blowing up. My actual work email was getting password reset notifications that I didn't request. Someone was trying to log into my GitHub account. My Slack showed someone had changed my status message to something weird. That's when I realized the password reset page was fake."

"What did you do next?"

"I ran to our actual IT security team. They told them everything. They locked my account immediately, forced a real password reset, checked the logs to see what the attacker accessed, and started investigating. Uncle Alan, they got in. For those thirty seconds before IT locked everything, someone had access to my work account."

Jake's voice cracked. "I gave them my password. I literally handed it to them. After everything you taught me, after all the training we did, after all the times I thought 'I'm too smart to fall for phishing,' I just... gave it to them."

This is the moment I've been dreading for years. Not because I expected Jake to fail, he was one of my best students. But because I know that phishing doesn't work by attacking ignorance. It works by attacking emotion, urgency, and the split-second decisions we make when we're busy, stressed, or scared.

Chapter 16: Phishing & Social Engineering

"Jake, listen to me very carefully. You didn't fail because you're careless or stupid. You encountered a sophisticated, targeted spear-phishing attack designed specifically to exploit your company's systems and processes. The email came during work hours when you were already logged into company systems. It created urgency that bypassed your normal caution. It replicated your company's visual design perfectly. This wasn't a poorly written scam from a stranger, this was professional-grade social engineering."

"But I should have caught it," Jake said. "I should have checked the sender's address more carefully. I should have verified with IT before clicking. I should have, "

"Yes," I interrupted. "You should have. And next time you will. But right now, we need to focus on damage control and learning from this, so it never happens again."

We spent the next two hours on the phone. Jake's company's security team handled the immediate response, they locked his account within sixty seconds of his report, forced company-wide password resets for his entire team, investigated what data the attacker accessed while they had those thirty seconds of access, and started backtracking the attack to understand how the phishing email bypassed their filters.

Fortunately, the damage was contained. Jake's quick recognition and immediate reporting meant the attacker only had access for a fraction of a minute, not enough time to exfiltrate meaningful data or establish persistence in the systems. His company praised his response, not criticized it. They used the incident as a company-wide training opportunity.

But Jake was shaken for weeks afterward. "I keep replaying it in my mind," he told me a month later. "Every detail I should have noticed. The sender address that was slightly misspelled. The link URL that wasn't quite our actual domain. The fact that IT would never ask for your current password. All these things I know intellectually. But in that moment, when I was already stressed about a deadline and the email created panic, I just... acted without thinking."

"That's exactly how phishing works," I said. "It doesn't attack your knowledge. It attacks your emotional state and your automatic responses. The best defense isn't just knowing about phishing, it's building habits that protect you even when you're scared, busy, or distracted."

Why This Chapter Matters More Than Technical Defense

For fifteen chapters, I've taught you technical defenses. Strong passwords that computers can't crack. Two-factor authentication that requires physical possession. Credit freezes that block account opening. Network security that stops digital intrusion. Breach monitoring that detects compromises. Legal protections that provide recourse.

All of that is essential. All of that works. But all of it can be bypassed by a single moment of human error.

Phishing works by exploiting the gap between what you know intellectually and how you behave under pressure. You know you shouldn't click suspicious links. But when an email claims your bank account has been compromised and you need to verify your identity immediately or lose access to your money, knowledge alone doesn't always protect you. Your amygdala, the ancient part of your brain responsible for fear response, takes over. You act before thinking.

In my thirty years protecting military systems, I learned that the most secure technical defenses could be defeated by social engineering. We had biometric access controls, encrypted communications, intrusion detection systems, physical

Chapter 16: Phishing & Social Engineering

security layers, and compartmentalized information. Millions of dollars in security technology.

And I watched all of it get bypassed by an adversary who called our reception desk, claimed to be from IT, said there was an urgent problem with the phone system, and talked the receptionist into reading him a network configuration password over the phone. Thirty seconds on the phone defeated years of technical investment.

That's why this chapter focuses exclusively on the human attack surface, phishing emails, phone pretexting, text message scams, social media manipulation, and all the other ways criminals exploit human psychology rather than technical vulnerabilities.

Because your judgment is your last line of defense. When phishing bypasses your spam filter, when attackers spoof a trusted sender, when a message creates enough urgency to override your caution, your ability to recognize manipulation and pause before acting determines whether you stay secure or become compromised.

This chapter teaches you to become a human firewall, the security layer that catches threats technical defenses miss.

⚠ THREAT ALERT

Phishing doesn't exploit technical vulnerabilities. It exploits human psychology.

Attackers use urgency to bypass careful thinking, authority to discourage questioning, fear to trigger immediate action, greed to cloud judgment, and curiosity to motivate clicking. Understanding these manipulation tactics is your primary defense.

The Psychology of Manipulation: Why Smart People Fall for Phishing

After Jake's incident, I spent time analyzing why the phishing attack worked so effectively on someone who knew better. What I found reinforced everything I'd learned from decades studying adversary tactics: phishing succeeds because it's designed by people who understand human psychology better than most psychologists do.

Let me break down the manipulation tactics that make phishing so effective, using real examples I've seen fool intelligent, careful people.

Urgency: The Clock That Bypasses Thinking

The email Jake received didn't ask him politely to consider resetting his password at his convenience. It created artificial urgency: "URGENT: Security Breach - Password Reset Required." It claimed his account would be locked if he didn't act immediately. It implied that every second of delay increased risk.

That urgency was deliberate and calculated. When humans face time pressure, our decision-making shifts from the prefrontal cortex, the rational, analytical part of our brain, to the amygdala, the reactive, emotional part. We stop analyzing and start acting.

I've seen this work on everyone from teenagers to executives. My neighbor, a surgeon who makes life-or-death decisions under pressure daily, fell for a phishing email claiming his daughter's school account was being closed for non-payment and would affect her grades unless he paid immediately. He clicked the link and entered his credit card information before noticing inconsistencies that would have been obvious if he'd taken thirty seconds to think.

The defense against urgency is a pause protocol. Whenever an email, text, or call creates urgency, "act now," "immediate action required," "your account will be locked", that's your signal to slow down, not speed up. Legitimate urgent communications can wait two minutes for verification. Fraudulent ones can't survive that verification.

Authority: The Voice That Discourages Questioning

Jake's phishing email appeared to come from his company's IT security team. That perceived authority made him less likely to question its legitimacy. We're conditioned from childhood to trust authority figures, parents, teachers, bosses, law enforcement, government agencies. Phishing exploits that conditioning ruthlessly.

I've watched sophisticated phishing attacks impersonate the IRS, claiming you owe back taxes that must be paid immediately to avoid arrest. The FBI, saying your identity was used in a crime and you need to verify your information to clear your name. Bank security departments, stating unusual activity requires immediate password verification. Company executives, ordering urgent wire transfers to unfamiliar accounts.

My brother Mike's construction company almost lost twenty-three thousand dollars to CEO fraud, a phishing email appearing to come from the company owner, sent during a day when the actual owner was traveling internationally, requesting an immediate wire transfer for an urgent acquisition. The email replicated the owner's communication style perfectly, used his personal email signature, and created urgency around a time-sensitive opportunity. Mike's accountant almost sent the wire before calling the owner directly to confirm.

Authority is powerful because questioning it feels uncomfortable. If your boss's boss emails you asking for something, you don't want to be the person who made them wait while you verified it was really them. If a government agency contacts you, you don't want to ignore what might be a legitimate legal issue. Phishing weaponizes that discomfort.

The defense against authority is verification through separate channels. If someone claiming authority requests sensitive information or action, you verify through a different communication method than the one they used. The email claims to be from your bank? Call the bank at the number on your card, not the number in the email. The text claims to be from your boss? Call them directly, don't reply to the text. Legitimate authority won't be offended by verification. Fraudulent authority will.

Fear: The Emotion That Demands Action

Fear is the most powerful manipulation tool in phishing because it bypasses rational thought entirely. Jake's email triggered fear by claiming a security breach had occurred and his account was at risk. My father-in-law Frank has received countless phishing calls claiming his Social Security number was suspended due to suspicious activity, suspended Social Security sounds terrifying if you rely on those benefits.

Fear of losing money. Fear of legal problems. Fear of account compromise. Fear of missing important opportunities. Fear of embarrassing yourself. Phishing attacks are engineered to trigger specific fears that motivate immediate action.

I've seen fear-based phishing convince a retired veteran that his VA benefits were about to be terminated unless he verified his information immediately. Convince a mother that her son was arrested abroad and needed money wired for bail. Convince a business owner that his website would be shut down for terms of service violations unless he re-verified his payment information right away.

The physiological response to fear, increased heart rate, tunnel vision, urgency to act, is exactly the wrong state for

Chapter 16: Phishing & Social Engineering

making careful security decisions. But that's when phishing attacks land.

The defense against fear is recognizing it as a manipulation tactic. When a communication makes you afraid, that fear itself is information. Legitimate companies and agencies don't use fear as their primary communication method. Scammers do. The presence of fear, your account will be locked, you'll lose money, you'll face legal consequences, your reputation will be damaged, should trigger skepticism, not immediate action.

Trust: The Relationship That Lowers Guards

The most sophisticated phishing attacks exploit existing trust relationships rather than impersonating strangers. When my mother's email was compromised in Chapter 13, the attackers didn't just send random phishing to strangers. They read through months of her correspondence, identified her closest contacts, learned the communication patterns and topics she discussed with each person, and sent targeted phishing to those specific people using information gleaned from legitimate emails.

Three of her contacts almost sent money not because they were careless, but because the request came from someone they trusted using communication styles and referencing details they expected. The email looked exactly like my mother's normal messages because it was written by someone who'd read hundreds of her normal messages.

This is why compromised accounts spread so quickly. Each compromised email or social media account becomes a trusted platform for attacking everyone in that person's network. When your friend's Facebook account messages you, you trust it. When your colleague's work email requests something, you comply. Trust disables the skepticism that would catch phishing from strangers.

My daughter Sarah's best friend had her Instagram compromised. The attacker sent direct messages to everyone on her friend list asking them to vote for her in an online contest by clicking a link and entering their Instagram credentials. Sarah almost did it, the message came from her best friend, mentioned an inside joke only they would know (which the attacker read in previous DM conversations), and seemed completely legitimate. She stopped only because we'd recently discussed this exact attack vector.

The defense against trust exploitation is verification even for trusted contacts, especially when they request unusual actions. Your friend messages you asking for money or requesting clicks? Call them on the phone. Your boss emails an urgent request outside normal procedures? Verify through a separate channel. Trust is valuable, but verification is necessary.

Scarcity: The Opportunity That Demands Speed

Phishing doesn't always create fear. Sometimes it creates greed or FOMO, fear of missing out. Limited-time offers. Exclusive opportunities. Deals expiring soon. Scarcity manipulation convinces you that if you don't act immediately, you'll lose something valuable.

I've watched educated people fall for phishing emails offering cryptocurrency investments with guaranteed returns, but only if they invest within the next three hours. Exclusive pre-sales for popular products that require immediate payment to secure allocation. Refunds for taxes or services that will be forfeited if not claimed by clicking a link and verifying information.

My nephew's college roommate fell for a phishing text offering a free iPhone 15, he just needed to pay shipping by entering his credit card information within the next hour. The artificial scarcity created urgency that bypassed his normal caution about free offers. He realized it was a scam after he'd already entered his card details, fortunately catching it quickly enough to cancel the card before fraudulent charges appeared.

Scarcity exploits the same psychological mechanism as urgency, it demands speed that prevents careful evaluation. If you have to decide right now or lose the opportunity forever, you make worse decisions than if you can take time to think.

The defense is understanding that legitimate opportunities aren't structured to prevent thinking. Real companies don't create artificial urgency that forces immediate decisions without time for consideration. If an offer is only valid for the next hour, it's probably designed to prevent you from thinking clearly.

Types of Phishing: Recognizing the Attack Vectors

Phishing attacks come through every communication channel you use. Understanding the specific characteristics of each type helps you recognize them regardless of the manipulation tactics being employed.

Email Phishing: The Original and Still Most Common

Jake's attack was email phishing, fraudulent emails designed to look legitimate, usually attempting to steal credentials or install malware. Email phishing ranges from mass campaigns sent to millions of addresses to highly targeted spear-phishing sent to specific individuals.

The emails I see most frequently impersonate banks and financial institutions, requesting account verification or claiming unusual activity. They mimic shipping companies like FedEx, UPS, or Amazon, claiming a delivery requires action or payment. They pretend to be streaming services like Netflix or Spotify, saying your payment failed and account will be suspended. They spoof government agencies like the

IRS or Social Security Administration, claiming problems requiring immediate attention.

The technical indicators that identify email phishing are relatively consistent. The sender address usually looks legitimate at first glance but contains subtle differences when examined carefully, maybe it's paypal-security@paypal-secure.com instead of the actual paypal.com. The sender display name might look correct, but the actual email address revealed by clicking or hovering is completely different.

Links in phishing emails often use URL shorteners that hide the actual destination, or they create domain names that look similar to legitimate ones, paypa1.com using the number one instead of the letter L, app1e.com using the number one instead of the letter L, or gooogle.com with an extra O. Hovering over links before clicking reveals these discrepancies.

The writing quality in mass phishing campaigns is often poor, grammatical errors, awkward phrasing, formatting inconsistencies. Though increasingly, AI-generated phishing has eliminated this indicator. Professional spear-phishing, like what Jake encountered, is often indistinguishable from legitimate communication.

My mother receives dozens of phishing emails monthly. Most are obvious, poorly written emails claiming she won lotteries she never entered, requests from foreign princes needing help moving money, notifications about packages from companies she doesn't use. But occasionally she receives sophisticated ones that would fool most people if they weren't paying careful attention.

Last month, she got an email appearing to be from her health insurance company. It used the correct logo, proper formatting, and claimed she needed to update her information in their patient portal or her coverage would lapse. The sender address looked legitimate at first glance. The link went to a

Chapter 16: Phishing & Social Engineering

website that perfectly replicated her insurance company's login page.

She caught it by checking the actual sender address carefully, noticing one letter was wrong. She called her insurance company directly at the number on her insurance card. They confirmed they'd never sent that email and reported it to their fraud team.

That's the defense in action, verification through separate channels before taking action on any request for sensitive information.

SMS Phishing (Smishing): The Text That Seems Legitimate

Text message phishing, called smishing, has exploded in the past few years because open rates for texts are much higher than for emails. People read texts within minutes. They respond to texts quickly. Texts feel more immediate and trustworthy than email.

I've seen smishing attacks claiming package delivery issues requiring immediate action, purporting to be from banks requesting account verification, impersonating government agencies like the post office or IRS, spoofing retailers claiming rewards or coupons are waiting, and pretending to be contacts who've been in accidents and need urgent help.

The challenge with smishing is that sender information is easily spoofed. A text can appear to come from your bank's legitimate number or from a contact in your phone, but be sent by attackers using number spoofing technology. The same verification principle applies, if a text requests sensitive information or urgent action, verify through a separate channel before responding.

Linda got a smishing attack last week. Text from what appeared to be her bank's fraud department claiming unusual charges on her account, with a phone number to call immediately. She almost called the number in the text before remembering our training. She called the number on the back of her card instead. The bank confirmed they'd never sent that text and had no unusual activity on her account. If she'd called the number in the text, she would have been connected to scammers ready to steal her information.

The sophistication is increasing. I've seen smishing attacks that appear to be part of existing text conversations, inserted between legitimate messages from companies or contacts. I've seen attacks that perfectly replicate official government messages with realistic formatting and language. The key defense is never calling numbers or clicking links from unexpected texts, regardless of how legitimate they appear.

Voice Phishing (Vishing): The Call That Creates Pressure

Phone-based social engineering attacks, called vishing, combine the authority of a direct phone call with high-pressure tactics that prevent careful thinking. The caller claims to be from a trusted organization and needs immediate information or action.

Frank gets vishing attempts regularly, calls claiming to be from the Social Security Administration saying his benefits are suspended, from the IRS saying he owes back taxes, from tech support companies claiming his computer has viruses, from credit card fraud departments reporting unauthorized charges. The calls use fear and urgency to push immediate action.

The sophistication is remarkable. Some vishing operations use AI voice cloning to impersonate people you know, your boss, your family members, your colleagues. I've heard recordings of these AI-generated calls that are nearly indistinguishable from the real person. Without knowing to listen for subtle audio artifacts and verify through other channels, most people would be fooled.

Chapter 16: Phishing & Social Engineering

My friend Dave's mother received a vishing call from someone claiming to be her grandson, saying he'd been arrested while traveling and needed bail money wired immediately. The voice sounded exactly like her grandson, same vocal patterns, same speech mannerisms, even using family nicknames. She almost sent five thousand dollars before her husband suggested calling their grandson's actual phone number. The grandson answered immediately, safe at home, completely unaware his grandmother had just been targeted by AI voice fraud.

The defense against vishing is never providing sensitive information or taking urgent action based solely on inbound phone calls. If your bank calls claiming fraud, hang up and call them back at the number on your card. If a family member calls requesting money, verify through a different method, text them, call them back at their known number, or use your family code phrase from Chapter 11.

Legitimate organizations won't pressure you for immediate information. Legitimate emergencies can withstand two minutes of verification. If a caller gets angry or aggressive when you want to verify their identity, that's confirmation they're not legitimate.

Social Media Phishing: The Friend Request That Isn't

Social media platforms create unique phishing opportunities because they're built on trust networks. An attacker who compromises one account gains apparent trustworthiness with everyone in that person's network.

The attacks I see most frequently involve compromised accounts messaging friends with investment opportunities, job offers, or requests for help. They include fake profiles impersonating real people to build trust before requesting money or information. There are romance scams where attackers build relationships over months before requesting financial help. Quiz and survey scams collect personal information disguised as entertainment. They also use fraudulent ads for products that look legitimate but are actually credential-harvesting sites.

My wife's cousin had her Facebook compromised. The attacker sent messages to all her friends sharing a link to her "new online business" and offering discounts to friends and family. The link led to a fake shopping site that collected credit card information but never delivered products. Seventeen people entered their card information before the cousin regained control of her account and warned everyone.

The warning signs for social media phishing include unusual messages from contacts, especially those requesting money or promoting opportunities. Friend requests from people you're already friends with suggest someone is creating duplicate accounts. Links shortened or disguised in posts or messages should raise suspicion. Messages referencing information that doesn't match your actual relationship with the person indicate potential compromise. Profiles with very few friends, recent creation dates, or minimal activity might be fake.

The defense is verification before trusting social media communications, even from known contacts. If a friend messages about an opportunity, call them to verify before clicking links. If you receive a duplicate friend request, message the person through your existing connection before accepting. Never enter financial information on sites reached through social media links without verifying legitimacy through separate channels.

QR Code Phishing (Quishing): The Modern Trojan Horse

QR code phishing is relatively new but growing rapidly. Attackers place fraudulent QR codes over legitimate ones in public spaces, or send them in emails and texts, directing victims to phishing sites when scanned.

I've seen fake QR codes placed over parking meter payment codes, attached to restaurant tables over legitimate menu codes, included in phishing emails claiming to be authentication requests, and posted on social media as shortcuts to deals or content.

The challenge with QR codes is that you can't see where they lead until after scanning. Your phone camera reads the code and asks if you want to visit the URL, but you have only a brief moment to evaluate that URL before confirming. Most people just tap "open" without thinking.

My daughter Sarah almost fell for a Quishing attack at a parking garage. She scanned what she thought was the official payment code, was directed to a site that looked exactly like the parking company's payment portal, and entered her credit card information. She realized something was wrong only when she got a text from her card company flagging the charge as suspicious. The QR code had been a sticker placed over the legitimate code, directing to a fraudulent payment site.

The defense is treating QR codes with the same skepticism as any other link. Before confirming the URL after scanning, actually read it and verify it matches the expected domain. For parking, payments, and menus, consider typing URLs directly instead of scanning when possible. Be especially cautious of QR codes in unexpected places or sent through email and text where verification is impossible.

415

🔒 FORTIFY PROTOCOL

The Two-Second Pause Protocol:

Every phishing attack depends on you acting quickly without thinking. The most effective defense is deceptively simple: pause for two seconds before clicking, calling, or responding.

When you receive an unexpected email requesting action, pause for two full seconds. During that pause, ask yourself these questions. Do I have an account with this company? Was I expecting this communication? Does this create unusual urgency? Can I verify this through a separate channel?

When you receive a text asking you to call a number or click a link, pause for two full seconds. Ask whether you recognize the sender, whether the request matches normal patterns, whether you can call back using a known number instead of the one provided, and whether the message creates artificial urgency or fear.

When you receive a phone call claiming to be from an organization you do business with, pause for two full seconds before providing any information. Ask whether you initiated this call or whether it was inbound, whether the caller can provide information proving legitimacy, whether you can hang up and call back through official channels, and whether the request seems consistent with normal procedures.

This two-second pause interrupts the automatic response that phishing exploits. It creates space for rational evaluation instead of emotional reaction. It's not foolproof, but it's remarkably effective because it prevents the instant click that most phishing attacks depend on.

Chapter 16: Phishing & Social Engineering

Real-World Training: The Monthly Phishing Drill

After Jake's incident, I revised my family's security training to include monthly phishing drills. Not theoretical discussions about what phishing looks like, but actual practice recognizing and responding to realistic examples.

The drill is simple. Once per month, usually over dinner or during our Sunday family check-in, I present three examples of real communications. Two are legitimate emails, texts, or scenarios that could reasonably occur. One is phishing. Everyone has to identify which is which and explain their reasoning.

The examples come from actual phishing attempts I've encountered or from excellent phishing simulation services. I preserve the exact formatting, writing style, and details. The only modification is removing actually dangerous links, replacing them with obvious fake placeholders.

Last month's drill included three email examples. First, a message from Amazon confirming an order Sarah actually placed, with correct order number, items, and delivery date. Second, a password reset notification from Netflix stating that someone requested a password change, this was legitimate, as my wife had actually requested it after forgetting her password. Third, a nearly perfect fake from "PayPal" claiming suspicious activity on her account and requesting login to verify.

My son immediately identified the PayPal one as phishing. "The sender address is wrong, it's paypal-security@paypalinc.com instead of paypal.com. And PayPal wouldn't ask you to log in through an email link to verify activity. They'd ask you to log in through their main site."

Sarah caught a more subtle detail. "Also, I don't even have a PayPal account. So, any email from PayPal is automatically suspicious."

417

That's the level of analysis we're building through monthly practice. The ability to spot red flags quickly, to verify sender information carefully, to recognize when requests don't match normal procedures, and to realize when you shouldn't have received the communication at all.

The drill evolves monthly. We practice recognizing text message phishing, voice call scripts, social media scenarios, QR code risks. We discuss recent real attacks that have targeted people we know. We share phishing attempts we've encountered during the month. We celebrate catches, times when someone recognized phishing and avoided it.

Mike adopted this drill for his construction company. Once a month at the crew meeting, he presents examples and has his team identify phishing. He's made it competitive, the person who correctly identifies all the examples first gets lunch on him that day. His team has gotten remarkably good at spotting phishing, which matters because construction companies are frequently targeted with fraudulent supplier invoices and payment requests.

The value of monthly practice is that it builds instinctive recognition. The first few times, everyone has to think carefully through each indicator. After six months, the recognition becomes automatic. After a year, people are catching phishing in real life before it causes problems.

Jake now runs similar drills with his roommates. Sarah does them with her friend group. My wife started doing them at her book club after one member got scammed. The practice spreads, which makes everyone safer.

Chapter 16: Phishing & Social Engineering

The Evolution: AI-Enhanced Phishing and What's Coming

Everything I've taught you about recognizing phishing, poor grammar, awkward phrasing, obvious formatting errors, generic greetings, is becoming less reliable because artificial intelligence has transformed phishing sophistication dramatically in the past two years.

The old indicators that helped you spot phishing, spelling errors, grammatical mistakes, awkward phrasing, have largely disappeared. AI-generated phishing is grammatically perfect, stylistically appropriate, and contextually relevant in ways that older phishing never was.

I've analyzed dozens of AI-generated phishing emails over the past year. They're written in perfect English with natural phrasing and appropriate tone. They replicate company communication styles accurately. They reference current events and seasonal contexts correctly. They don't trigger the "something seems off" feeling that helped people catch older phishing.

More concerning, AI enables highly personalized spear-phishing on a scale. Attackers can scrape your social media, analyze your communication patterns, identify your interests and concerns, and generate phishing tailored specifically to you. What used to require days of manual research per target now happens automatically in seconds.

Voice cloning technology has advanced to the point where ten seconds of audio can be turned into a convincing voice model. The vishing attack on Dave's mother using her grandson's cloned voice? That's not rare anymore. It's becoming routine. Attackers scrape voice samples from social media videos, TikTok posts, YouTube videos, or public recordings, then generate phone calls that sound exactly like your family members or colleagues.

Video deepfakes are approaching the same threshold. While not yet common in phishing attacks, the technology exists to create convincing video calls impersonating people you know. Imagine a video call from your boss requesting urgent action, showing their face and voice in real-time, but completely fabricated. That's not science fiction; it's technology available today and likely to be weaponized soon.

The psychological impact of these advanced attacks is significant. When you can no longer trust that an email sounds right, that a voice sounds like your family member, or that a video call shows who it claims to show, every communication becomes suspect. The mental burden of constant verification is exhausting.

But the fundamental defenses remain effective. The two-second pause still works because even perfect-seeming phishing still relies on urgency and emotional manipulation. Verification through separate channels still works because attackers can fake the communication method they control but can't fake other channels. Family code phrases still work because AI can clone voices but can't read your mind to know the secret phrase you established.

The key is understanding that surface-level indicators, writing quality, voice characteristics, visual appearance, are no longer reliable. You need to verify through independent channels and trust procedures rather than appearances.

When my daughter Sarah received what appeared to be a video call from her boss last month asking her to urgently transfer funds to a new vendor account, she didn't trust that the video looked right and the voice sounded right. She ended the call and called her boss back on his known cell phone number. It was a deep-fake attempt, her boss had never made that call, but attackers had used video scraped from company

Chapter 16: Phishing & Social Engineering

presentations and voice samples from recorded meetings to create a convincing fake.

She caught it not because she detected technical flaws in the fake, she couldn't, but because she followed procedure: verify urgent requests through separate channels, never act on a single communication alone, and trust processes more than appearances.

That's how defense against AI-enhanced phishing works. You can't out-detect AI. But you can out-process it through verification procedures that AI-generated phishing can't bypass.

SITREP: The Phishing Landscape 2025-2026

The phishing environment has evolved dramatically and will continue evolving rapidly. Understanding current trends helps you calibrate your defenses appropriately.

AI has made phishing indistinguishable from legitimate communication at the surface level. Grammatical perfection is now standard rather than exceptional. Contextual relevance is automated and accurate. Personalization that once required extensive research now happens automatically. The old rule "obvious errors mean phishing" is dead, phishing is now often error-free.

Multimedia phishing using voice, video, and interactive elements has moved from experimental to operational. Voice cloning for vishing attacks is routine and highly effective. Video deepfakes for business email compromise are emerging and will become common within two years. Interactive phishing sites that replicate entire login experiences perfectly are standard practice.

Social media remains the primary intelligence source for targeted phishing. Every public post, every photo, every comment provides information attackers use to personalize attacks. The more you share publicly, the more sophisticated the phishing targeting you becomes. Privacy settings matter more than ever, not just for keeping information private, but for reducing the attack surface for personalized phishing.

Mobile phishing is increasing because phone screens make verification harder. It's difficult to carefully examine sender addresses on small screens. URL verification before clicking is nearly impossible. Separate-channel verification is less convenient on phones, making it more likely people skip this step. Mobile security often lags desktop security, creating additional vulnerabilities.

The volume of phishing continues to increase exponentially. Most people receive multiple phishing attempts daily across email, text, and calls. The sheer volume creates fatigue that makes people more likely to miss indicators or skip verification.

But law enforcement capacity remains limited. Most phishing originates outside US jurisdiction. Individual cases are too small for federal resources. Local police lack technical capability and jurisdiction. Recovery focus on victims defending themselves rather than catching perpetrators.

What this means practically is that you're largely on your own for defense. Technical filters catch some phishing but miss increasingly sophisticated attempts. Verification procedures remain your most reliable defense. Skepticism and the two-second pause are more critical than ever.

Chapter 16: Phishing & Social Engineering

Success Stories: When Training Works

Let me share four real examples from my extended family and friends where phishing training prevented what would have been devastating compromises.

Frank, my father-in-law, received a call claiming to be from the Social Security Administration stating his benefits were suspended due to suspicious activity. The caller had his Social Security number, his date of birth, and his home address, all public information from data brokers, lending credibility. The caller said to reinstate benefits, Frank needed to verify his identity including his Medicare number and bank account for direct deposit.

Six months earlier, Frank would have provided everything asked. He trusted authority. He feared losing benefits he relied on. The caller sounded professional and had information that seemed to prove legitimacy.

But after family security training, Frank recognized the fear manipulation. He told the caller he'd call the Social Security Administration directly to resolve the issue and hung up. He called the real SSA at the number on his benefits card. They confirmed they'd never called him, his benefits were active and not suspended, and the call was a scam attempt.

That two-minute verification saved Frank from potentially losing thousands of dollars and compromising multiple accounts.

Linda received an email appearing to be from her credit card company claiming unusual activity on her account. The email looked perfect, correct logo, proper formatting, professional language, legitimate-seeming sender address. It requested she log in through the provided link to verify recent charges.

She'd received dozens of similar emails over the years that were legitimate, her credit card company does send fraud alerts that require verification. This one looked identical to those legitimate emails.

But Linda had learned to verify through separate channels. She didn't click the link in the email. She opened her banking app directly and checked for alerts. None existed. She called the fraud number on the back of her card. They confirmed they hadn't sent any email and had no unusual activity on her account.

The email was perfectly crafted phishing. Without the training to verify independently, she would have entered her login credentials on the fraudulent site, giving attackers full access to her account.

Sarah received a text message appearing to be from a colleague asking her to review and sign an urgent document. The text included a link to what looked like DocuSign. Sarah and this colleague frequently exchange documents for signature, so the request was entirely plausible and the timing wasn't unusual.

Sarah almost clicked the link. But she'd practiced the two-second pause. During that pause, she noticed the link URL wasn't actually docusign.com, it was docusiqn.com with a Q instead of a G. She texted her colleague directly asking if she'd sent a document. The colleague responded she hadn't sent anything.

The attacker had compromised someone else's phone or was spoofing the number, researched Sarah's work relationships through LinkedIn, identified a colleague she regularly exchanged documents with, and crafted a contextually appropriate phishing text. Without the two-second pause and careful URL inspection, Sarah would have entered her credentials on the fake DocuSign site.

Jake, after his initial phishing incident, encountered a second attempt three months later. This time, an email claimed to be from his company's HR department requesting updated tax withholding information through a linked form. The email came during tax season when such requests are common. It appeared to come from an internal email address and used his company's HR portal design perfectly.

Jake didn't immediately recognize it as phishing, it was that well crafted. But he'd learned not to trust appearances. He didn't click the link. He opened a separate browser window, logged into the actual HR portal directly, and found no request for updated information. He forwarded the email to his company's security team.

They confirmed it was a spear-phishing attempt targeting multiple employees. The email appeared internal but actually came from a compromised former employee account. If Jake had entered his information through the fake form, attackers would have gained enough personal details to file fraudulent tax returns in his name.

These four examples share common elements. Each person encountered sophisticated phishing that would have fooled most people. Each recognized manipulation tactics despite technically excellent execution. Each verified through separate channels rather than trusting surface appearance. Each avoided compromise because of training and practice, not because the phishing was obviously fake.

That's what success looks like, not catching every phishing attempt instantly, but having procedures that protect you even when you can't immediately identify the threat.

Teaching Your Circle: Spreading the Defense

After you've practiced phishing recognition yourself for several months, you become capable of teaching others. This is important because your security is interconnected with your community's security. When your family member falls for phishing, their compromised account attacks you. When your coworker's credentials are stolen, your company's systems become vulnerable.

Teaching phishing defense requires different approaches for different people. What works for tech-savvy adults doesn't work for children or elderly relatives. Effective teaching matches the method to the audience.

For young children, focus on the concept of "stranger danger" applied digitally. Unknown numbers calling shouldn't be answered. Messages from people they don't know shouldn't be opened. Requests for information should always involve a parent. Keep it simple and concrete rather than technical.

For teenagers, emphasize the sophistication of attacks and the reputational consequences. Show them real examples of how phishing targets their age group through social media. Discuss romance scams, job scams, and fake friend requests. Make them understand that falling for phishing isn't just a security issue, it can affect their college applications, job prospects, and friend relationships if their accounts are used to attack others.

My daughter Sarah teaches phishing defense to high school students at a local community center. She shows them real examples of Instagram account compromises, fake job offers targeting students, and college application scams. She makes it relevant to their world rather than abstract. Her program has reached hundreds of students, several of whom have reported avoiding scams because of her training.

Chapter 16: Phishing & Social Engineering

For elderly relatives, focus on common scams targeting their demographic and build confidence in verification procedures. Government impersonation scams, tech support fraud, grandparent scams, and investment fraud. Teach them specific verification steps for each type, like always calling back through official numbers rather than using numbers from calls or emails. Assure them that legitimate organizations expect and appreciate verification.

Frank teaches phishing awareness at his veterans' organization. He shares real examples targeting veterans, like fake VA benefits calls and fraudulent military charity requests. He's created a simple laminated card listing verification procedures for common scams. His group has caught dozens of phishing attempts because of these trainings.

For colleagues and coworkers, focus on business email compromise and company-specific threats. Use real examples from your industry. Practice recognizing fraudulent invoices, fake executive requests, and compromised vendor communications. Make it part of regular team meetings rather than separate training sessions.

Mike runs brief phishing discussions during Friday afternoon crew meetings at his construction company. Five minutes, one example, team discussion about how to spot it. His crews now routinely catch fraudulent supplier invoices and fake payment requests that would have cost the company thousands.

The key to effective teaching is making it concrete rather than abstract, relevant rather than generic, and practiced rather than just discussed. People don't learn phishing defense from lectures. They learn it from seeing examples, making judgments, getting feedback, and gradually building instinctive recognition through repeated practice.

Mission Complete

By the end of this chapter, you should understand that phishing exploits human psychology more than technical vulnerabilities. The manipulation tactics of urgency, authority, fear, trust, and scarcity work because they trigger emotional responses that bypass rational thinking.

You should be able to recognize phishing across all common attack vectors including email, SMS, voice calls, social media, and QR codes. You should understand the specific indicators for each type while knowing that surface indicators like grammar and formatting are becoming less reliable with AI-generated phishing.

You should have adopted the two-second pause as an automatic response to unexpected communications requesting action. That pause creates space for rational evaluation instead of emotional reaction.

You should know how to verify through separate channels rather than trusting single communications, regardless of how legitimate they appear. Call back using known numbers. Log in through direct URLs rather than email links. Confirm with contacts through different platforms before acting on their requests.

You should be conducting monthly phishing drills with your household, practicing recognition with real examples. You should be building instinctive skepticism that protects you even when individual attacks are too sophisticated to consciously analyze.

You should be teaching phishing defense to your circle using age-appropriate and context-relevant methods. Children, teenagers, elderly relatives, and colleagues all need different approaches. Effective teaching builds their capability to defend themselves and spreads protection throughout your community.

Chapter 16: Phishing & Social Engineering

Call to Action

Schedule your first monthly phishing drill this week with your household or team. Don't wait until you feel completely prepared, start practicing now. Use examples from your own inbox or from phishing simulation sites. Three examples, two legitimate and one fake. Discuss the indicators. Build recognition through practice.

Create a family or team verification protocol for common scenarios. How do you verify urgent requests from executives or family members? What's the procedure when messages request money or sensitive information? Write it down. Make it specific. Practice until it's automatic.

Share one story from this chapter with someone who needs it. Your elderly parent who's vulnerable to vishing. Your teenager who's active on social media. Your coworker who almost fell for business email compromise. Teaching reinforces your own learning and spreads the protection.

Add verified contact numbers to your phone contacts now. Your bank's fraud line. Your credit card company's customer service. Your IT security team at work. Label them clearly so you can find them instantly when you need to verify a suspicious communication.

Reference Materials: Use the Phishing Recognition Checklist, Common Scam Examples, and Verification Protocol Template in the appendices to build your recognition skills and teach others.

Next: Chapter 17 provides the closing orders that integrate everything you've learned into sustained defensive practice, case studies of both success and failure, and your final mission brief for maintaining security for life.

Chief Palmer notes that the human attack surface is the hardest to defend because it requires constant vigilance rather than one-time technical implementation. "In thirty years, I never saw an impenetrable technical defense," he says. "But I saw plenty of people who trained themselves to recognize manipulation and verify before acting. That training, that discipline, that two-second pause, that's what wins against social engineering. The strongest firewall is the human who refuses to be rushed into making decisions."

Chapter 17: Closing Orders - Your Mission Continues

⏱ 30 minutes to read | A lifetime to practice

CALL SIGN: FORTRESS SECURE, THE MISSION NEVER ENDS. THE VIGILANCE CONTINUES.

I stood in my garage on a cold Saturday morning in January, looking at three decades of military documentation stacked in boxes against the wall. Security manuals from the 1990s. Incident reports from the 2000s. Training materials from the 2010s. Operational procedures that had protected some of the most sensitive facilities in the United States Air Force.

My wife stood in the doorway with coffee, watching me sort through the boxes. "Are you really going to get rid of all of this?"

"Most of it," I said, pulling out a thick binder labeled "Operational Readiness Inspection Procedures, 1997." The pages were yellowed, the terminology outdated, the specific threats long since evolved past recognition. "The threats change. The technology changes. The procedures have to change with them."

"But doesn't all that experience still matter?"

I set the binder down and picked up another, this one from 2022, just before my retirement. "The experience matters. The principles matter. But holding onto old procedures when the battlefield has changed? That's how you lose."

I'd been working on the final chapter of this book for three weeks, trying to figure out how to end it properly. How do you conclude a book about security when security never concludes? How do you write closing orders when the mission continues indefinitely?

The answer came while sorting through those boxes. You don't teach people to follow 1997 procedures in 2026. You teach them principles that adapt to whatever 2027, 2030, or 2040 brings. You give them a foundation strong enough to build on as threats evolve. You show them both what success looks like and what failure looks like so they understand the stakes.

That's what this final chapter does. It brings together everything you've learned, shows you real examples of sustained success and catastrophic failure, and gives you the tools to adapt your fortress as the battlefield changes around you.

Because the mission never ends. The vigilance continues. And the principles you've learned will protect you for the rest of your life if you maintain them with the same discipline, you built them.

Chapter 17: Closing Orders

The Integration: How All the Pieces Work Together

For sixteen chapters, I've taught you individual components of security. Strong passwords. Two-factor authentication. Credit freezes. Network security. Breach monitoring. Recovery procedures. Legal protections. Phishing defense. Maintenance discipline. Each chapter focused on a specific defensive layer.

But real security isn't sixteen separate techniques. It's an integrated system where each layer supports the others, and weakness in one area is covered by strength in another.

Let me show you what I mean by using a real compromise attempt against my family last year, and how the layered defenses worked together to prevent damage.

It started when my wife received an email that appeared to be from our health insurance company. The email was professionally written, used the correct logo and formatting, and claimed she needed to update her payment information in their patient portal, or our coverage would lapse. The sender's address looked legitimate at first glance.

She almost clicked the link in the email. But she'd practiced the two-second pause from Chapter 16. During that pause, she noticed something felt wrong. She couldn't articulate exactly what, just a vague sense of wrongness. So, she didn't click. Instead, she called me over.

I examined the email carefully. The sender's address was subtly wrong. The real insurance company uses anthem.com. This email came from anthem-benefits.com. Similar enough to pass a quick glance, different enough to be fraudulent.

I checked the link destination by hovering over it without clicking. It went to anthem-portal.net, not the actual company website. Definite phishing.

433

But here's where the layered defense became interesting. I logged into Have I Been Pwned to check if my wife's email address had appeared in any recent breaches. It had. A small forum she joined years ago for a hobby was compromised three weeks earlier. Her email address and an old password were exposed.

That breach was the intelligence source for the phishing attack. The attackers knew she had health insurance through Anthem because she'd mentioned it in forum posts. They knew her email address from the breach. They crafted a targeted phishing attempt using that information.

If the breach monitoring from Chapter 4 had been working properly, she would have received an alert about that forum breach three weeks earlier and could have changed her password immediately. But the breach monitoring had failed. The forum breach was discovered but notifications weren't sent properly due to a technical error.

If she'd clicked the phishing link and entered her login credentials on the fake portal, several other defensive layers would have prevented full compromise. Her password manager from Chapter 1 meant she was using a unique, strong password for the insurance portal that wasn't reused anywhere else. Even if attackers captured it, they couldn't use it to access other accounts.

Her MFA from Chapter 2 meant that even with the password, attackers couldn't log into her actual insurance account without the authentication code from her phone. The phishing site couldn't capture that because MFA codes are time-sensitive and specific to individual login attempts.

Her credit freeze from Chapter 10 meant that even if attackers gained enough personal information from the insurance account to attempt identity theft, they couldn't open new accounts in her name.

Chapter 17: Closing Orders

The monitoring systems from Chapter 4 meant that any attempt to use compromised information would trigger alerts on multiple platforms. Bank notifications would catch fraudulent charges. Credit monitoring would flag suspicious applications. Breach alerts would catch if credentials appeared in future breaches.

The legal protections from Chapter 15 meant that if fraud occurred despite all the technical defenses, she had clear remedies for recovery and could enforce her rights against companies that failed to protect her.

In the end, none of those backup layers were needed because the two-second pause from Chapter 16 caught the attack at the first stage. But if that first defense had failed, five other defensive layers would have limited or prevented damage.

That's what integrated defense looks like. Not a single perfect barrier, but multiple overlapping layers where the strength of one compensates for weakness in another. The breach monitoring failed to alert her about the compromised forum, but phishing defense caught the resulting attack. If phishing defense had failed, password management would have limited damage. If password management had failed, MFA would have blocked access. If MFA had failed, credit freezes would have prevented identity theft.

The fortress you've built through sixteen chapters works the same way. Every chapter added a defensive layer. Together, those layers create a security system where no single point of failure can compromise everything you're protecting.

Marcus's Story: When the Fortress Falls

I need to tell you about Marcus because his story illustrates what happens when someone builds strong initial defenses but fails to maintain them. Marcus isn't a real person. He's a composite of several people I've known who made similar

435

mistakes with similar consequences. I'm presenting his story as a single narrative to show you clearly what progressive security decay looks like and where it leads.

Marcus was one of my early students when I started teaching digital security to civilians after retiring from the Air Force. He came to one of my first workshops at the local library, took copious notes, asked excellent questions, and implemented everything I taught with impressive speed and thoroughness.

Within three weeks of the workshop, Marcus had set up a password manager with strong unique passwords for all 47 of his accounts. He enabled two-factor authentication everywhere was available. He froze his credit at all three bureaus. He set up breach monitoring through Have I Been Pwned. He configured his home network properly with guest network separation. He documented everything in an organized binder.

Marcus's fortress was strong. I used him as an example when teaching others. "This is what proper implementation looks like," I'd say, showing his documentation to my classes.

But Marcus didn't maintain what he built.

It started small. His password manager subscription came up for renewal eight months after initial setup. The renewal email looked like spam to him. He was busy with work. He deleted it thinking he'd deal with it later. A week later, his password manager access was suspended due to non-payment.

Marcus didn't notice immediately. He had his passwords saved in his browser on his laptop, so he could still access everything. The password manager was just an additional security layer he didn't think he needed for daily use. He told himself he'd renew it eventually. Eventually never came.

Three months passed. Marcus's work laptop died and had to be replaced. When he set up the new laptop, his saved browser passwords didn't transfer over. He needed his password

Chapter 17: Closing Orders

manager to access his accounts. But when he tried to log in, he discovered his account had been deleted after 90 days of non-payment.

He still had his emergency backup of the password manager vault on an external hard drive. But when he tried to access it, the file was corrupted. He'd never tested his backup. He didn't know it had failed.

Marcus panicked. He had 47 accounts and couldn't access any of them because he'd followed my advice about making passwords impossible to remember. He spent an entire weekend using password reset procedures to regain access, creating new passwords and writing them down on paper because he didn't have a working password manager anymore.

The passwords he created during that stressful weekend were weaker than the originals. Not terrible, but not the 20-plus-character random strings his password manager had generated. And because he was using paper notes and typing from them, he started reusing variations of the same base password for accounts he considered less important. "Amazon2024!" for Amazon. "Netflix2024!" for Netflix. "Spotify2024!" for Spotify.

The pattern was obvious and exploitable, but Marcus was exhausted from the recovery process and convinced himself these passwords were good enough.

Six months later, Marcus got a breach notification. A shopping website he'd used once was compromised. The breach exposed his email address and password. Because he'd reused that password pattern across multiple shopping sites, attackers were able to access four of his accounts using slight variations of the exposed password.

Marcus didn't notice the breach notification immediately. It went to his email during a busy work week and got buried under hundreds of other messages. By the time he saw it two weeks later, attackers had already used his compromised shopping accounts to attempt fraudulent purchases on three different sites. Two were caught by the merchants' fraud detection systems. One went through, charging his credit card $487 for electronics shipped to an address in Florida.

Marcus reported the fraudulent charge to his credit card company. They reversed it without issue. But the incident shook his confidence. He decided to take security seriously again.

He downloaded a free password manager and spent another weekend changing all his passwords to strong unique ones. He verified his two-factor authentication was still enabled everywhere. He checked his credit freeze status. Everything was secure again.

For about four months.

Then Marcus started skipping the monthly maintenance checks I'd taught in Chapter 14. He was busy. Life got in the way. He figured everything was fine since he wasn't having any problems. Monthly checks became quarterly checks became "I'll do it when I remember."

A year passed without Marcus running a single security check. During that year, several things degraded without his knowledge.

His home router firmware became outdated. Three critical security vulnerabilities were discovered and patched by the manufacturer, but Marcus never installed the updates because he never checked. His router was running software so vulnerable that simple automated scripts could gain access.

One of his old email addresses appeared in two separate data breaches. He didn't know because he'd stopped checking Have, I Been Pwned regularly. The compromised credentials included enough personal information to enable targeted phishing attacks.

Chapter 17: Closing Orders

His phone number appeared on multiple data broker sites after he'd moved to a new address. He'd spent considerable effort removing his information two years earlier, but the brokers had re-listed him with updated details. He didn't know because he'd stopped running quarterly data broker removal.

The combination of these degraded defenses created an exploitable attack surface that eventually got exploited.

Marcus received a sophisticated phishing email appearing to come from his bank. It claimed unusual activity on his account and requested immediate verification by clicking a link and logging in. The email was perfectly crafted, using information from the data breaches to personalize it with his actual account history and recent transaction patterns.

Marcus had stopped practicing the phishing drills I'd taught. He hadn't reviewed red flags or verification procedures in over a year. When he received this email during a stressful afternoon, he clicked the link and entered his credentials without the two-second pause that would have saved him.

The phishing site captured his banking username and password. Within minutes, attackers were attempting to log into his actual bank account. His MFA stopped them initially. They couldn't get the authentication code from his phone.

But Marcus had made a critical error during his rushed password recreation after the password manager failure. He'd reused his banking password as his email password. The attackers tried his captured banking credentials on his email account. It worked.

With access to his email, they could now bypass his banking MFA. They requested a password reset for his bank account through the legitimate process. The reset link came to his email, which they controlled. They clicked it, set a new password, and added their own phone number for MFA.

439

By the time Marcus realized what was happening the next morning, attackers had transferred $8,700 from his checking account to an external account at another bank. They'd attempted to open a line of credit in his name, which was blocked by his credit freeze. They'd tried to access his investment accounts, which failed because those had different passwords.

Marcus's bank reversed the fraudulent transfer after a two-week investigation. He didn't lose money. But he lost two weeks of sleep, hours upon hours dealing with fraud reports and security reviews, his sense of security, and his trust in his own judgment.

"I don't understand how this happened," Marcus told me when he came to me for help recovering. "I did everything you taught me. I set up all the defenses properly. I was so careful."

"You built the fortress correctly," I told him. "But you didn't maintain it. Security isn't a project you complete. It's a practice you sustain. Your initial setup was excellent. But a fortress that isn't patrolled, isn't inspected, isn't maintained will eventually fall."

Marcus spent a month rebuilding his security with renewed commitment to maintenance. That was three years ago. He hasn't had another incident since because now he understands that the setup phase is just the beginning. The real work is the ongoing maintenance that keeps your defenses effective as threats evolve and circumstances change.

The Palmer Family: Sustained Success

Let me show you what sustained success looks like by describing my own family's security over the past five years since I retired and implemented Fortress Shield principles with everyone.

Chapter 17: Closing Orders

My immediate family consists of my wife, my adult son, my adult daughter Sarah, my brother Mike, my sister Linda, my mother, and my father-in-law Frank. Seven people across three generations, different technical skill levels, different risk profiles, different lifestyles. What they have in common is consistent security maintenance and the results that come from that discipline.

My wife and I run monthly security checks together on the first Saturday of every month. We spend about 45 minutes reviewing password manager health reports, checking financial statements, auditing social media privacy settings, and verifying our subscriptions and accounts. We run quarterly security reviews covering network scans, firmware updates, data broker removal, and credit freeze verification. We conduct an annual comprehensive security assessment covering everything in detail.

In five years of monthly maintenance, we've caught 11 problems before they became crises. We found a compromised password from a data breach within a week of exposure and changed it before any unauthorized access occurred. We discovered a forgotten subscription charging us $14.99 monthly for a service we stopped using two years earlier, recovering over $350. We caught privacy settings on Facebook that were reset to public by a platform update, before we posted sensitive travel information. We identified an unknown device on our home network that turned out to be a neighbor's teenager who'd somehow obtained our guest network password.

Each of these problems was minor because we caught them early. Without monthly maintenance, each could have escalated into something significantly worse. The compromised password could have led to account takeover. The forgotten subscription was wasting hundreds per year. The public privacy settings could have exposed information used for targeted phishing. The unauthorized network access could have been a more serious intrusion.

My daughter Sarah, whose identity theft recovery I detailed in Chapter 3, has maintained perfect security discipline for three years since that incident. She runs her monthly maintenance religiously on the second Sunday of every month. She's caught two breach notifications early and changed passwords immediately. She's identified three phishing attempts before clicking. She's had zero security incidents since implementing sustained maintenance.

More importantly, Sarah's psychological relationship with security has transformed. In the first year after her identity theft, she was vigilant to the point of anxiety. Every email seemed suspicious. Every phone call triggered worry. She was exhausted by constant hypervigilance.

But sustained maintenance changed that. By checking regularly, she knows the current state of her security. She doesn't worry about unknown problems because she has procedures that would catch problems. The quarterly checks give her confidence that everything is secure. She's moved from anxious hypervigilance to calm vigilance, where security is routine practice rather than constant worry.

My son moved to Seattle for work two years ago. Living alone in a new city, he's had to maintain his own security without immediate family support. I was worried he'd let things slide once he was on his own. But he's kept up with monthly maintenance, participates in our quarterly family security summits via video call, and has caught several problems through his own vigilance.

Last year, he received a sophisticated phishing attempt impersonating his company's IT department, similar to Jake's incident from Chapter 16. He recognized it immediately because of the monthly phishing drills we've been running as a family for years. He didn't just avoid falling for it, he

Chapter 17: Closing Orders

reported it to his actual IT security team so they could warn other employees and identify the attack vector. His company praised his response and used it as a training case.

My brother Mike, who runs a construction company, has implemented Fortress Shield security for his entire business. All eight of his employees use password managers. They conduct monthly phishing drills during team meetings. They verify financial requests through separate channels. They maintain proper network security at the office.

In four years of sustained practice, Mike's company has avoided three business email compromise attempts that could have cost tens of thousands of dollars. They've caught two fraudulent supplier invoices before payment. They've identified and removed malware from an employee laptop within hours of infection, before it could spread to company systems. Mike estimates that sustained security maintenance has saved his company at least $75,000 in prevented fraud, probably more.

My sister Linda, whose card fraud started her security journey, has maintained her defenses for three years. She's had two additional fraud attempts on her cards, both of which she caught within hours because of her habit of checking her bank app regularly. Both were resolved quickly with zero losses. She's taught her own children about security, and her teenage son recently avoided a social media phishing attack because of that training.

My mother, now seventy-eight, maintains the security systems I helped her set up after her email compromise four years ago. She's not technically sophisticated, but she follows procedures religiously. She checks her accounts weekly. She verifies unexpected communications through phone calls. She reports suspicious emails to me immediately rather than trying to handle them alone. She's encountered probably 20 phishing attempts over four years and hasn't fallen for a single one because she applies the two-second pause and verification procedures consistently.

My father-in-law Frank, who's seventy-two, has maintained his security for three years since I helped him after his router compromise. His quarterly router firmware updates, network scans, and verification procedures have kept his home network secure. He runs a monthly security discussion at his veterans' organization, teaching fellow veterans about scams targeting their demographic. He's helped five other veterans avoid fraud through that teaching.

Across my extended family, seven people maintaining sustained security for an average of 3.5 years each. Total time investment: approximately 30 minutes monthly per person, three hours quarterly, five hours annually. That's roughly 48 hours per person per year, or 336 hours total for the family annually.

What has that 336 hours of annual maintenance prevented? At least four account compromises. At least three identity theft attempts. At least six significant fraud attempts. Hundreds of successful phishing recognitions. Probably dozens of smaller problems we caught so early we didn't even register them as threats.

The estimated financial impact of prevented fraud and compromise across the family is easily over $100,000 during this period. That's not speculation. That's adding up the specific incidents we caught and estimating their cost if they'd succeeded.

But the value isn't just financial. It's psychological. Everyone in my family has confidence that their security is maintained. They're not worried about unknown threats because they have procedures that catch threats. They're not stressed about digital security because it's routine practice, like brushing teeth or checking tire pressure.

They sleep well. They travel without anxiety about accounts being compromised while they're away. They use technology confidently rather than fearfully. That peace of mind is worth more than any dollar amount saved.

That's what sustained success looks like. Not perfect security, there's no such thing. But consistent practice that catches problems early, prevents most attacks from succeeding, and creates confidence through verified protection rather than hoped-for security.

🔒 FORTIFY PROTOCOL

Your Sustainment Battle Rhythm:

This is your complete maintenance schedule integrating everything from 16 chapters into sustainable practice. Follow this rhythm and you replicate my family's sustained success.

Daily practice requires about five minutes total spread throughout your day. While having morning coffee, check your password manager notifications for any breach alerts. When receiving unexpected communications, apply the two-second pause before clicking, calling, or responding. During routine financial checks, scan transactions quickly for anything unfamiliar. These habits become automatic after three months of consistent practice.

Weekly maintenance takes about 15 minutes every Sunday evening or Monday morning. Scan your home network with Fing to verify you recognize all connected devices. Check that your backups ran successfully and have adequate storage space. Review any security alerts from monitoring services. These weekly checks catch problems within days rather than months.

Monthly practice requires about 45 minutes on the first weekend of each month. Run your password manager health report and act on weak, reused, or breached passwords immediately. Review financial statements from all accounts for unauthorized charges. Audit social media privacy settings for changes made by platform updates. Verify MFA is functioning on critical accounts by testing one. These monthly reviews catch degradation before it becomes exploitable.

Quarterly maintenance takes about two to three hours during the first weekend of January, April, July, and October. Run a mini–Red Team ORI focusing on high-risk areas. Update firmware for your router and IoT devices. Complete another cycle of data broker removal since they continuously re-add you. Verify credit freeze status at all three bureaus. Pull one credit report on a rotating schedule. These quarterly inspections identify gaps that monthly maintenance might miss.

Biannual tasks require about two hours in January and July. Rotate critical passwords even if they haven't been breached as an extra precaution for your most sensitive accounts. Verify all recovery methods and backup codes are current and accessible. Test your backup restoration process with a random file to confirm backups actually work. These semi-annual checks ensure your emergency procedures function when needed.

Annual maintenance takes about four to five hours spread across January. Conduct a full Operational Readiness Inspection as described in Chapter 12. Pull all three credit reports and review them thoroughly. Complete a comprehensive account inventory including accounts you rarely use. Refresh family security training with updated threat examples. Review the latest annual edition of Fortress Shield for new threats and updated procedures. These annual reviews adapt your defenses to evolving threats and changing circumstances.

Chapter 17: Closing Orders

This schedule seems extensive written out completely, but it totals approximately 45 to 50 hours per year, less than one hour per week on average. Distributed across the year as described, it never feels overwhelming. Most months require only one 45-minute session plus weekly 15-minute checks. The heavier quarterly and annual work happens predictably on a schedule you control.

The key is calendar integration. Put every task on your actual calendar with reminders. Don't rely on memory or motivation. Treat security maintenance like dentist appointments or car maintenance, scheduled obligations you honor because they're important, not optional tasks you do when you feel like it.

Adapting to Evolution: The 2027 Threat Landscape

Everything I've taught you in this book is accurate as of early 2026 when I'm writing these words. But threats evolve constantly. The phishing techniques that work today will be augmented or replaced by more sophisticated approaches tomorrow. The tools I've recommended will improve or be superseded by better options. The legal protections might be strengthened or weakened by new legislation and enforcement priorities.

Your fortress must adapt to these changes without abandoning its foundation. Let me show you how to do that by walking through my predictions for the next two to three years and how you should prepare.

Artificial intelligence will make phishing essentially indistinguishable from legitimate communication at the technical level. By 2027, AI-generated emails will be grammatically perfect, contextually appropriate, and personalized using information scraped from social media and data breaches. Voice cloning will be routine in vishing attacks.

Video deepfakes will become common in business email compromise targeting executives.

The defense against AI-enhanced phishing isn't better detection. You won't reliably detect it. The defense is better verification procedures through independent channels. The two-second pause matters more than ever. Family code phrases become critical when voices and videos can be faked. Procedural verification becomes more important than appearance-based verification.

Data breaches will continue to accelerate in frequency and scale. By 2027, assume that every major company you've done business with will experience at least one significant breach within a three-year period. Your email addresses, passwords, personal information, financial history, health records, and biometric data will all be compromised at some point.

The defense isn't preventing breaches at companies you have no control over. It's ensuring that each breach exposes only that specific account and doesn't cascade into compromise of everything else. Unique passwords through password managers. Broad MFA implementation. Credit freezes that block new account fraud. Rapid breach response when notifications arrive. These defenses turn breaches from catastrophic compromises into minor inconveniences.

Deepfake technology will create authentication challenges that current systems aren't designed to handle. When voices, faces, and behavioral patterns can all be faked convincingly, traditional identity verification breaks down. Expect to see more fraud targeting financial institutions, remote work authentication, and family emergency scams using cloned voices and faces.

The defense is establishing out-of-band verification methods that deepfakes can't bypass. Family code phrases that only real family members know. Predetermined authentication procedures at work that don't rely on recognizing someone's face or voice. Callback procedures using known contact information rather than numbers provided in the communication.

Privacy regulations will continue to expand globally but enforcement will remain uneven. California, Colorado, Virginia, and other states have comprehensive privacy laws. The European Union has GDPR. Other countries are implementing similar frameworks. These give you more rights over your personal data, but exercising those rights requires understanding what they are and actively invoking them.

The defense is staying informed about your privacy rights in your jurisdiction, using data broker opt-out procedures regularly since rights without action provide no protection, and supporting privacy legislation in your state that strengthens consumer protections. Privacy rights are strongest where consumers actively exercise them and demand enforcement.

Quantum computing may eventually threaten current encryption methods, though this is further out than 2027. When quantum computers become powerful enough, they could potentially break the encryption protecting password managers, financial transactions, and secure communications. This isn't an immediate threat, but it's on the horizon.

The defense is waiting until the security community provides clear guidance on quantum-resistant encryption methods, being prepared to migrate to new encryption standards when they become necessary and not panicking about theoretical future threats while neglecting current practical security. Quantum computing threats are years away from practical exploitation. Current threats are here now.

Social media will become an even more important intelligence source for targeted attacks. Every post, photo, check-in, and like provides information attackers use to personalize phishing and social engineering. The tension between sharing your life publicly and maintaining security will intensify.

The defense is privacy settings that limit public visibility of sensitive information, regular privacy audits to catch platform changes that reset your settings, consideration before posting details that could enable social engineering, and understanding that convenience and visibility always trade off against security. You choose where on that spectrum you want to be based on your risk tolerance.

The specific tools I've recommended throughout this book will evolve. Password managers will add features or change business models. Breach monitoring services will improve or decline. Credit freeze procedures will be streamlined or complicated by regulatory changes. Network security tools will advance with new capabilities.

The defense isn't loyalty to specific tools but rather understanding the functions those tools perform and migrating to better options as they emerge. Don't stick with a tool because it's what I recommended in 2026 if something significantly better becomes available in 2028. Evaluate tools based on current capabilities, not historical recommendations.

This is why I release updated annual editions of Fortress Shield. Not to sell more books, though I appreciate readers who buy updated versions, but because annual updates are genuinely necessary. Each edition covers new threats that emerged since the previous year, updated tool recommendations as services improve or decline, revised legal guidance as laws and enforcement priorities shift, and updated procedures as best practices evolve.

Chapter 17: Closing Orders

Getting the new edition each year, reading the "What's Changed" summary chapter, and updating your battle plans accordingly keeps your fortress adapted to current threats rather than last year's threats.

Your Final Orders: The Mission Continues

We've reached the end of this book but not the end of your security practice. The mission continues. The vigilance continues. The discipline continues. Let me give you your final orders, the standing guidance that carries you forward from here.

First, you will maintain what you have built. The fortress you've constructed through sixteen chapters is strong but requires upkeep. You will follow the sustainment battle rhythm without exception. You will schedule all maintenance tasks on your calendar and honor those commitments as you would any other important obligation. You will not convince yourself that maintenance is optional when life gets busy. The busier you are, the more important maintenance becomes because that's when attackers exploit neglect.

Second, you will adapt to evolving threats without abandoning foundational principles. New attack methods will emerge that I haven't covered in this book. New technologies will create vulnerabilities I didn't anticipate. You will learn about these new threats through news, security bulletins, community discussion, and annual book updates. You will adapt your specific procedures while maintaining the core principles of strong passwords, multi-factor authentication, credit protection, network security, monitoring, and verification.

Third, you will help others build their own fortresses. Security is not competitive. Your neighbor being more secure doesn't make you less secure. In fact, the opposite is true. The more people in your community understand these principles, the safer everyone becomes. You will teach your family. You will help your friends. You will share what you've learned with colleagues and neighbors. You will contribute to collective defense rather than hoarding knowledge.

Fourth, you will practice humility about your own security. You are not now immune to compromise simply because you've read this book and implemented its recommendations. Sophisticated attacks will get through. Phishing will eventually fool you despite your best efforts to recognize it. Breaches will expose your information despite strong passwords and MFA. You will respond to these incidents with the procedures you've learned rather than panic or despair. You will learn from each close call and each compromise to strengthen your defenses going forward.

Fifth, you will maintain perspective about security's place in your life. Security is important but it's not everything. It serves your life rather than dominating it. The goal is not paranoid hypervigilance where you're constantly anxious about digital threats. The goal is confident practice where security is routine, manageable, and integrated into normal life. You brush your teeth daily without anxiety about cavities. You check your mirrors when driving without fear of accidents. Security maintenance should feel the same, important routine practice that enables you to live confidently.

Sixth, you will stay connected to the Fortress Shield community. The battle plans in the appendices include information for joining the online community forum where readers share experiences, warn about new threats, ask questions, and support each other. You will participate in that community, whether actively posting or passively reading. You will contribute when you have knowledge to share. You will ask when you need help. You will understand that security is a team effort and communities that defend together succeed together.

Chapter 17: Closing Orders

Seventh, you will get the annual edition when it releases each January. This isn't just a sales pitch. Security information ages rapidly. Threat landscapes shift. Tools evolve. Legal frameworks change. The 2026 edition you're reading now will still contain valuable principles in 2030, but its specific tool recommendations and procedure details will be outdated. Annual updates keep your knowledge current. Consider the annual edition an ongoing investment in your security education, like annual training in any professional field.

Eighth, you will trust the process even when results aren't immediately visible. Security maintenance prevents problems you'll never know about. You'll never meet the criminals who moved on to easier targets because your defenses were too strong. You'll never see the phishing attempts your spam filter caught before they reached your inbox. You'll never know about the identity theft attempts blocked by your frozen credit. The absence of crisis is itself proof of success, even though it's tempting to interpret lack of visible threats as evidence that threats don't exist.

Ninth, you will celebrate your security successes without becoming complacent. When you catch a phishing attempt before clicking. When you identify a compromised password from a breach alert within hours. When your verification procedures prevent a fraud attempt. When your family member avoids a scam because of your training. These are victories worth acknowledging. But each victory should reinforce your practice rather than convince you that you can relax your vigilance.

Tenth, you will forgive yourself for inevitable mistakes without abandoning the system. You will eventually click a phishing link you should have caught. You will sometime reuse a password out of convenience. You will occasionally skip a monthly maintenance session because life got overwhelming. These failures don't mean the system doesn't work. They mean you're human. You will recover from each mistake, learn from it, and continue the practice rather than giving up because you weren't perfect.

These are your standing orders. They continue until the end of your digital life, which means effectively forever in the modern world. Security isn't a phase you go through. It's a lifelong practice that protects you and everyone connected to you.

The mission never ends. But unlike military missions that have definite completion points, this mission is sustainable. It doesn't require heroic effort or constant sacrifice. It requires steady, consistent, manageable practice integrated into normal life.

You can do this. Thousands already have. You've made it through 16 intensive chapters of security education. You've built comprehensive defenses layer by layer. You've practiced skills and procedures. You've invested time and effort into protection that will serve you for decades.

Now you maintain what you've built. That's the mission. It's not glamorous. It won't feel dramatic most of the time. But it works. It protects you. It gives you confidence. It enables you to use technology without fear.

The fortress stands. Your mission is to keep it standing.

After Action: Five Years from Now

Let me end where we began, with a vision of your future. Not the worst-case scenario if you ignore everything in this book. Not the best-case scenario if you implement everything perfectly and never make mistakes. But the realistic scenario if you follow the core guidance consistently with normal human imperfection.

It's five years from now. You're having coffee on a Saturday morning when your phone buzzes with a breach notification.

Chapter 17: Closing Orders

One of your passwords appeared in a newly discovered breach database. You open your password manager, check which account was affected, verify the password is unique and wasn't reused anywhere, and change it to a new random 24-character string. Total time: three minutes. No panic. No crisis. Just routine incident response.

Later that day, your elderly parent calls. They received a phone call claiming to be from Medicare saying their benefits were suspended. They almost gave their Social Security number to the caller. But they remembered your training about verification through separate channels. They hung up and called you instead to confirm it was a scam. You praise their good judgment and remind them they did exactly right. Another successful defense because you taught your family to think critically about unexpected communications.

During the week, your teenage daughter shows you a message on Instagram. Someone claiming to be a modeling agent wants to schedule a photoshoot and needs her personal information to send a contract. She's excited but also skeptical because you've taught her about social media scams. Together you verify the agency is real by looking them up independently and calling their published number. Turns out it is legitimate, a real opportunity. But she knew to verify first, and now she trusts the opportunity because verification confirmed it.

At work, your colleague mentions she's about to wire a large payment to a vendor based on an email request from the CEO. You ask her if she verified the request through another channel. She hasn't. You suggest calling the CEO directly just to confirm. She does. The CEO never sent that email. Your intervention just saved your company from business email compromise that would have cost tens of thousands of dollars. Your security awareness protected more than just yourself.

That evening, you run your monthly security check. Password manager health report shows three weak passwords from old accounts you rarely use. You update them. Financial statements show a $2.14 charge from a company you don't recognize. You call your credit card company and report it as potentially fraudulent. They investigate and confirm it was a test charge before a larger fraudulent attempt. They issue a new card. Crisis avoided because you caught it early.

Over the weekend, you help your neighbor set up a password manager after they mentioned being overwhelmed by trying to remember dozens of passwords. You show them the basics, help them migrate their first 10 accounts, and explain how breach monitoring works. They're grateful and relieved. You've extended protection beyond your own household.

This is your life five years from now if you maintain what this book has taught you. Not stress-free, there are still threats and incidents. Not effortless, you still do regular maintenance. But manageable, confident, routine. Security is simply how you operate, like checking your mirrors before changing lanes or looking both ways before crossing the street. Important habits that keep you safe without dominating your thoughts or creating constant anxiety.

You sleep well because you know the current state of your security. You travel confidently because your monitoring systems alert you to problems. You use technology fully because your defenses protect you. You help others because you understand these principles well enough to teach them.

You've been maintaining your fortress for five years. You've caught dozens of problems early before they became crises. You've avoided several major compromises that would have happened without your vigilance. You've taught at least 10 people in your circle, who've taught others in turn, creating ripples of protection through your community.

Chapter 17: Closing Orders

Your total time investment over five years is about 250 hours. That's less than one hour per week averaged across the entire period. In exchange for those 250 hours, you've prevented thousands or tens of thousands of dollars in fraud, protected your identity and reputation, maintained peace of mind, and contributed to your community's security.

Was it worth it? You already know the answer.

Closing Thoughts from Chief Palmer

Thirty years ago, I took an oath to support and defend. That oath technically expired when I retired from the Air Force in 2024. But the commitment behind it never expires.

For three decades, I defended critical military systems against sophisticated adversaries with massive resources. I protected nuclear command facilities. I secured classified networks. I built defenses for installations that could not be allowed to fail under any circumstances.

The stakes were different then. National security. Military operations. Lives of service members depend on the security of systems I was responsible for protecting.

But in retirement, I've learned that protecting your family's financial security, your identity, your ability to operate in the digital world without fear or compromise is also high stakes. Different scale, perhaps. But it is not less important to the people whose lives are affected.

You've invested time in reading this book. You've learned principles I spent 30 years refining. You've built defenses that would have impressed my military commanders. You've taken responsibility for your own security and the security of those you care about.

That matters. It matters more than you might realize.

Every person who implements these principles is one fewer victim for criminals to exploit. Every family that maintains these defenses is one more network of people who can recognize and resist manipulation. Every community that adopts these practices becomes harder to attack and easier to defend.

You're not just protecting yourself. You're contributing to collective defense that makes society marginally more secure for everyone.

I'm proud of you for making it this far. Reading 17 chapters of dense security instruction isn't easy. Implementing the recommendations is even harder. Committing to maintenance for years or decades is hardest of all.

But you've started. That's the crucial first step.

Now you continue. Daily habits. Weekly checks. Monthly maintenance. Quarterly reviews. Annual updates. Year after year. Adapting to new threats. Teaching others. Learning from mistakes. Celebrating successes.

The mission never ends. But you're equipped for it now. You have knowledge, tools, procedures, community, and confidence.

Your fortress stands. Keep it standing.

That's your mission. That's your responsibility. That's your contribution to a more secure world.

Chapter 17: Closing Orders

Thank you for your service in defending your family. The mission continues.

Fortress Shield 2026. Mission Briefing Complete. Sustainment Underway.

Good luck. Stay vigilant. Stay safe.

Chief Master Sergeant Alan Palmer, USAF (Ret.) January 2026

Mission Complete

You have reached the end of formal instruction. Everything that follows in the appendices is reference material, battle plans, templates, worksheets, and resources for ongoing practice. You now possess comprehensive knowledge of personal digital security comparable to what I taught airmen protecting military facilities. You understand the threat landscape and how criminals operate. You've built layered defenses that protect passwords, accounts, credit, network, devices, identity, communications, and family.

You know how to detect breaches through monitoring and alerts. You can recover from compromises using documented procedures. You understand your legal rights and how to enforce them. You recognize phishing and social engineering across all attack vectors. You have maintenance schedules that keep your fortress effective as threats evolve.

Most importantly, you understand that security is ongoing practice rather than completed project. You have realistic expectations about what protection means, it's not invulnerability but rather rapid detection, contained damage, and swift recovery when attacks succeed.

You're ready. Not perfect, perfection is impossible. But prepared, equipped, and capable of sustained defense.

Your Next Actions

This week, schedule all your maintenance tasks on your actual calendar with reminders. First Saturday monthly maintenance. First weekend of January, April, July, October quarterly reviews. First two weeks of January annual comprehensive inspection. Make these scheduled commitments you honor like dentist appointments or work meetings.

Review the battle plan appendices and organize them for quick reference. Create a digital folder on your computer. Print critical reference materials for physical backup. Store freeze PINs and recovery codes in your password manager. Make sure your family knows where to find these resources.

Run your first post-instruction security check using the complete ORI worksheet from Chapter 12. Document your current security posture honestly. Identify any gaps or areas of weakness. Create a plan to address them over the next month. Schedule your second ORI for three months from now.

Teach one person this month about security using principles from this book. Your parent, your child, your sibling, your friend, your neighbor, your colleague. Pick the person who needs it most and who will be most receptive. Start simple. Show them one meaningful improvement they can make this week. Build from there.

Join the Fortress Shield community forum using information in the appendices. Introduce yourself. Share what you've implemented. Ask questions about anything that's unclear. Read recent posts to see what threats other readers are encountering. Contribute when you have knowledge to share.

Order or preorder the 2027 annual edition when it becomes available next January. Mark your calendar to check for it. Updated editions keep your knowledge current with evolving threats and changing tools.

Chapter 17: Closing Orders

Share one lesson from this book on social media or with your broader circle. Not the entire book, just one concept that clicked for you. The two-second pause. Credit freezes. Phishing recognition. Maintenance discipline. Whatever resonated most. Your post might protect someone who needs to hear it.

You are now a defender. Act like one.

Reference Materials

The appendices that follow contain specialized guidance for helping others implement Fortress Shield principles:

Appendix A: Guided Setup for Helping Parents and Elders provides step-by-step instructions adapted for less technical users. This appendix includes simplified language and patient procedures for teaching elderly relatives, large-print checklists and verification procedures they can follow independently, strategies for overcoming resistance and building confidence, and common pitfalls when helping older adults with technology.

Appendix B: Teen Starter Pack: Essential Digital Defense offers age-appropriate security training for teenagers including social media privacy fundamentals, recognizing scams targeting their demographic, managing peer pressure around account sharing, and building healthy digital security habits early.

Appendix C: Fortress Shield Reference Materials contains quick-reference guides for common security tasks, one-page emergency response procedures you can print and store, key terminology and definitions, and recommended reading for deeper understanding of specific topics.

These appendices supplement the main text with specialized guidance for teaching security to specific groups who need adapted approaches.

Strategic Defense Plans: Your Free Companion Resource

The practical implementation materials you need to execute everything in this book are available as a separate free PDF download titled **Strategic Defense Plans**. This companion resource is deliberately separated from the main book for three important reasons that serve you better.

First, the Strategic Defense Plans PDF contains live URLs, specific tool instructions, fillable forms, and printable checklists that don't work well in audiobook or e-reader formats. By keeping these materials in a separate PDF, you can access them on your computer or print them while listening to or reading the main book on any device. You get the best format for each type of content.

Second, security information ages rapidly. URLs change. Tools evolve. Forms get updated. While I update the main Fortress Shield book annually every January, the Strategic Defense Plans PDF receives semi-annual updates in January and July. You get current procedures and working links twice per year without buying a new book. When a major tool changes its setup process or a data broker changes its opt-out procedure, you receive updated instructions within onths rather than waiting a full year.

Third, the semi-annual updates include threat alerts covering new scam techniques that have emerged in the past six months, tools that have improved or declined and should be reconsidered, legal changes affecting your rights and procedures, and real-world case studies from the Fortress Shield community. These briefings keep you current with the evolving battlefield without overwhelming you with constant notifications.

Chapter 17: Closing Orders

What Strategic Defense Plans Contains:

Battle Plan Quick Reference Guides provide step-by-step procedures for every major security task including password manager setup for Bitwarden, 1Password and alternatives, MFA implementation with authenticator apps and backup codes, credit freeze procedures for all three bureaus with current URLs, network security configuration for common routers, breach response protocols for different compromise types, and data broker opt-out procedures with current submission forms.

Templates and Forms give you ready-to-use documents including credit dispute letters citing FCRA, debt collector cease communication letters citing FDCPA, CFPB complaint forms with proper formatting, attorney consultation checklists, breach documentation logs, and family code phrase worksheets.

Maintenance Resources include calendars and checklists covering daily security habit reminders, weekly network scan procedures, monthly password manager health check guides, quarterly ORI worksheets, and annual comprehensive review templates.

Contact Lists and URLs provide current information for Consumer Financial Protection Bureau complaint portal, state Attorney General consumer protection offices, credit bureau freeze and dispute contacts, Have I Been Pwned and breach monitoring services, recommended password managers with affiliate-free links, and network security tools with setup tutorials.

Family Training Materials adapted for different groups including phishing recognition exercises for children, social media security guides for teenagers, comprehensive training presentations for adults, and simplified procedures for elderly relatives with large-print formatting.

Emergency Response Procedures offering one-page quick reference guides for account compromise, financial fraud, malware infection, identity theft, and phishing incidents you can print and store with emergency documents.

How to Get Your Free Strategic Defense Plans PDF:

Visit **FortressShieldBook.com/plans** and enter your email address. You will receive immediate download access to the current Strategic Defense Plans PDF. Your email address joins the Fortress Shield community list, which receives semi-annual updates every January and July with the latest version of Strategic Defense Plans including updated URLs, revised procedures, and current threat briefings. You also receive announcements when new annual editions of Fortress Shield are published, typically each January, so you know when updated guidance is available.

I will never spam you. I will never sell your email address. You will receive exactly two security updates per year plus annual book announcements, nothing more. You can unsubscribe anytime with one click. This is professional security communication, not marketing noise.

The Strategic Defense Plans PDF is approximately 75 to 100 pages of pure reference material. Forms you can fill out. Checklists you can print. URLs you can click. Step-by-step instructions with screenshots where helpful. Everything is designed for practical application rather than reading.

Download it before you start implementing it. Print the sections you need. Keep it accessible on your computer. Use it alongside this book as you build your fortress. Update it twice per year when new versions arrive.

Why This Matters:

I've watched too many people read security books, understand the principles, but fail at implementation because they didn't have the practical tools to execute. They knew they should

Chapter 17: Closing Orders

freeze their credit but didn't have the URLs or phone numbers. They understood password managers but couldn't figure out which one to choose or how to set it up. They wanted to dispute fraudulent charges but didn't know what language to use in the letter.

Strategic Defense Plans solves this implementation gap. Every procedure in the main book has a corresponding battle plan in the companion PDF. Every concept has a practical checklist. Every template you need is included and ready to use.

Don't skip this resource. It's not optional bonus material. It's the operational component of your security system. The main book is your training manual. Strategic Defense Plans is your operations manual. You need both.

Semi-Annual Updates Keep You Current:

The January update, delivered in the first week of January, covers the previous year's major threats and provides updated tools and procedures for the new year. It reviews significant breaches from the past 12 months and lessons learned. It announces the new annual book edition and summarizes what has changed. It updates all URLs, forms, and contact information for the current year.

The July update, delivered the first week of July, covers mid-year threat landscape changes and provides urgent updates that can't wait until January. It includes new phishing techniques observed in the first half of the year. It revises tool recommendations if significant changes occurred. It offers case studies and success stories from community members.

Each update is five to ten pages of focused, actionable information. No filler. No marketing. Just current intelligence about threats and defenses. Read it in 15 minutes twice per year and stay current with evolving security landscape.

Fortress Shield - 2026 Edition

Get Started Now:

Go to **FortressShieldBook.com/plans** right now, before you forget, before you move on to something else before you convince yourself you'll do it later. Enter your email. Download Strategic Defense Plans. You'll have it immediately.

Then come back and finish this chapter, knowing that all the practical implementation tools are waiting for you when you're ready to execute.

Your fortress stands. Strategic Defense Plans are the blueprint that keeps it standing.

Next: The remaining sections of this chapter continue with practical guidance for sustained security practice, but first, ensure you have the tools you need. Visit **FortressShieldBook.com/plans** now if you haven't already. I'll wait.

Your fortress stands. These are the maintenance manuals that keep it standing.

Final Note: If this book helped you, if these principles protected you, if this knowledge gave you confidence, share it. Security knowledge becomes more valuable the more widely it's distributed. Every person you help becomes part of the collective defense that makes everyone safer.

Thank you for trusting me to teach you. Stay safe out there. And, if you want to thank me...For an Author, nothing says thank you more than providing a review where you purchased this material. Reading reviews of my work truly makes my day, and I read every one.

Chapter 17: Closing Orders

Fortress Shield: The Civilian's Guide to Digital Defense by Chief Master Sergeant Alan Palmer, USAF (Ret.) 2026 Edition

"The mission never ends. The vigilance continues. The fortress stands."

Appendix A: Guided Setup for Helping Parents and Elders

Mission Time: 90 minutes | Essential

Mission Overview

Objective: Assist a parent, grandparent, or older friend who finds technology overwhelming but needs reliable digital protection.

Supplies Required: Printed copy of this guide, their devices including phone, computer, and tablet, plus access to their email and phone for receiving verification codes.

Mission Prep: Setting Expectations

Before touching any device, have this conversation. Tell them this isn't about being tech-savvy, and remind them that these criminals fool cybersecurity experts regularly. Explain that you're making them a harder target so criminals move on to someone else. Let them know you'll show them each step, and they don't need to remember the technical details. Most importantly, assure them that when they have questions later, they should call you because that's what you're here for.

Print and bring this complete guide for their reference, a blank emergency contact sheet you'll fill in together, and simple instruction cards for everyday tasks they'll need to perform.

Step 1: Password Manager Setup

⏱ 20 minutes | Essential

Objective: Establish a single master credential and teach confidence with the tool.

Start by explaining what a password manager does in terms they understand. It's a secure digital vault that remembers all their passwords so they only need to remember one master password. Like having one key that opens a safe containing all their other keys. This makes their accounts more secure while actually making their life easier.

Choose Bitwarden because it's free, reliable, and has excellent customer support. Open a browser and go to bitwarden.com together. Click "Get Started" and walk them through creating an account using their primary email address, the one they check most often.

Creating the master password is the most important step. Don't rush this. Help them choose something memorable but strong. A good approach is combining three or four random words with a number and symbol they'll remember. "Coffee!Mountain!Sunrise!2024" works well. Have them write it on paper temporarily while they practice typing it several times. Once they can type it from memory reliably, destroy the written copy together.

Install the browser extension by clicking the extension icon in their browser, searching for Bitwarden, and clicking "Add to Browser." Then install the mobile app from their phone's app store. Show them how to log in on both devices using their master password.

Test the system with an account they use frequently, probably email or Facebook. Have them log out of that account, then use Bitwarden to log back in. Watch them do it themselves rather than doing it for them. This builds confidence through actual practice.

Set up recovery options carefully. Add your phone number or email as a trusted emergency contact. Save the recovery codes in a physical location they can access, like the same drawer where they keep their insurance papers. Write down where these recovery codes are stored on their emergency contact sheet.

Before moving to the next step, confirm they can log into Bitwarden on their phone and computer without your help. Have them demonstrate it while you watch. This verification prevents problems later.

Step 2: Critical Account Updates

🕐 **30 minutes | Essential**

Objective: Secure the three most important accounts: email, banking, and primary social media.

Start with email because it controls password resets for everything else. Log into their email account and go to security settings. The location varies by provider, but look for "Settings" then "Security" or "Privacy and Security." Change the password using Bitwarden to generate a strong random password. Have Bitwarden save this new password immediately. Enable two-factor authentication if available, using their phone number to receive codes. Save backup codes in Bitwarden's secure notes section.

Move to their primary bank account next. Many older adults use the same bank they've used for decades and trust it completely, which makes them particularly vulnerable to phishing that impersonates their bank. Log into their online banking portal and navigate to security settings. Change the password using Bitwarden to generate a new one. Enable two-factor authentication, usually called "enhanced security" or "secure access" by banks. Save the new credentials in Bitwarden under a clear name like "First National Bank Login."

Verify they can log into both email and banking using Bitwarden before continuing. Have them log out and back in on their own while you watch. This repetition builds muscle memory.

If they use Facebook, Twitter, or another social platform regularly, secure that account too. Go to account settings, find security options, change the password through Bitwarden, and enable two-factor authentication if available. Save everything in Bitwarden with a clear, recognizable name.

For each account, take a moment to review recent activity if the platform provides it. Check for login locations they don't recognize or devices they don't remember using. If anything looks suspicious, log those devices out immediately and note it for monitoring.

Appendix A: Guided Setup for Helping Parents/Elders

Step 3: Credit Freezes

⏱ 25 minutes | Essential

Objective: Prevent criminals from opening credit accounts in their name.

Explain credit freezes in plain terms. A credit freeze locks their credit file so even they can't open new credit accounts without first unfreezing it. This stops identity thieves from opening credit cards, loans, or other accounts in their name. It doesn't affect their existing credit cards or loans at all. Those keep working normally. It also doesn't hurt their credit score. It just prevents new accounts from being opened.

Tell them they'll need to do this at three separate websites, one for each credit bureau. Yes, it's annoying that there are three different companies. Yes, they all should talk to each other but they don't. That's just how the system works.

Start with Equifax at equifax.com. Look for the link that says "Freeze Your Credit" or similar language. They'll need to create an account first if they don't have one. Use their primary email address and let Bitwarden generate a strong password. Save the login immediately in Bitwarden. They'll need to provide their Social Security number, date of birth, and address. This is legitimate and necessary. Walk through the freeze setup together. When it's complete, Equifax will provide a PIN number. Save this PIN in Bitwarden in the secure notes for the Equifax account. Without this PIN, unfreezing later becomes very difficult.

Repeat the entire process at Experian.com. Create account, use Bitwarden for the password, provide verification information, activate the freeze, and save the PIN in Bitwarden. The process is similar but the website layout is different. Be patient.

Repeat once more at TransUnion.com. Same process, different website. Create account, generate password, activate freeze, save PIN.

After completing all three, verify with them that each freeze is active by logging back into each site and checking freeze status. All three should show "Frozen" or "Active Freeze" or similar language.

Explain what happens when they need credit in the future. If they want to apply for a credit card, car loan, or mortgage, they'll need to temporarily unfreeze their credit first. They log into the bureau's website, enter their PIN, and unfreeze for a specific time period like one day or one week. After the credit check is complete, they can refreeze immediately. The whole process takes about five minutes once they're familiar with it.

Write down on their emergency contact sheet that their credit is frozen at all three bureaus and the login information is in their password manager. This reminds them months from now when they've forgotten about the freezes.

Step 4: Monitoring Setup

⏱ **10 minutes | Recommended.**

Objective: Enable breach alerts and continuous awareness.

Explain what breach monitoring does. Companies get hacked all the time. When that happens, email addresses and passwords are stolen and shared online. Breach monitoring services watch for their information in these stolen databases and alert them immediately so they can change passwords before criminals use them.

Go to haveibeenpwned.com together. This is a free service run by a respected security professional. Enter their primary email address in the search box and click "pwned?" The results will probably show several breaches. This is normal. Almost everyone's email appears in at least one breach.

Review the breach results together without causing panic. Each breach shows what information was exposed. Usually it's email addresses and passwords. Sometimes it includes other information like phone numbers or dates of birth. For each breach shown, check if they still use that password anywhere. If yes, change it immediately using Bitwarden. If no, make a note but don't worry about it.

Subscribe to breach notifications by clicking "notify me" and entering their email address. They'll receive an email asking them to confirm the subscription. Open their email together and click the confirmation link. Now they'll receive alerts whenever their email appears in a new breach.

Set up their phone to notify them about these emails. Go to their email app settings and make sure notifications are enabled for their primary email account. When they receive a breach alert, they should change that password within 24 hours.

Step 5: Basic Habits Training

⏲ 15 minutes | Essential

Objective: Reinforce safe online behavior through practice.

The most important habit is the two-second pause before clicking any link. When they receive an email, text, or message with a link, they should pause for two full seconds before clicking. During that pause, ask themselves three questions. First, was I expecting this message? Second, does the sender's address look legitimate? Third, if there's any doubt at all, can I go to the website directly instead of clicking this link?

Practice this together with real examples from their inbox. Find a legitimate email from their bank and examine it together. Look at the sender's email address carefully. Hover over any links without clicking to see where they actually go. Point out that legitimate emails from their bank come from addresses ending in their bank's actual domain name.

Then show them a phishing example if there are any in their spam folder. Point out the red flags. Generic greeting like "Dear Customer" instead of their name. Urgent language trying to scare them into acting quickly. Links that go to weird domains that aren't the actual company. Grammar or spelling errors that a real company wouldn't make.

Create a simple verification rule for them. If any email or text asks them to log into an account, take action on an account, or provide sensitive information, they should not click links in the message. Instead, they should open their browser, go to the company's website directly by typing the URL or using a bookmark, log in through the real site, and check if there's actually a problem. Real problems will show up when they log in the legitimate way. Fake problems only exist in phishing emails.

Practice this verification process with their bank. Show them how to bookmark their bank's login page. Then if they receive an email claiming to be from their bank, they can click their bookmark instead of clicking any link in the email.

Teach them about phone scams too. If someone calls claiming to be from the IRS, Social Security Administration, their bank, or any government agency and asking for personal information or demanding immediate payment, that's a scam. Real government agencies and banks don't operate that way. They should hang up and call the organization back using a phone number from their insurance card, bank statement, or official website. Never use a phone number the caller provides.

Appendix A: Guided Setup for Helping Parents/Elders

Walk through one practice scenario. "Let's say you get an email that says your Amazon account has been compromised and you need to verify your password immediately by clicking this link. What do you do?" Guide them through the correct response: pause, recognize the urgency as a red flag, don't click the link, open Amazon directly by typing amazon.com or clicking a bookmark, log in through the real site, check if there's actually a problem.

Follow-Up Schedule

Week 1 Check-In: Call them or visit within a week to confirm the password manager is working and they're using it successfully. Verify they can access their email and bank accounts without problems. Ask if they've had any suspicious emails or calls and how they handled them. This check-in catches any setup problems early while you can still fix them easily.

Month 1 Review: After a month, the password manager should feel more automatic. They should be comfortable logging in and trusting it to remember their passwords. If they're still struggling, schedule another in-person session to practice more.

Month 3 Confidence Check: By three months, they should feel confident enough to help others recognize scams. If they're sharing their knowledge with friends or warning family members about suspicious emails, the training worked.

Emergency Contact Sheet

Fill this out together and print it. They should keep it with other important documents like insurance papers and medical information.

Fortress Shield - 2026 Edition

Emergency Contact Sheet
(Fill Out Together)

Mission Purpose: Ensure a quick, accurate response if a cybersecurity or identity-related emergency occurs.

Category	Contact Name / Department	Phone Number	Email or Website	Notes / Account Info
Primary Tech Support				
Secondary Tech Support (Family / Friend)				
Bank Fraud Hotline				
Credit Card Fraud Hotline				
Credit Bureau – Equifax				
Credit Bureau – Experian				
Credit Bureau – TransUnion				
Password Manager Support				
Email Provider Support				
Mobile Carrier Support				
Internet Provider Support				
Local Police (Non-Emergency)				
FTC Identity Theft Hotline				
Social Security Administration (Fraud)				
Other Important Contacts				

- Emergency Instructions:

- Keep this sheet printed and stored in a visible, safe location (inside a folder or desk drawer).

- Update phone numbers annually.

- Never store passwords on this sheet — only contact references.

- When a breach or suspicious event occurs, call your Primary Tech Support first.

Appendix A: Guided Setup for Helping Parents/Elders

What to Do If:

Suspicious email or text: Don't click anything. Call your primary contact above before taking action.

Can't log into account: Open password manager and look up the correct password. If still having trouble, call your primary contact.

Receive call asking for personal information: Hang up. Call the organization back using a number from your official statement or card.

Think you clicked something bad: Disconnect from internet immediately. Call your primary contact for help.

Success Indicators

You'll know the setup worked when you observe these signs over time. After the first week, they log in using their password manager without calling you for help and they feel calm rather than anxious about online accounts. After the first month, using the password manager feels automatic and they're confidently accessing their accounts daily. After three months, they're sharing scam warnings with friends and helping others recognize suspicious emails. That's when you know they've internalized the training and become part of the collective defense.

When They Get Stuck

These are the most common problems you'll hear about and how to solve them quickly over the phone.

If they say they can't remember their master password, remind them where they wrote it down during setup. If they destroyed that note, use the recovery process you set up with your email as the trusted contact. Walk them through account recovery step by step. This is why you saved recovery codes in a physical location.

If the password manager isn't working, ask them to check if the browser extension is enabled. Sometimes browser updates disable extensions. In their browser, click the extensions icon and make sure Bitwarden shows as active. If it's disabled, click to enable it.

If they're locked out of an account, retrieve the password from Bitwarden and try logging in together over the phone. If that doesn't work, use the account's password reset process. Get the reset email, click the reset link, let Bitwarden generate a new password, and save it.

If they're getting too many breach alerts and feeling overwhelmed, help them prioritize. Only worry about breaches for accounts they still use actively. Old accounts they haven't touched in years can be ignored or closed entirely. Focus their attention on protecting active accounts.

Emotional Support Guidelines

Remember that technology anxiety is real and often connected to feelings of aging or becoming irrelevant. Your approach matters as much as the technical instruction.

Tell them regularly that this is complicated stuff and they're doing great. Security challenges everyone, including experts. Tell them everyone makes mistakes, even you, and mistakes are how we learn. Remind them that you're helping because they're important to you and helping them stay safe matters to you personally. This emotional support builds confidence as much as the technical training does.

Mission Complete

The objective isn't perfection. It's confidence. If they feel calmer about using technology, safer in their online activities, and willing to call you when they're unsure about something, the mission has succeeded. They don't need to understand how everything works. They just need to trust the system you've built together and know you're there to help when needed.

Appendix B: Teen Starter Pack - Essential Digital Defense

⏱ 20 minutes | Essential

Reality check: you're more likely to have your identity stolen than crash your car, but nobody teaches digital self-defense in driver's ed. These four moves take just 20 minutes total and prevent most of the problems you'll face online.

Move 1: Password Manager Setup

⏱ **5 minutes | Essential**

Threat: Weak, reused passwords make you an easy target. One compromised password means multiple compromised accounts.

Defense: Let trusted software remember impossible-to-crack passwords for you. Your brain remembers one master password. The software remembers everything else.

Execute: Go to bitwarden.com and sign up with your email address. When creating your master password, make it memorable but secure. Something like Coffee!Mountain!Sunrise!2024 works because it combines random words with a number and symbol you'll remember. Install the app on your phone and the browser extension on your computer. Test it by saving your Instagram login, signing out completely, then signing back in using Bitwarden to autofill your credentials.

Result: Every account now has its own uncrackable password you never have to remember. Each password is 20-plus random characters that would take millions of years to crack. But you only need to remember one.

Pro Tip: Use your fingerprint to unlock the password manager. It's faster than typing and safer because biometrics can't be phished or stolen like passwords can.

Move 2: Freeze Your Credit

⏱ 5 minutes | Essential

Threat: Criminals can open loans or credit cards in your name using stolen personal information. They rack up debt, you deal with collections and damaged credit for years.

Defense: Lock your credit files so even you need permission to open new accounts. Identity thieves can have your Social Security number, your address, your mother's maiden name, and still can't open accounts because your credit is frozen solid.

Execute: Visit Equifax.com and create an account. Enable the credit freeze through their security settings. Save your login credentials in Bitwarden immediately. Repeat this entire process at Experian.com and TransUnion.com. Yes, you have to do all three separately. Yes, it's annoying. Yes, it's worth it.

Result: Identity thieves cannot open new accounts in your name even if they have your personal data. The fraud attempt fails at the credit check stage before any account is created.

When needed later: Temporarily unfreeze online in about 30 seconds when you need to apply for credit, then re-freeze after

Appendix B: Teen Starter Pack

the application goes through. The whole process is quick once you're familiar with it.

Move 3: Breach Alerts

⏲ 3 minutes | Essential.

Threat: Companies are constantly hacked. Stolen emails and passwords circulate on criminal forums for months before you find out. Meanwhile, attackers are testing your credentials on every site they can think of.

Defense: Receive alerts within hours when a data breach includes your accounts. Fast notification means you can change passwords before criminals have time to exploit them.

Execute: Visit haveibeenpwned.com and enter your email address to check for breaches. You'll probably find several. This is completely normal and doesn't mean you did anything wrong. It means companies you trusted got hacked and exposed your information. Click "Notify Me" at the top of the page and confirm via email. Now you'll get alerts whenever your email appears in a new breach database. If the results show breaches, change those passwords immediately using your password manager to generate strong random replacements.

Result: You'll know about breaches faster than most criminals can exploit them. The notification-to-action time is measured in hours instead of months.

Move 4: Link Awareness

⏲ 2 minutes to learn | Essential.

Threat: Clicking fake links that steal credentials or install malware. These attacks work because they exploit urgency and trust to bypass your normal caution.

Defense: A two-second pause before clicking any link. That pause interrupts the automatic response and creates space for rational evaluation.

Execute: When you receive any message with a link, pause for two full seconds before clicking. During that pause, ask yourself three questions. Was I expecting this message? Does the sender's actual email address or phone number look legitimate, not just the display name? When in doubt, can I go directly to the website instead of clicking the link?

Result: Phishing fails because you think before you click. The criminals' psychological manipulation doesn't work when you give yourself two seconds to recognize it.

Examples of suspicious messages: "Your account will be closed unless you verify immediately" creates artificial urgency. "Congratulations! You've won a prize you didn't enter" exploits greed. "Emergency: A family member needs money" manipulates fear and concern. All of these use emotional manipulation to bypass rational thinking.

Your New Superpower Status

Let me show you where you stand compared to most college students. Most students use the same password for everything, or maybe three passwords they rotate through. Their credit is wide open to identity thieves who could open accounts tomorrow if they wanted. They click first and think later, assuming that obvious scams are the only real danger. They discover security problems months later when debt collectors start calling or their bank account is empty.

But you're different now. You have unique passwords for everything, generated randomly and impossible to crack. Your credit is locked down like Fort Knox, frozen at all three bureaus. You pause and verify before clicking anything

Appendix B: Teen Starter Pack

suspicious. You get instant alerts about security problems, often before criminals can exploit them.

You're now harder to hack than most adults. You have defenses that many executives and professionals don't have. That's not an exaggeration. Security experts regularly test corporate environments and find senior managers using weak passwords, reused credentials, and no credit monitoring. You're ahead of them.

Monthly Maintenance

⏱ 10 minutes each month | Recommended.

Once per month, probably the first weekend, run through these quick checks to catch problems before they escalate. Open your password manager and check the security report for compromised passwords. If any passwords appear in breaches, change them immediately. Remove yourself from two or three data broker sites by searching your name, finding the sites that list you, and using their opt-out pages. The sites constantly re-add you, so this is ongoing work. Verify your credit freezes are still active every three months by logging into each bureau and checking freeze status.

That's it. Twenty minutes of setup, ten minutes of monthly upkeep, and years of protection. The time investment is minimal. The protection is substantial.

When Friends Ask for Help

Share this starter pack with anyone who wants protection. Every friend you help strengthens your own digital circle because when their accounts are secure, they can't be compromised and used to attack you. Security is collective, not individual.

Here are the questions they'll ask and the answers that work.

"Won't this make life complicated?" Only for the first week while you're getting used to the password manager. After that, it's actually easier than trying to remember passwords or using the same password everywhere. Autofill is faster than typing.

"What if I forget my master password?" Write it on paper until you've memorized it, then destroy the note. Practice typing it several times per day for the first week. By the end of the week, it's muscle memory.

"What if I need credit?" Unfreeze online in about 30 seconds, apply for whatever you need, then re-freeze afterward. Most credit applications happen online anyway, so you can unfreeze, apply, and re-freeze all in one sitting.

"Isn't this paranoid?" Identity theft is more common than car accidents for our age group. According to Javelin Strategy & Research, people under 30 are the most targeted age group for identity fraud. You wear a seatbelt even though you probably won't crash. This is the digital equivalent.

Advanced Moves

Once you've mastered the four essentials and maintained them for three months, consider these additional protections for even stronger security. Use email aliases for different types of accounts. One email for shopping, another for social media, a third for official accounts like banking and taxes. This compartmentalization limits damage when one email is compromised. Enable two-factor authentication everywhere using authenticator apps like Authy or Google Authenticator rather than SMS codes. Apps are more secure because they can't be hijacked through SIM swapping. Use a VPN when traveling or using public Wi-Fi in coffee shops, airports, or hotels. Public networks are easy targets for packet sniffing and man-in-the-middle attacks.

However, start with the four essentials. They prevent most real-world attacks and build the foundation for everything else. Don't overwhelm yourself trying to implement advanced security before mastering the basics.

Success Stories

Jake at Colorado State dealt with malware on his laptop during sophomore year. He learned these principles while cleaning up the infection, implemented everything systematically, and now mentors his entire dorm on cybersecurity. He's the person everyone calls when they get suspicious emails.

Sarah works as a forensic accountant tracking financial crimes. She uses these same principles professionally because they're not just personal security. They're professional security standards that scale from individual protection to corporate defense.

Emma graduated last year after recovering from identity theft her freshman year. Someone opened three credit cards in her name before she even knew what credit freezes were. After spending six months cleaning up that mess, she implemented everything in this guide and now teaches digital safety to incoming freshmen. She turns her painful experience into protection for others.

Your story is next. You're the friend others call when they get suspicious emails or want to protect themselves. You're the person who pauses before clicking and catches phishing that fools others. You're building security habits now that will protect you for decades.

Fortress Shield - 2026 Edition

Mission Complete

Scammers look for easy targets. They want people with reused passwords who click without thinking and have unlocked credit just waiting to be exploited. That's not you anymore. You're a hard target now. You make criminals work too hard for too little payoff, so they move on to easier victims.

Stay sharp. Update monthly. Help your circle stay protected. The fortress stands because you built it.

Appendix C: Fortress Shield Reference Materials

⏱ 1 hour total+ | Essential

OBJECTIVE: ESTABLISH, MAINTAIN, AND RECOVER YOUR DIGITAL DEFENSES USING CLEAR, REPEATABLE PROCEDURES.

Print these pages and keep them handy.

Quick Start Checklist - Week 1 Priority

⏱ **1 hour total | Essential**

Objective: Build your digital perimeter in six days.

Day 1: Foundation (15 minutes)

Start with the password manager because it's the foundation for everything else. Install Bitwarden or Proton Pass on both your phone and computer. Create a strong master password using three or four random words combined with numbers and symbols. Import any passwords your browser has been saving so everything's in one place. Test the system by logging into one account using the password manager. Set up recovery codes and add a trusted contact who can help if you get locked out.

Day 2: Credit Protection (10 minutes)

Freeze your credit at all three bureaus. Go to Equifax.com, Experian.com, and TransUnion.com one at a time. Create accounts and activate freezes. Save each login and PIN in your password manager immediately. Verify you received email confirmations from each bureau showing your freeze is active.

Day 3: Breach Alerts (5 minutes)

Visit haveibeenpwned.com and subscribe for notifications using your primary email address. Understand that alerts are normal responses to external breaches you have no control over. When alerts arrive, respond calmly by changing the affected password within 24 hours.

Day 4: Browser Hardening (10 minutes)

Enable automatic updates in your browser settings so security patches are installed without manual intervention. Turn on privacy settings including HTTPS-Only Mode which forces encrypted connections to websites. Add your password manager extension to your browser so autofill works seamlessly.

Day 5: Scam Awareness (10 minutes)

Practice the Two-Second Rule by pausing before clicking any link in emails or texts. Review examples of scam messages together with family or friends so you can recognize patterns. Discuss what makes messages suspicious such as urgency, fear tactics, or requests for sensitive information.

Day 6: Verification (10 minutes)

Confirm all systems work by testing each one. Log into your password manager on both devices. Check that your credit freezes show as active at all three bureaus. Verify breach monitoring is sending you notifications by checking for the confirmation email. Print the emergency contact sheet and

Appendix C: Fortress Shield Reference Materials

store it in a secure, accessible location like the drawer where you keep insurance papers.

Monthly Maintenance Routine

⏱ 15 minutes | Recommended

Objective: Maintain readiness and detect threats early through consistent checking.

Start your monthly maintenance by opening your password manager and running the security report. Look for passwords flagged as weak, reused across multiple sites, or appearing in known breaches. Change these immediately, letting the password manager generate strong random replacements. Run a manual check at HaveIBeenPwned.com by entering your email address to see if any new breaches have occurred that weren't automatically reported. Act on any alerts by changing affected passwords within 24 hours.

Verify your credit freezes remain active by logging into all three bureaus and checking freeze status. This catches any technical glitches or unauthorized changes. While you're doing security checks, take five minutes to audit your installed apps and software. Uninstall anything you haven't used in the past three months because unused apps are potential security vulnerabilities. Update everything that needs updating including your operating system, browser, and critical applications.

Finally, back up your essential documents to offline storage like an external hard drive or USB drive. Keep this backup disconnected from your computer except during the backup process. Ransomware can't encrypt backups it can't access.

Fortress Shield - 2026 Edition

Oh-No Playbook - Emergency Response

⏱ As needed | Critical

Objective: Restore control, contain damage, and recover securely when something goes wrong.

Incident Response Steps

Lost Device

When you lose your phone, tablet, or laptop, time is critical but panic doesn't help. Take a deep breath and move through these steps methodically. Log into your password manager from another device using your master password. Change your master password immediately before anyone can access the lost device. Use the Find My Device feature for iPhone or Android to locate, lock, or remotely erase your device. Notify your bank and email provider about the lost device so they can monitor for suspicious activity. If the device contained work information, notify your IT department immediately.

Account Compromised

If you discover someone has accessed one of your accounts without authorization, immediate action limits the damage. Reset the password immediately using your password manager to generate a new strong random password. Enable two-factor authentication if you haven't already so this doesn't happen again. Check recent account activity for unauthorized transactions, messages, or changes to account settings. Alert friends or family if they might receive suspicious messages from your compromised account. Review what information the attacker could have accessed and secure related accounts that might be vulnerable.

Phishing Link Clicked

If you realize you clicked a suspicious link, assume compromise and act defensively. Disconnect from the internet

Appendix C: Fortress Shield Reference Materials

immediately by turning off Wi-Fi or unplugging your ethernet cable. This prevents malware from communicating with command servers or spreading to other devices. Run a full antivirus scan using updated security software. Change the password for any account you logged into after clicking the link. Monitor your email for suspicious password reset requests over the next few days.

Emergency Contacts

⏱ Keep printed copy nearby | Essential.

Keep these numbers accessible in printed form because digital devices fail during emergencies. Store this sheet with other critical documents in a physical location you can access even if your computer and phone are compromised.

Bank Fraud Hotline: 1-800-555-0101

Credit Card Fraud Hotline: 1-800-555-0110

Equifax: 1-800-349-9960

Experian: 1-888-397-3742

TransUnion: 1-888-909-8872

FTC Identity Theft Hotline: 1-877-438-4338

Social Security Fraud: 1-800-269-0271

Local Police (Non-Emergency): _____

Primary Tech Support: _____

Physical Emergency Kit

⏱ 10 minutes setup | Recommended.

Create a physical backup of critical information that remains accessible even during digital emergencies. Print copies of all reference materials from Appendices A through C. Store them in a waterproof, fire-resistant envelope or small safe. Include a backup USB drive with encrypted copies of essential documents like tax records, insurance policies, and account information. Label the envelope clearly as "FORTRESS SHIELD - EMERGENCY KIT" so family members can find it if you're incapacitated. Update this kit annually when you update your other security systems.

Recovery Time Expectations

⏱ For planning purposes

Understanding realistic timeframes helps you plan responses and set appropriate expectations. Lost device recovery takes one to two hours depending on whether you can locate and recover the device or need to replace it entirely. Password reset and account recovery typically requires 30 to 60 minutes including verification steps and enabling additional security. Identity theft response takes one to three business days for the initial report filing and freeze activation, though full recovery can take months. Credit freeze setup at all three bureaus takes about 10 minutes per bureau, totaling 30 minutes for complete protection.

Mission Complete

You've built resilience into your defenses through preparation and documentation. Keep this printed reference with your emergency kit because paper never crashes, doesn't require passwords, and works even when power fails. Update it annually from new book editions to ensure procedures remain current as tools and threats evolve.

Service Recommendations and Disclaimers

5 minutes | Essential

Objective: Review service transparency, verify vendor independence, and ensure reader awareness of limitations.

Recommended Services Reference

The tools and providers mentioned throughout Fortress Shield were selected based on four criteria: security, privacy, cost-effectiveness, and accessibility. No compensation, sponsorship, or affiliate arrangements exist between the author or publisher and any vendor listed in this book. These recommendations reflect genuine professional assessment without financial incentive.

For password management, this book recommends Bitwarden, Proton Pass, and 1Password based on their security track records, transparent operations, and user-friendly implementations. For private email and storage, Proton Mail, Tutanota, and Skiff offer strong encryption and privacy protections. For breach monitoring, Have I Been

Pwned, Firefox Monitor, and Proton Sentinel provide reliable alerts about compromised credentials. For VPN services when traveling or using public networks, ProtonVPN, Mullvad VPN, and Mozilla VPN maintain strong no-logs policies and transparent operations. For browser security, Firefox, Brave, and DuckDuckGo Browser prioritize user privacy over advertising revenue. For device protection, the book recommends using built-in operating system security tools supplemented by browser extensions like uBlock Origin and Privacy Badger.

These recommendations are current as of publication but should be verified annually since technology companies change ownership, modify privacy policies, and alter pricing structures regularly.

Information Sources

Information in Fortress Shield draws from publicly available data provided by trusted organizations with established track records in cybersecurity and consumer protection. The National Institute of Standards and Technology provides technical security standards and best practices developed through extensive research and industry collaboration. The Federal Trade Commission offers consumer protection guidance based on enforcement actions and complaint data. The Cybersecurity and Infrastructure Security Agency publishes threat assessments and security recommendations for both government and civilian infrastructure. Additional research draws from privacy-focused organizations including Proton's security research team, the Mozilla Foundation's privacy initiatives, and the Electronic Frontier Foundation's digital rights advocacy.

Readers are encouraged to verify current information independently since technology and vendor practices evolve rapidly. What's accurate today may change tomorrow as new

Service Recommendations and Disclaimers

threats emerge, companies are acquired, or regulations are updated.

Technology Evolution Notice

All recommendations reflect the state of available tools and services as of early 2026. The cybersecurity landscape changes constantly. Companies get acquired and change their privacy policies. New vulnerabilities are discovered in previously trusted tools. Better alternatives emerge that didn't exist when this edition was published. Regulatory environments shift as new laws are enacted or enforcement priorities change.

Readers should recheck each listed service annually to ensure current pricing, ownership structure, and privacy policies align with your needs and values. The Strategic Defense Plans PDF companion resource provides semi-annual updates in January and July covering significant changes to recommended tools, but your own periodic verification adds an additional layer of assurance.

Legal and Compliance Notices

Nothing in Fortress Shield constitutes legal, financial, or professional cybersecurity advice. The author is a retired military cybersecurity professional sharing educational information based on three decades of experience, not a lawyer, financial advisor, or licensed security consultant. All examples and procedures are provided for educational and informational purposes only. They represent general guidance that may not apply to your specific situation.

Readers are responsible for confirming compliance with applicable laws in their jurisdiction. Federal laws including the Fair Credit Reporting Act govern how you can dispute credit information and what rights you have regarding credit reports. State privacy laws including the California Consumer Privacy Act and Virginia Consumer Data Protection Act provide specific rights over personal data that vary by state. International privacy regulations including the European Union's General Data Protection Regulation may apply if you live outside the United States. Other state, federal, and international laws may be relevant depending on your circumstances.

When in doubt about legal requirements or your rights under specific laws, consult a qualified attorney in your jurisdiction. This book provides general education, not legal counsel.

Educational Purpose Statement

Fortress Shield provides guidance for individual users and families seeking to strengthen their personal cybersecurity posture. The book addresses common threats facing civilians in everyday life, not specialized threats facing corporations, government agencies, or high-value targets. The procedures outlined are simplified to make them accessible and actionable for readers without technical backgrounds. They cannot cover every variation of device configuration, operating system version, service implementation, or threat scenario.

Technology changes faster than books can be updated. By the time you read this, some specific procedures may have changed slightly as companies redesign interfaces or modify workflows. The core principles remain valid, but the exact steps may require adaptation. Use your judgment and common sense when implementing recommendations. If something doesn't work exactly as described, look for the functional equivalent in current interfaces rather than abandoning the protection entirely.

Service Recommendations and Disclaimers

Fortress Shield Community Standards

Readers are encouraged to share knowledge responsibly and help others establish strong digital safety practices. Teaching others what you've learned multiplies protection throughout your community and makes everyone safer. However, redistribution of this guide must be done ethically. You may share this book in full with attribution to the author and publisher. You may not excerpt substantial portions, modify the content, or claim authorship of materials you didn't create.

If you want to share specific techniques or procedures with others, teach them in your own words based on your understanding, or recommend they get their own copy of the book for complete context. Partial information can be more dangerous than no information if it gives people false confidence without full understanding.

Contact and Corrections

Despite extensive review, errors occasionally appear in published works. If you discover a factual error, broken URL, outdated procedure, or misleading information, please report it so it can be corrected in future editions. Contact the publisher through the official website at FortressShieldBook.com/contact or email admin@ValueStreamLearningGroupLLC.com with specific details about the error including page number, section title, and the nature of the problem.

Verified corrections will be published in the next annual edition and included in semi-annual Strategic Defense Plans updates when the correction is time sensitive. Not all suggestions will result in changes, as some represent differences of opinion about best practices rather than factual errors. The author and publisher evaluate all feedback carefully and incorporate improvements where appropriate.

Acknowledgments and Copyright

To every reader applying these principles, you're part of the Fortress Shield community now. Your commitment to protecting yourself and helping others strengthens collective defense for everyone. Thank you for taking security seriously and for contributing to a safer digital environment through your vigilance and your willingness to teach others.

This book reflects the contributions of many people beyond the author. My wife, who tolerated countless evenings of writing and provided patient feedback on explanations that were too technical. My children, who let me use their security experiences as teaching examples. My extended family, who became test subjects for these procedures and provided honest feedback about what worked and what didn't. Fellow veterans who shared their experiences protecting critical systems. Readers of early drafts who identified confusing sections and suggested improvements. All of you made this book better than I could have made it alone.

Copyright Notice

Copyright 2025, 2026 SPIRE Value Stream Press, an imprint of Value Stream Learning Group, L.L.C. All rights reserved.

No part of this publication may be reproduced, stored in a retrieval system, or transmitted in any form or by any means including electronic, mechanical, photocopying, recording, or otherwise, without prior written permission of the publisher, except for brief quotations embodied in critical reviews or articles, or for educational use in accordance with fair use doctrine.

For permission requests, contact the publisher at the address above or through FortressShieldBook.com.

About the Publisher

SPIRE Value Stream Press publishes practical guides for personal and professional development with emphasis on operational excellence, continuous improvement, and sustainable practices. Visit ValueStreamLearningGroupLLC.com for additional titles and resources.

About the Author

CMSgt Alan Palmer, USAF (Ret.), served his country for more than three decades in the United States Air Force. His career began in the Security Forces, where he guarded B-52 bombers in extreme weather and served at Cheyenne Mountain and Schriever Air Force Base in Colorado Springs, two of the most secure and demanding duty stations in the na`tion.

As technology transformed the battlefield, Palmer transitioned from physical defense to digital protection, leading teams responsible for safeguarding mission-critical networks and communications. Rising to the rank of **Chief Master Sergeant**, he became one of the Air Force's most respected senior enlisted advisors in the field of cybersecurity.

Now retired, **Alan Palmer** lives in Colorado Springs, Colorado, where he continues to serve in a new way, educating, mentoring, and empowering everyday people to take control of their digital safety. His writing reflects the same principles that guided his Air Force career: integrity, vigilance, and the belief that protecting others is a lifelong duty.

When not writing or consulting, Alan enjoys Colorado's mountain trails, time with family, and the quiet satisfaction of knowing that every reader who applies what they learn is one more civilian, better protected against the threats of the modern world.

"Protect what matters. Prepare for what's next."

www.ingramcontent.com/pod-product-compliance
Lightning Source LLC
Chambersburg PA
CBHW050059170426
43198CB00014B/2385